Flexible Rigidities

*Industrial policy and structural adjustment
in the Japanese economy 1970–80*

Flexible Rigidities

*Industrial policy
and structural adjustment
in the Japanese economy
1970–80*

Ronald Dore

Stanford University Press
Stanford, California

Stanford University Press
Stanford, California
© *1986 Ronald P. Dore*
Originating publisher:
  The Athlone Press, London
First published in the U.S.A. by
  Stanford University Press, 1986
Printed in Great Britain
Cloth ISBN 0-8047-1328-6
Paper ISBN 0-8047-1465-7
First paperback printing, 1988

Contents

Acknowledgements

A substantial part of this volume is based on a monograph which I wrote with contributions by Professor Kōji Taira of the University of Illinois, and which was recently published by the International Labour Office, Geneva, under the title *Structural adjustment in Japan, 1970–82*. I am grateful to all those involved in planning the research on which that monograph was based for much stimulus and enlightenment.

It will be obvious from what follows how much I also owe to all those friends in the Japanese textile industry who helped me to some understanding, at least, of their problems and achievements. I would also like to thank those at the Institute of Development Studies where the work was begun, and at the Technical Change Centre where it was finished, who gave their help and support, but most notably those who worked so nobly with messy drafts and bumbling tapes to produce an intelligible typescript: Julia Broomfield, Pat White and Maria Spoors, especially the last who also took on the job of improving my grammar while making sure the typescript got accurately into print.

Introduction

'It is not,' said Adam Smith, 'from the benevolence of the butcher, the brewer, or the baker, that we expect our dinner, but from their regard to their own interest.'

The trouble with the Japanese is that they have never really caught up with Adam Smith – in spite of the fact that a British publisher with a new scholarly work on Smith or Ricardo can expect to sell half the edition in Japan. They don't *believe* in the invisible hand. They believe – like Mao unleashing the Cultural Revolution and all other good Confucianists – that you cannot get a decent moral society, not even an efficient society, simply out of the mechanisms of the market powered by the motivational fuel of self-interest, however clever, or even divinely inspired, those mechanisms may be. The morality has got to come from the hearts, the wills and motives, of the individuals in it. The butcher and the brewer have *got* to be benevolent. They need to have a conscience about the quality of the meat and the beer they supply. They need to care.

The individualistic West – and let there be no doubt about the great material achievements which its individualism has brought over the last four or five centuries – made egoism the touchstone of its economic morality – indeed of the morality applicable to the whole range of behaviour beyond relations with family and friends. Even nationalism – patriotism – as exemplified by Mrs Thatcher in the Falklands, becomes a kind of ego-projection. Even the basic rules, the minimal constraints on sharp practice necessary even for a market system to operate have themselves to be justified in terms of self-interest. 'Honesty is the best policy.' The Japanese *might* say something similar – 'caring is the best policy' – caring about quality and service. That, indeed, was the message of the £8m campaign launched by the Department of Industry in 1983 to improve quality assurance standards in British industry, a sign that the Japanese demonstration of the relation between quality and competitiveness is being taken seriously.

But the Japanese do not say 'caring is the best policy'. They say 'caring is a duty'. Being conscientious about the quality of his work, assiduous in service to the customer or his firm, is the individual's way of repaying his debts to society. It is an essential part of being a good citizen. And as for individuals, so for the business firm. Of course they believe that in *the long run* it is also best policy. Suppose that a supplier is in trouble. For a couple of years, you go on buying from him in spite of having to pay him higher prices than are being offered by a firm around the corner in order to keep him out of the bankruptcy courts. It will pay off in the end. He'll be so morally indebted, for one thing, that you'll be able to squeeze him when *you're* in trouble. These advantages the Japanese are very well aware of. But the self-interest of 'best policy' is not the way they naturally talk about the emphasis on quality and honestly delivering the goods on time. One hears much more about 'serving society'.

That does mean that the hypocrisy quotient is higher in Japanese than in British life. But it also means that, while the Japanese sententiousness that makes the British cynic snort *is* sometimes self-serving and hypocritical, it is *also* sometimes for real – and sometimes half and half in the curious mixed-up way that human motives do get confused in practice in any society.

At any rate the Japanese economic system works on the assumption that the 'serving society' sentiments *are* for real. That is why the large Japanese firms whose export products have become household words abroad found their employment system on a belief in original virtue, not original sin. They base their work systems on the assumption that their workers can be *trusted* to be just as concerned as the managers are about conscientious testing procedures, about making sure that no faulty car is allowed to pass and damage the company's reputation for reliability abroad. Similarly, the firm which pays higher prices to keep its supplier out of bankruptcy believes he can be *trusted* to reciprocate X years hence if the situation demands it.

All economies in practice, notwithstanding Adam Smith, contain a fair proportion of such trust relationships, as opposed to arm's-length contractual relationships. The Japanese economy just moves a good deal further in that direction than most. 'Trust relationship versus arm's-length contractual relationship' is one way of putting it. 'Relational contracting versus spot contracting' (Goldberg 1981) and 'customer relations as opposed to auction market relations' (Okun 1974) are others. And what Hirschman calls 'voice and loyalty' as opposed to 'exit and entry' relationships are yet another. Japanese consumers do shop around for the 'best buy' refrigerator. Much 'spot contract' transacting of that kind goes on in Japan no differently from elsewhere. But with their fishmonger and greengrocer Japanese consumers are more likely to have a relational contract. And in the employment relationship, the extent to which loyalty and long-term commitment are expected to play a part is well known. One might measure where an employment relation stands between the 'spot' and the 'relational' extremes by the frequency with which the employee looks at the job advertisements and wonders whether he might not do better elsewhere. By that criterion, employment relations for a large part of Japan's 'lifetime-committed' employees fall squarely towards the relational end of the continuum.

The same applies in the market for intermediate goods – the transactions already referred to between large engineering firms and their sub-contracting suppliers, between final goods producers and the suppliers of their industries. Japanese automobile companies each buy their steel, through the same trading companies and from the same two or three steel companies, in proportions that vary very little from year to year. The price is set by the biggest seller and the biggest purchaser in annual bargains which the others follow. For several years certain kinds of Brazilian and Korean steel have been available more cheaply than domestic products, but it was a long time before they made any significant penetration of the market because the trading companies which handled the steel companies' sales hesitated to jeopardize their established customer relations by dealing in them.

These established customer relations ramify throughout the economy, and impart what we would call a sluggishness to every kind of market – for loan finance, for insurance, for equity capital as well as for labour and producers' goods. They are at their strongest in hierarchical relations. The more dependent firm – and especially, as with a part supplied to a local automobile company, say, where the dependence is 'structural' and not much affected by fluctuations in the supply–demand balance – has to give stronger guarantees of quality and service and loyalty to retain the mutual obligation of the relation. And the vertical element of inequality and dependence in the employee relation is clear enough – the employee probably needs the firm more than the firm needs the employee. But these obligated customer relationships operate importantly in situations of equal and mutual dependency, too – as between steel-maker, trading company and car firm, for example.

If all this is true, the economist is likely to ask, how can it be that the Japanese economy operates with apparent efficiency? If there is so little market competition, how can the forces of supply and demand establish a set of relative prices which allocates goods efficiently or gives the right signals to producers? Surely, all this fine talk of trust and mutual obligation amounts to a lot of feather-bedding and protection of the inefficient? How can one get growth out of an economic system like that?

There are several answers to that. One is that – and the international oil market is a case in point – markets dominated by relational contracting can still respond fairly quickly to changes in demand/supply conditions if there is a tiny spot market fringe. Another is the answer Harvey Liebenstein has been offering for years – that the allocative efficiency brought by a competitive market is in the end less important than what he calls X-efficiency – the efficiency that comes from everybody in the system being keen to do his or her job conscientiously, and actually having the knowledge and skill to do it well. And it is precisely *these* qualities which trust relationships with their emphasis on quality and service promote.

Well, supposing you are right, the orthodox economist may grudgingly say; that may explain the static efficiency of a system, but how can such an economy be dynamically efficient? If economic activity is encompassed within a rigid set of long-term relationships which do not easily respond to price signals, how do you ever get change?

It is a question of very wide general interest, for it is the kind of question constantly being asked about European and North American economies. Trade union monopolies, the unwillingness of unions to accept redundancies and changes in work practices, the growth of government regulations, protection for declining industries, are all blamed for making our economies 'rigid', for their lack of 'dynamism'. Lester Thurow writes of America as becoming a 'zero sum society', a web of government regulation which cannot be untangled because every restraint of X's activity protects the interests of Y, and Y is always politically mobilized to defend the status quo.

And defence of the status quo was no principle for the running of any economy in the 1970s when most of the Organization for Economic Co-operation and Development (OECD) countries faced a triple challenge. The sharpest and most obvious was the hop, skip and jump of relative energy prices. The second was the increase in inflation rates, exacerbated by the oil price rise, but starting long before that and associated with the decline in the power of competitive forces even to hold back increases in wage rates, much less to cut wages. Getting control over inflation came increasingly to dominate economic policy and the search for the recipe to combine inflation control with growth is still on. The third was the rise of the newly industrialized countries (NICS). The four Asian NICS, with Brazil and Mexico in particular, began, in their accumulation of capital and technical sophistication, to reach levels at which their still cheaper labour costs enabled them to penetrate the domestic markets of the OECD countries and the Third World markets of their exporters – especially in the labour-intensive textile, leather goods, ship-building, etc., branches of industry.

'Rigidity' came into all three. Adjustments to oil price changes meant primarily a redistribution of income – among countries, obviously, and within countries between those who use a lot of energy and those who do not. Where everyone thinks he has an inalienable right to his place in the relative income scale – thinks that the distribution is a rigid 'given' and is prepared to fight to preserve his right, adjustment takes a long time. The second, the challenge of inflation, is variously attributed to the inability of governments flexibly to control public spending, faced as they are by a rigidly unyielding structure of demands by pressure groups, or to their inability to control the leap-frogging of wage claims by unions which have substituted trade-union monopoly for competitive labour markets.

As for the third, the challenge of adjustment to the rise of the NICS, the economic efficiency answer was obvious. The decisive shift in the pattern of comparative advantage meant that the OECD countries must let their declining labour-intensive industries go to the wall. With the consumer surplus their citizens could gain from buying cheaper Korean shirts, they would increase the volume of demand for other more sophisticated products; Korea would use its export earnings to buy more capital goods from the OECD countries. These increases in demand would more than compensate for the loss of employment and output in textiles. Thus, too, would the humanitarian obligation of the rich countries, their duty to respond to the Third World's demand for 'trade not aid', be simultaneously fulfilled. But again it was the rigidities of existing structures, the ability of industry associations and trade unions to organize successful demands for protection of the status quo – in particular the success of the trade unions in making (Japanese-type) job-tenure security close to being an inalienable human right, making 'hire and fire' employment systems morally suspect – which blocked the efficient solution.

So, rigidities led to stagflation. So, with Mrs Thatcher and Mr Reagan showing the way, it has become orthodoxy in OECD circles that only by restoring to markets their competitive vigour can the dynamism of the world's leading economies be restored. 'Monetarist' may be what the new orthodoxy is usually called, but 'marketist' better describes its inspiration.

Why on earth, then, should Japan, an economy which almost flaunts its rigidities as a matter of principle, be the most successful among the OECD countries at dynamically adjusting to the three challenges – absorbing the oil-price rises, controlling inflation at a low figure, and shifting the weight of its industrial structure decisively away from declining to competitive industries?

That is what this book is about – the answer to that paradox. After a brief survey of the major characteristics of the economy, chapter 2 charts the changes in economic structure over the decade, chapters 3 and 4 examines the 'adjustive behaviour' in turn of businessmen, workers and their unions, and government, and the next three chapters offer a case study of the textile industry.

The details of the Japanese recipe for dynamic adjustment can wait until then. At the most general level, the message, as I see it, is this. Don't stand against the tide of history. Accept that there are good technical-efficiency reasons for oligopoly sometimes. Accept that it does make for a better *quality* of human relations at work if people are not hired and fired at will and that the improved quality of personal relations is a luxury our societies can now afford to indulge in *as well as* having potential efficiency pay-offs. Accept that the realities of international competition demand more active state intervention and hence the preemption of a lot of investment decisions by bureaucratic rather than market processes. Accept all these things, but make them work. Accept, for instance, that the virtual disappearance of competitive labour markets requires political control over wages and think how you can create the consensus that make incomes policies possible. Work out principles for the dividing lines between open competition and oligopoly–oligopsony bargaining, and devise schemes to make sure that the latter is not at the expense of the public and consumer interest. Give up simple notions of a clear cut distinction between the state's minimal regulation of the legal framework and the free market operations of business within that framework, and accept that workable arrangements require a lot of corporatist bargaining in which the state represents a residual public interest against the contending interests of organized – not market-atomized – parties. Accept, further, that a sense of community of interest and social solidarity, and hence of national purpose, provides a useful, even necessary, basis for making these new processes of corporatist bargaining work flexibly, for making them work to produce beneficial change, not the stalemate which arises when the priority of established rights and 'what I have I hold' are the only decision principles that all parties can agree on. And accept, in consequence, that while no heterogeneous European nation can aspire to the beehive-like homogeneity of Japanese society, the chances of developing the sense of common purpose and social solidarity which make 'rigidities' flexible *are* much affected by social institutions. That is why the sense of common purpose is likely to be strongest in a society with decent and temperate industrial relations, with a distribution of income and wealth which is widely considered equitable, and with patterns of authority within organizations which subordinates can accept as functionally necessary, not as exemplifications of a pattern of class domination.

For a country like Britain, a lot to expect.

1 An eventful decade

1
Adjustment: The agenda and the instruments

It was not without justification that the OECD 1979 Report on the impact of the newly industrialized countries referred to Japan as the forerunner of the NICS (OECD, 1979). The Japan of the 1980s is the product of two decades of faster growth than the world had ever seen until the even faster growth of some of the Asian NICS began a decade or so later. Japan is unquestionably an industrial power of the first rank – with its dollar GNP per capita rapidly approaching that of the USA as the yen climbs up towards its purchasing-power parity level, and well ahead of Britain and Italy, if still lagging behind Sweden and West Germany. Its total size of GNP – thanks to its large, 115-million population – is second only to that of the USA among market economies.

In terms of relative factor prices *too*, her pattern of comparative advantage in world trade with respect to labour-intensive, capital-intensive, or skill-intensive goods is roughly that of the other advanced industrial countries (if anything lying more with capital- and skill-intensive production than the OECD average). But – and this is important for understanding her adjustment to her contemporary situation – it is not much more than a decade ago that Japan was being forced into trade-induced structural adjustment because she evoked protectionist reactions to her exports of *labour*-intensive goods as a *low*-wage-cost competitor.

Hence it is that measures of, for example, state adjustment aid to the textile industry, now invoked to cushion the impact of Chinese or Korean low-wage competition, are in direct line of descent from the measures taken when production had to be cut back in the late sixties in response to American insistence on export restraints to protect domestic producers from floods of 'unfairly competitive' cheap Japanese textiles. Indeed, the last global negotiations over trade in textiles leading to the renewed Multi-Fibre Arrangement (MFA), Japan figured still as a textile exporter, the potential recipient rather than the imposer of quotas.

But more important than such direct institutional continuity is the way in which the whole experience of rapid growth over the

Table 1.1   Some dimensions of change 1960–80

	1960	1973	1980
Per capita product (1975 prices)	100	493	593
Manufacturing output	100	462	564
Composition of GDP* by economic activity:			
agriculture, forestry, fisheries	14.7	5.9	3.9
mining	1.6	0.7	0.6
manufacturing	29.0	35.1	36.8
construction	5.7	8.7	8.1
tertiary	49.0	49.6	50.6
	100.00	100.00	100.00
Employed labour force (1960 = 100)	100	120	127
Composition of employed labour force:			
primary: agriculture, forestry, fishing	32.6	13.4	10.9
secondary: mining, construction,			
manufacturing	29.2	36.6	33.5
tertiary	38.2	49.9	55.7
	100.00	100.00	100.00

* For 1960: NDP at factor cost
Source: KY, 1981–2, pp. 14–17, 194–7, 69, Yomiuri Nenkan, 1969, p. 850.

last twenty years, and the rapidity of Japan's transformation in recent decades, shifting her from the status of a backward country claiming special dispensation to protect its infant industries from competition to that of a leading industrial power, has diffused throughout the nation – among trade unionists and production workers as well as among managers and bureaucrats – a *general* conception of the inevitability and even desirability of continuous structural adjustment, of positive adjustment as a positive good. A good many Japanese think naturally in the imagery of the ladder-model of the world economy according to which Korea, say, now occupies the rung which Japan occupied fifteen years ago and stands in the same relation to Japan on a higher rung today as Japan did to the USA then – partly because most of them can remember what it was like to be on that rung fifteen years ago. Partly, also, it is because the ladder model has long been well established in the thinking of the Japanese economic profession – Colin Clark's *Conditions of Economic Progress* was a favourite book in the 1950s – and it has been generally diffused in a number of simple slogan-phrases, mostly originating in the reports of government committees, which have gained wide-spread acceptance and had a considerable impact on those business decisions which shape the structure of production. Thus, the 1960s were declared, in Japan, to be the decade in which Japan was developing 'the heavy and chemical industries'. A report of 1971 spoke of the end of that era – urged, even, increased reliance on imports for such products – and hailed the need to concentrate on development of 'the knowledge-intensive industries'.

But the movement of the countries of the South 'up the ladder' – the accumulation of capital and skills in lower-wage countries – has been only one of the exogenous changes affecting investment, recruitment, training and production decisions in Japanese firms – only one of the factors that the Japanese economy has been adjusting to. Several other major contextual changes have been generally seen by those taking business decisions as calling for adjustment – as requiring, in other words, not just accommodation to the fluctuations of the business cycle, but decisions which in their cumulative effect have led to change in the Japanese industrial structure. These contextual changes may be briefly listed, roughly in chronological order of their appearance.

Environment

The first was an efflorescence of concern with environmental pollution and the quality of life. This was not the result of any particular triggering incident, but rather of the cumulation of a number of factors: the rapid onset of the automobile age brought a rapid thickening of urban smog; one or two famous cases of poisonous industrial pollution attracted widespread attention; internationally notions of development were affected by the UN's slogan for the Second Development Decade, 'balanced social and economic development' (the phrase 'social development' gained general currency in Japan in 1963 after it was used in a report of the government's Population Problems Council). The take-off of the environmental movement in the United States in the late 1960s also had its effect. By the end of that decade, it had become a recurring cliché of public discussion that Japan had developed its productive infrastructure too fast at the expense of her social infrastructure and the quality of life. There was much talk of the need for increased public expenditure, and a flurry of experimentation with the devising of measures of Net National Welfare.

In concrete terms this had several consequences. Politically effective protest against pollution led to the enactment of quite stringent emission standards which affected cost structures and stimulated certain kinds of machine-building industry. Expenditure on pollution control investment by private firms covered by the Ministry of International Trade and Industry (MITI) investment survey increased nearly nine times from Y62 bn. to Y917 bn., from 2 per cent to 15 per cent of total investment between 1968 and 1974. (KY, 1981, p. 129). Secondly, finding sites for raw material processing and chemical industries with high pollution potential, which had become increasingly difficult for physical and cost reasons (the Pacific Seaboard had already become the area with the highest density of economic activity in the world) became even more difficult for reasons of local amenity-protecting opposition. This was one of the major motives for the 1971 declaration by the Industrial Structure Council – a declaration which reflected large sections of business opinion – that Japan should consider increasing reliance on imports of heavy and chemical industry products (albeit that they expected them to be the products of Japanese firms located abroad) and concentrate at home on 'knowledge-intensive' branches of production: computers, robotics, VLSI, fine chemicals, industrial housing, business machines, fashion goods, electronic music, high quality printing, etc. This was a declaration which affected not only government decisions on support for R & D and various other fiscal and financial decisions, but also business decisions concerning research, investment and location.

The oil-shock

Japan's rapid industrialization in the 1960s had been based on cheap oil and no other industrial economy was quite so dependent on imported oil for its energy as Japan. (In 1977 oil accounted for 44 per cent of Japan's total imports compared with 21 per cent in France and even less in Germany and the UK). That it was the Japanese who coined the term 'oil-shock' for the quadrupling of oil prices in 1973 is not, therefore, surprising. In the short term, Japan staged a rapid recovery from the inflation induced by the oil-price rise and the earlier commodity boom. After general consumer price rises of 12 per cent and 21 per cent in (calendar) 1973 and 1974, (the last a year of negative real income growth), by 1976 the economy was back to 6 per cent inflation and 5 per cent growth. The 3 per cent cut in GNP which the oil price rise represented had been absorbed and distributed (the holding back of wage increases played a major part) and exports had been increased to meet the oil bill.

Beyond such questions of economic management, however, the increase in the cost of energy – particularly the second round of 1979 – had important lasting consequences with long-term impact on the industrial structure. Industries which were heavy users of energy, and those like the chemical and fertilizer industries which used oil products as raw material, faced a loss of competitiveness *vis-à-vis* those who did not have to pay international prices for their energy (aluminium smelters at large hydroelectric sites, for instance, or steel producers sitting on large domestic coal deposits) or for their naphtha (Indonesian producers of urea from natural gas, for example). By and large these were also the industries which were most pollution-prone so that the oil-price effect tended to reinforce the environmental effect.

Lower growth prospects

The third occasion for long-term adjustment was the general acceptance of the idea that in an energy-constrained world economy it was no longer possible for Japan to resume her pre-1973 growth trajectory. In the mid-1970s it became the received wisdom in Tokyo that Japan could and should aim for something like 5 per cent growth rates until 1990. This gearing-down of expectations had the greatest effect on the internal structure of companies; they could no longer invest at rates earlier projected and, indeed, some industries – synthetic fibres, electric arc smelting, etc. – found that their large investments in the mid-1970s, planned in the optimistic early 1970s, had left them with excess capacity which it took several years to absorb or dispose of. The prospect of slower output growth in the future, combined with pressure to raise the retirement age beyond 55 as a result of growing social concern with the rapidly rising age of the population, made it impossible to maintain the pyramidical age-authority structures which had hitherto been fed by annually increasing cohorts of school and university leavers. Recruitment numbers had to be reduced, and whereas output growth had exceeded labour-productivity growth until 1973, thereafter the relationship was reversed and the total in manufacturing employment began to fall. Smaller and more stable recruitment quotas implied also a shortage of promotional opportunities for mid-career managers – not enough Indians for the available chiefs – which added to the incentives for establishing overseas operations.

At the same time, the end of employment expansion in manufacturing, not fully compensated by expansion in services, had clear consequences for the adjustment process: nothing so eases the pain of phasing out a few particular industries than a general dynamic of expansion, and nothing more increases the pain than rising unemployment – though in Japan's case unemployment has still, until 1983, been kept to around 2 per cent of the labour force, with only a 1 per cent fall in participation rates, 1973–80, fully in line with long-run trends.

The place of the plant construction industry in the industrial structure was also obviously adversely affected, although some compensation was found in exports. The rapid expansion of the plant export industry (from \$4bn. in 1974 to \$12bn. in 1979) dates from this time.

Likewise, in so far as Japan's growth had derived some of its stimulus from export expansion (though exports were only 9 per cent of GNP in 1973), and particularly in so far as one of the major parameters involved in creating the consensual view that Japan could not expect high growth rates was pessimism about the growth of world markets, plans for expansion of industries relying largely on exports (the electrical industry, for instance) were also set back.

Reactions against Japanese exports

Pessimism about export prospects originally based on growth of world purchasing power was reinforced in the late 1970s and early 1980s by the fear of protectionism further reducing export possibilities. The mounting criticism of Japan's 'aggressive' (read 'successful') export drive in the United States and Europe, and the voluntary restrictions placed on exports of, e.g., automobiles to both markets can thus be counted a fourth exogenous change which has called for adjustment – though one which in its effects is not easily distinguished from the last.

The major consequences for the industrial structure have been (a) to cut back plans for expansion in certain mass consumer-goods industries (and some capital-goods industries such as machine tools), (b) to accelerate plans for export-substituting overseas investment in Europe and America, and (c) to give extra incentives to firms to 'move up market', to products where they can be protected against the protectionism of European and American domestic producers by sheer product superiority – a concern reflected at the national level in plans to provide government support for 'next generation' technology.

Before trying to look in more detail at the way in which the economy has adjusted to these challenges, in particular at the employment aspects of adjustment, and especially at the way in which adjustment to all the other factors has interrelated with the form of adjustment which concerns us most – adjustment to the rising manufacturing export capacity of developing countries – it will be useful to set out a few salient characteristics of the Japanese economy which has been doing the adjusting.

Major characteristics of the Japanese economy

Perhaps the most striking characteristic of the Japanese economy is its combination of some of the world's most technologically advanced industries with some of the hallmarks of its recent past as an 'underdeveloped country'. On the one hand, in 1980, over half the world's industrial robots were working in Japan. On the other, although both capital and output are highly concentrated in industry and services, and agriculture contributes less than 5 per cent of GNP, it is an agriculture which is still structured in tiny two-to-three acre homesteads, and still involves 15 per cent of the nation's households, even if the bulk of them (in 1980, 65 per cent) now derive less than half of their income from agriculture and only 11 per cent of the labour force, predominantly older workers and two-thirds of them women, are actually engaged in agricultural work.

The persistence of family enterprise is marked also in other parts of the economy – and very important, as we shall see, precisely in those labour-intensive sectors most subject to competition from developing countries. Still, in 1981, only 72 per cent of the employed labour force were in wage or salary employment: 28 per cent were self-employed, or employers or family workers, and even if agriculture and forestry are excluded from the calculation the figure was still 21 per cent.

A good proportion of the employees also work in small enterprises (16 per cent in firms with less than ten workers in 1971, 18 per cent in 1979) which are often, in terms of the social character of the employment relation, extensions of family enterprises. At the opposite pole, the large-scale enterprises which dominate manufacturing and communications and parts of the service trades were employing increasing proportions of the total employees until about 1970, but stable or declining proportions since. (About 35 per cent of the workers in private firms are in firms with more than 300 workers.) The 'Japanese employment system', as it is operated in those firms, is well known for its distinctive features: a strong preference for recruitment straight from school or university and a strong taboo – reinforced by fears of sanctions from the union – against dismissing workers for reasons of redundancy; a wage system based very largely on seniority increments within categories defined by educational qualifications; rather clear, though not formally prescribed, seniority qualifications for promotion within job groups with merit selection among the qualified, (e.g. in the managerial hierarchy, the age for appointing directors may never vary from the 50–55 band, though not every manager aged 55 becomes a director); wage bargaining on a predominantly enterprise-by-enterprise basis between managers and an enterprise union which embraces all categories of employees, including younger managerial staff without line responsibilities; considerable training investments, the rentability of which is assured by lifetime employment; concentration of at least a third of cash wage payment in the form of twice-yearly bonuses, also union-bargained but varying a little more according to current profitability than wages do; a substantial portion of labour costs paid in kind as housing, medical, recreational facilities and subventions.

The system is one which appears to generate a measure of loyalty and commitment to the firm's success, and a dynamism and willingness to accept or promote change which compensates for the inflexibility of wage costs and the age restrictions on merit appointments which strike many Western observers as flagrantly flouting all received principles of capitalist rationality.

The meta-enterprise pattern of organization is complex. Enterprises combine together in three ways. There are, first, groups of firms, made up of a major firm and its satellites, possibly tied by capital ownership and the strategic 'posting' of the major firm's staff to the satellite 'colonies', but at least by long-standing trading relationships – contracts for the purchase of parts or intermediates, exclusive dealerships and rights for further processing, etc. All the major manufacturing firms like Hitachi, Toyota, Kubota have such *keiretsu* – such satellite clusters. Secondly, there are groups of firms of relatively equal status, usually including a major bank as an important component, which maintain continuous liaison over major matters of corporate strategy, and give each other marginal preferences in inter-firm transactions. These latter groups, like the Mitsubishi and Mitsui groups, were formed on the basis of the informal personal relations between managers dating from a time when the core firms were part of the integrated *zaibatsu* conglomerates, dominated by a central holding company, which were compulsorily dissolved in 1946–7. More will be said about the functioning of these two types of groups, and about their importance – for technological development, for quality maintenance and also for the possibilities of import penetration – in chapters 3 and 6.

The third form of grouping is of the greatest importance for adjustment matters, whether it be a matter of adjusting to energy prices or import competition: namely the industry associations. These are well-organized and often have good business research sections and officials of some authority. They play an important role in joint R & D projects sponsored by the state in industries thought to be of major importance for industrial policy. In the highly oligopolized industries they often provide a forum for the co-ordination part of the delicate balance between conspiracy and competition which the oligopolists maintain. They are the principal instrument through which recession cartels can be formally arranged by MITI; they are often the channel for 'administrative guidance' from the Ministry; and/or a means for individual firms to get the information necessary for them to assess the even-handedness of the guidance the Ministry offers to individual firms.

The effectiveness of these associations and their operations reflects a strong sense, evidently shared by top managers, of membership in 'the industry' as a community. This is a function of the well-known 'groupishness' manifest in so many other spheres of Japanese life, a willing propensity to accept the constraints and comforts of group membership – a consequence partly of the almost direct organizational continuity between feudal guilds and modern industrial associations and partly of the fact that genuine conglomerates are very rare in Japan: most firms are firmly located in 'their' industry without dual loyalties.

The highly organized nature of the Japanese economy, serving in many ways to lend inertia to relations between firms and their suppliers is an often cited 'non-tariff barrier' which reduces the penetration into the Japanese market of manufactured goods, other than the small range of capital goods in which Japan is still not competitive, and some luxury prestige consumption items. So it is that in spite of an extreme poverty of natural resources – only enough land to provide 40 per cent of basic grains and 60 per cent of the value of total food consumed, forests to provide less than a third of timber consumption, a little poor-quality coal, minor deposits of a few minerals, hydroelectric resources to provide 5 per cent of energy needs – Japan's foreign trade ratio is still low: her economy is still a good deal less integrated with that of her neighbours than European economies are with theirs. At some points, indeed, exports have been the most dynamic sector, giving some substance to the characterization 'export-led growth', and certainly export growth was a major policy goal right through the 1950s (export tax relief ended in 1962). But the surpluses which accumulated towards the late 1960s were first reduced by yen appreciation (correction, most would say, of the earlier policy of under-valuation of the yen) and later – twice – by the impact of higher oil prices. The overall increase in the export ratio – from 9 per cent of GDP in the 1960s to 14–16 per cent in the mid-1970s and then to 19–20 per cent after the second oil crisis – did little more than cover the cost of dearer oil imports. There were small balance of payments deficits in 1979 and 1980. The momentum of export growth plus easier oil prices changed that picture somewhat in the 1980s, bringing the prospect of a $40bn. ·trade surplus in 1984.

The making of policy

The feature of the Japanese economy which more than any other distinguishes it from the other seven summit-nation economies is the stable integrated nature of its politico-bureaucratic establishment. The Liberal Democratic Party has been continuously re-elected since 1955, and the constituent elements from which it was formed were in power since 1948. The opposition, once dominated by a Socialist Party, closely backed by the trade unions, is now fragmented into the New Liberal Club, a centrist break-away group from the Liberal Democratic Party (LDP); a Democratic Socialist Party which has strong support from Dōmei, the trade union federation covering the bulk of private industry and whose views on policy issues differ from that of the ruling establishment only about as much as the views of, say, the Nissan union differ (as they sometimes do) from those of the Nissan management; thirdly, a Socialist Party with a Marxist vocabulary, strong support from the public sector unions in the Sōhyō federation, and a more determined oppositional stance; a Communist Party which is similarly, if not more, 'alienated' and uncompromising in mobilizing indignation on civil rights, poverty and inequality issues and which competes with the fifth party, the Kōmeitō – a party originally of Buddhist organizational origin, not markedly different from the establishment in basic world view – for the votes of the poorer third of Japanese society, the workers in petty commerce and backyard industry, the old, the widowed, the divorced and the handicapped.

The degree of integration of the bureaucracy and the ruling party may be indicated by the surprise occasioned when a former bureau chief from the Economic Planning Agency (EPA), retiring around the age of 50 as convention required when one of his age mates was made vice-minister above him, went, not into one of the myriad of quangos maintained by the various ministries (and maintained partly because they provide such splendid sources of second jobs), nor into private industry, nor (admittedly a route more often trodden by Ministry of Finance or MITI than by EPA officials) into a safe constituency seat of the LDP, nor even, as some quirkish EPA intellectuals had been known to do, into academic teaching, but instead into association with the opposition – to head a research institute designed primarily to serve the Dōmei federation and the Democratic Socialist Party. A recent newspaper feature article recalls the circumstances of his translation in the autumn of 1978, at a time (known in Japan as the 'government-opposition-neck-and-neck period') when the opposition parties were making electoral gains and it looked possible that the LDP might lose its overall majority. Mr Sasaki, the official in question, who had done a lot of work on wage issues in the EPA, was invited out to a restaurant by the Dōmei leaders who explained that, with the looming possibility that there might actually be an opposition–coalition takeover of government, they badly felt the lack of real policy-making capacity, and would he be willing to head a research centre which was supported by, but independent of, the major trade union groups. He said he would think about it.

It was right in the middle of the neck-and-neck period. There was a certain perturbation in leading civil service circles as to what might happen if the period of permanent LDP rule should come to an end. And the EPA was no exception. When Sasaki discussed the approaches with the other senior members of EPA the general view was: there are possibilities of big changes in the political situation in the future. It would be not at all a bad thing for the EPA to have its pipe into the trade unions and the labour world. Sasaki should take up the offer.

The EPA also being a non-sectoral ministry, not having any obvious places, nor many of its own quangos, for its retired officials to parachute into . . . (*Nikkei*, 15 November 1984)

In the heady days of the 1945–8 post-war reforms, the Socialist Party had had a number of leaders recruited from the bureaucracy. Today, after a 30-year institutionalization of the patterns of political power, the establishment/non-establishment boundaries are so tightly drawn that migration across them is barely conceivable, except in the sort of circumstances just described.

In the politico-bureaucratic alliance, there is no question of the bureaucracy's intellectual dominance. Bureaucrats appear beside ministers to represent the government in the parliamentary committees where all the real work of the Diet is done, thus freeing ministers from the tiresome duty of actually mastering the details of legislation or administration. Politicians specialize rather in cultivating expansive and dominating personalities and an acute sense for the feelings and interests of constituents. Those among the bureaucrats who have both brains and dominant personalities move into the Party and, when they do so, have a better chance of becoming ministers than those who have graduated to the centre from local politics. From a third to a half of most cabinets have been composed of ex-bureaucrats. They have held the prime ministership for roughly 25 of the first 35 post-war years.

The dominant form of political conflict is rivalry between competing factions within the LDP. Factions are relatively formally organized networks of personal loyalties clustering around leading politicians competing for preferment. Conflict between them is rarely rooted in, or expressed in, differences of policy or ideology, though when there are unresolved policy issues opposing factions may become identified with opposing views – as when, in the rivalry between Messrs Nakasone and Kōmoto for the party leadership and prime ministership in 1982, the former was seen in the bureaucracy, at least, as more closely identified with the conservative Ministry of Finance views favouring retrenchment of government expenditure, the latter with the more expansionist views of MITI and the EPA. In practice, however, it would be hard for any observer of the subsequent actions of the Nakasone government to point to policies which would clearly have been different, had one of his rivals been successful. On the one issue on which Mr Nakasone did break out from the prevailing consensus – defence expenditure – he was quickly drawn back to moderation. Forceful leadership of the kind expected in the politics of more individualistic societies is not the Japanese style.

The management of the economy

The role of the politicians in the making of economic policy becomes, then, largely one of ratifying rather than shaping the consensus which emerges from the – very open and public – debates between the main 'organized interests'. In the matter of month-to-month 'conjunctural' management of the economy, the main 'organized interests' are the Ministry of Finance, the Bank of Japan and what is known as *zaikai* (with the EPA, MITI and the Party's Budget Committee playing minor roles). There is no easy translation for 'zaikai'. Literally it means 'financial circles', but whereas in the context of a Britain one would have to distinguish between the financial circles of 'the City' and 'industry', in Japan, because of the far greater involvement of the banks in industry (see chapter 3), Keidanren, the organization whose austere octogenarian leaders are the most powerful spokesmen of zaikai, is equally representative of financial as well as of manufacturing, and indeed commercial, interests.

The main monetary regulator is the Bank of Japan base rate plus the imposition of direct credit ceilings on the main lending banks, the city banks and the long-term investment banks. The main fiscal regulator is the acceleration and deceleration of public spending plans, which is made easier by the maintenance of a separate government investment account, the Fiscal Investment and Loan Plan, which is financed largely from state insurance funds and post office savings. The volume of expenditure it finances (until 1973 it was not subject to Diet scrutiny) has steadily risen from around 3 per cent of GNP in the 1950s to over 9 per cent in 1980.

Relatively little use is made of variation in taxes as a fiscal regulator except to save the raising of thresholds made necessary by inflation for periods when the economy is thought to need a boost. The tax take rose during the 1970s from 19 per cent to 24 per cent of GNP in 1981 (central from 13 to 16, local from 6 to 8) but with almost no change in the 70/30 ratio between direct and indirect taxation. The general acceptance, until 1980 at least, of the need for a long-run increase in government spending ruled out much use of tax reduction as a means to stimulate the economy. At the same time the constraints of the political competition limited the possibilities of increasing taxation in spite of a general consensus by the mid-1970s that indirect taxation had to be raised. The LDP majority was cut in the 1978 election and this was attributed to its leader's proposal to introduce a value-added tax. Since then, fingers burned, no would-be leader has dared to make himself unpopular by resurrecting the idea. The deficit has been covered by borrowing, sometimes to the tune of more than 30 per cent of government expenditure.

In addition to fiscal and monetary regulators the third arm of, if not month-to-month at least year-to-year, economic management is the 'control' over wages. This involves not formal incomes policies, but an institution with the unlikely name of the Spring Offensive. It consists, essentially, of a short, sharp 'annual round' of wage bargaining concentrated in a few weeks in March–April. The key element is the simultaneous contract settlement date throughout the private sector, and the creation in public consciousness of the concept of an annual 'norm' which *ex post* is the weighted average (weighted by numbers involved) *percentage* increase in wages and *ex ante* is what everyone expects the *ex post* figure to be. The trick lies in engineering convergence of these expectations. Bargaining is predominantly by enterprise, but partly by industry and, even where there is enterprise bargaining, industrial federations frequently co-ordinate the strategy of individual unions and encourage the strongest unions, in the most favourable position, to accelerate their schedule of one-day strikes in the hope that they will be norm-makers at a high figure. When enough of the giants have settled the television pundits declare that 'the peak of the Spring Offensive has passed', and their prediction that the average thereto established will not be very different from the final one becomes self-fulfilling as the remaining settlements are made by unions which see themselves primarily as norm-takers, their ambition being to come out on the norm or, if they are explicitly arguing a case for preferential – better than comparable – treatment, a little above it.

The key to the smooth working of the system, however, is the fact that all parties go into their disputes after months of national shadow-boxing – the first union statement to the effect that they cannot settle for less than x and zaikai statements that more than y would be unthinkable appear in the press in November. In the course of these months of publicized discussion a consensus emerges concerning the general range within which the average rate of increase is likely to fall, and the coercive effect of this consensus makes it largely self-fulfilling. Continuous newspaper comment, well-publicized 'quadri-partite' seminars (government, employers, unions and academics), authoritative statements by economic ministers, all play their part in creating the consensus. Other important ingredients of the system are the quite high level of macro-economic sophistication of union leaders and even union members in Japan, and the fact that bargains are enterprise bargains between managers and enterprise unions which acknowledge their stake in the success of the firm. The way the system worked to restrain, or rather eliminate, the wage-cost-push element in inflation in the second-half of the 1970s will be described in chapter 4.

If it would be hard to define very precisely the role of the government in the determination of wages in Japan, it is equally hard to define the role of government in the field of industrial policy which is the main concern of this book. It has been aptly said that left-wing British visitors come back from Japan convinced that they have seen a shining example of state planning; right-wing visitors return full of praise for the virtues of Japan's free-enterprise system. The wide variation even in academic economists' interpretations has been illuminatingly classified by Chalmers Johnson (1978, pp. 16–18, 1982, pp. 1–20), and more recently by Boltho (1985).

Johnson is certainly right in saying that the Japanese state, since 1870, has been a *developmental* state, and its guiding and controlling role has been, and consequently remains, greater than in other societies where night-watchmen states have only gradually and grudgingly acquired developmental functions. Within that developmental state control over the long-term growth and structure of the economy has been highly concentrated in a single ministry, MITI, whose powerful position is symbolized and reinforced by the fact that it ranks along with the

Finance Ministry as the most difficult of all ministries to enter, in a society where the prestige of the public service as a whole is such as to give it far more than its fair share of the brightest talent coming from the universities. Élite consciousness in a career service helps to create a strong work ethic with an emphasis on thorough enquiry, a premium on initiative and – thanks to a generalist tradition with postings every two or three years from one industry branch to another – an emphasis on a broader national view.

The practice of early retirement and transition to a second job – in the case of high-flyers sometimes into leading positions in business corporations – helps in various ways (the personal contacts between old colleagues, the 'anticipatory socialization' of middle-aged bureaucrats not unmindful of their future career choices) to create a 'bureaucratic industrial complex' within which the creation of the famous consensus becomes easy.

The concrete measures which this consensus supports will be described in more detail in chapter 5. Briefly, there is nothing very novel about most of the measures used by Japanese governments: preferential credits through government lending institutions, special tax concessions, subsidies and direct investment in industry through public or mixed public/private corporations. The less usual features are: first, direct investment is used somewhat more readily than in most countries (though not more than in a Labour Britain) and used not just for basic industries but for relatively small quick-response initiatives (like JECC, the mainframe computer leasing company) to foster particular strategic industries; secondly, raw material and export quota allocation systems of the wartime and post-war reconstruction periods survive in some industries and are revived as production allocation quotas in recession cartels, temporary arrangements sponsored by the Ministry. Thirdly, the Government has created and retained a wide range of licensing powers which are used not solely for the public-interest purpose for which they were originally intended but for broader purposes of guiding the evolution of the industrial structure – the control over technology imports, for instance, was justified by the need to conserve foreign exchange; it was used also to regulate (both stimulate and moderate) competition, and to control the relative volumes of investment in different industries. Finally, there is 'administrative guidance'. This can be imparted as informal discretionary conditions when granting licences transactions or allocating subsidies or loan funds. It may, however, be hung on no such regulatory peg and be, simply, consultative measures initiated by officials who seek to impose public objectives on the private objectives of individual firms – or rather to seek a reconciliation between the two.

The relevance of these government–industry relations to the adjustment process will be a matter for later discussion and illustration.

The structure of national expenditure

The high prestige and authority of the bureaucracy is only one sense in which Japan may be called a highly bureaucratized society. There are other senses too. The employment systems of the large business firms, for example, are of a kind typically associated, in Europe, with a civil service or army. Again, there is the matter of organizational styles. Firm written contracts, and litigation to enforce them, may play a very small part in Japanese, as compared with American business life – *market* relations depend a good deal on verbal trust as we shall see in chapters 3 and 6, but within *organizations*, the elaboration of explicit written rules for work procedures or conditions of employment, in management–union contracts, etc., is carried to a length rare in the West. The output of laws and regulations by government is also on a heroic scale. For nearly every industrial and social field at least one 'compilation of laws relating to' – education, or energy, or the steel industry – is published in annually revised editions. The survey activity and statistical services provided not only by government but even by small local producers' associations are of a rare quality and coverage.

It comes as something of a surprise, therefore, to find Japan is still a 'small government' society. Government final consumption as a proportion of GNP is still 10 per cent, in the same range as Thailand and Philippines (less, in fact, than the former) rather than in the 15–20 per cent range of France, USA, Canada or Australia, much less the 20–30 per cent range of West Germany, Britain and Scandinavia. This reflects a lesser government expenditure on defence and health and welfare activities (other than education) as compared with other economies – though with stronger family bonds and lesser crime problems, a lesser expenditure does not in all fields represent lesser levels of welfare enjoyed. (Also, the stock of hospitals and schools has been improved in recent years as government capital expenditure has slowly increased from 4 per cent of GNP in the late 1960s to 6 per cent in the late 1970s, and it has to be remembered that a stable proportion of GNP in an economy growing at 6 per cent represents twice as rapid a growth as a 1 per cent increase per annum in any economy growing at 2 per cent – even if a lot of that growth is absorbed in increased salary levels with little increase in service to the public.)

Private consumption has also been at a relatively low level compared with other societies. It is investment that has claimed a much greater share than in other economies: with rates consistently over 30 per cent, Japan has had the highest rate of investment of all the market industrial economies, and between 45 per cent and 50 per cent of that investment has been by private firms. With declining growth prospects corporation investment has fallen from the 18–19 per cent of GNP levels of the early 1970s, but was still running at a strong 15–16 per cent at the end of the decade, and soon got back to those levels as soon as the economy got into the recovery stage of what the economists count as the ninth post-war economic cycle from the trough of February 1982. A good deal of the fixed-capital formation has been financed by depreciation and reserves and retained profits of the corporations themselves, but household savings have also played a major role. Up to the oil crisis the household savings rate (which, it must be remembered, includes the business reserves of a lot of one-man businesses) was running at 14–16 per cent, typically providing 25–30 per cent of total savings. The uncertainties of life in 1974–5 pushed it up as high as 18 per cent (at the height of the inflation!), 47 per cent of total savings, but as confidence in the future gradually recovered (if, indeed, that is the explanation) the rate steadily fell back to 13–14 per cent at the end of the decade and the beginning of the 1980s – around 40 per cent of total savings.

Some of these funds are channelled through state savings and insurance schemes into public investment, or into the private sector via state banks. A high proportion is channelled into private investment through banks rather than the stock market. The resulting financial structure of enterprises, with high debt–equity ratios and distinctive patterns of share ownership, has consequences for enterprise strategies. In a nutshell it reduces shareholder pressure for short-term results and enhances the sense of the corporation as a body corporate – as a nexus of co-operative endeavour of the people who work in it.

These are some of the themes to be pursued in later chapters.

2
Structural change in the Japanese economy

Scope

The subject of this book is change and adjustment in the 'structure' of the Japanese economy. The word 'structure' can be made to mean almost anything, so it will be as well for the purpose of this chapter, to make clear what sort of 'structural changes' are intended. They are:

Changes in the composition of output as between major activities.
Changes in the composition of output within manufacturing.
Changes in the role of foreign trade in the economy, the composition of exports and imports.
Changes in the composition of the labour force and the distribution of employment between activities.
Changes in the organizational and control structures of business enterprises.
Changes in the distribution of income.
Changes in the mechanisms and co-efficients of savings, investments, technological innovation, demand creation, etc., which determine underlying growth rates.

Some of these changes are 'emergent', the cumulative, macroeconomic consequences of multiple individual decisions, as when older women increasingly decide to seek work, or wage settlements show a persistent, but possibly unperceived, pattern of differentials. The consequent structural change is willed as such by no one. It is rather the result of the working out of demographic changes, changes in values, living standards, ideals of equality, etc.

Those changes in behaviour might be called 'adjusting behaviour', but, to be pedantic for a moment about the term 'adjustment', I shall try to reserve the term 'structural adjustment' only for cases where some identifiable persons – in government or business organizations or trade unions – do see some

change in structure as desirable and seek to stimulate the economic behaviour which will produce it. Metaphorical talk of 'the
economy' adjusting to, say, a change in the terms of trade can
sometimes be useful shorthand, but can sometimes, also, mis-
leadingly suggest invisible hands and mysterious homeostatic
functions and thereby obscure the actual adjusting microbeha-
viour, or the macro-level interventions, which are at work.

Primary, secondary, tertiary

Table 2.1 gives EPA's figures for GNP by economic activity. (Where
possible all tables will show the beginning of the decade; 1973,
the last year of high growth; 1975, the bottom of the recession,
and the latest available year.)

Table 2.1 GNP by economic activity (Y1,000bn at calendar 1975 prices/
percentage of GNP)

	1970		1973		1975		1980	
Agriculture and fisheries	7.2	(6.1)	8.4	(5.7)	8.1	(5.4)	7.4	(3.9)
Mining	0.8	(0.7)	1.0	(0.7)	0.8	(0.5)	1.0	(0.5)
Manufacturing	35.1	(29.8)	47.0	(32.2)	44.3	(30.0)	69.5	(36.8)
Construction	11.0	(9.3)	14.2	(9.7)	14.3	(9.7)	15.3	(8.1)
Utilities	2.4	(2.0)	2.7	(1.9)	3.0	(2.0)	3.7	(2.0)
Commerce	15.9	(13.5)	21.6	(14.8)	21.9	(14.8)	27.4	(14.5)
Finance, insurance	5.0	(4.2)	8.1	(5.5)	8.3	(5.6)	11.0	(5.8)
Real estate	8.6	(7.3)	11.4	(7.8)	12.3	(8.3)	17.1	(9.1)
Transport, communications	7.4	(6.2)	8.7	(5.9)	9.5	(6.4)	11.9	(6.3)
Private services	14.1	(11.9)	16.5	(11.3)	16.3	(11.0)	19.8	(10.5)
Government services	10.5	(8.9)	11.7	(8.0)	13.0	(8.8)	15.6	(8.3)
Non-commercial services to households	1.6	(1.4)	1.9	(1.3)	2.2	(1.4)	3.0	(1.6)
Import duties	1.6	(1.4)	1.6	(1.1)	0.5	(0.3)	0.8	(0.4)
(minus) interest payments	4.4	(3.7)	6.9	(4.7)	7.3	(4.9)	9.4	(5.0)
Errors and omissions	1.0	(0.8)	−1.9	(−1.3)	0.6	(0.4)	−5.3	(−0.3)
	117.8	(100.0)	145.9	(100.0)	147.8	(100.0)	188.8	(100.0)

Source: KY, 1982, pp. 70–1

Corresponding figures for employment are:

Table 2.2   Employment by industrial branch (million persons/percentage of employed)

	1970		1973		1975		1980	
Agriculture and fisheries	8.86	(17.4)	7.05	(13.4)	6.61	(12.7)	5.70	(10.3)
Mining	0.20	(0.4)	0.13	(0.2)	0.16	(0.3)	0.10	(10.2)
Construction	3.94	(7.7)	4.67	(8.9)	4.79	(9.2)	5.48	(9.9)
Manufacturing	13.77	(27.1)	14.43	(27.5)	13.46	(25.8)	13.71	(24.7)
Commerce	10.06	(19.8)			11.23	(21.5)	12.51	(22.6)
Finance, insurance	1.11	(2.2)	12.42	(23.7)	1.36	(2.6)	1.58	(2.9)
Real estate	0.27	(0.5)			0.37	(0.7)	0.43	(0.8)
Transport, communications, utilities	3.53	(6.9)	3.72	(7.1)	3.63	(7.0)	3.83	(6.9)
Services	7.51	(14.8)	8.26	(15.7)	8.55	(16.4)	10.08	(18.2)
Government	1.61	(3.2)	1.80	(3.4)	1.96	(3.8)	1.98	(3.6)
	50.86	(100.0)	52.48	(100.0)	52.12	(100.0)	55.41	(100.0)

Source: KY 1982, p. 196 and RH 1981, Fuzoku 17 and 20

Japan is still experiencing the long-term shift in the balance of the industrial structure generally referred to as 'industrialization'. There are still considerably larger numbers of workers (of older age groups) locked into agricultural, forestry and fish production than are necessary to secure current levels of output with currently available capital and techniques. They do not easily transfer to other sectors, but on the other hand they are not replaced as they die or retire. Employment in these sectors, consequently, steadily declines. Agricultural output remained more or less constant through the decade which meant a declining share of that sector in total output, but still, since the share in employment was declining even more rapidly, a greater-than-average increase in productivity.

In spite of that increase, productivity remains low. Eleven per cent of the labour force produce 4 per cent of the national product. (The 400,000 – 0.8 per cent – employed in real estate 'produce' twice as large a 'contribution' to GNP.) Further transfer of labour from agriculture to other more profitable industries is generally seen as a structural adjustment to be aimed at, but not an objective which can easily be achieved except as the slow result of generation transition.

The problem to which that desired structural change would be

Table 2.3   Changes in percentage share 1970–80

	Output	Employment
Agriculture and fisheries	−2.2	−7.1
Mining	−0.2	−0.2
Construction	−1.2	+2.2
Manufacturing	+7.0	−2.4
Commerce	+1.0	+2.8
Finance and insurance	+1.6	+0.7
Real estate	+1.8	+0.3
Utilities	0.0	0.0
Transport and communications	+0.1	0.0
Services	−1.4	+3.4
Government	−0.6	+0.4

Source: Ap 2.1; 2.2

an adjustment is precisely the large productivity gap which requires, in order to maintain the incomes of conservative-voting farmers at parity with urban incomes, a high level of subsidy and protection. However, the cost of this protection is something the Japanese economy has got used to affording. The problem becomes acute in an international political form only, i.e. in the form of pressure from would-be exporters of agricultural products who see the protection of Japanese markets against imports as discriminatory. That pressure comes hardly at all from developing countries (unlike the case of e.g., the European beet industry), but predominantly from the USA and Australia over citrus fruits and meat. Reductions in the level of protection are contemplated solely in order to reduce the danger of retaliatory protectionist measures discriminating against Japanese exports to the United States.

But, with 'industrialization' still incomplete, the Japanese economy is already moving towards 'post-industrialism'. Manufacturing was still increasing its share of the national product at the end of the decade (after losing ground during the recession), but losing employment at least relatively (25 per cent of the labour force compared with 27 per cent at the beginning of the decade) and, although there has been some absolute increase in recent years when output grew faster than productivity, the total remained half a million below the 1973 peak in 1982. The slack has been taken up by the tertiary industries with two-and-three-quarter million extra workers being absorbed over the decade

Table 2.4   Growth in service employment 1972–8 (1,000 persons)

	Self-employed	Companies, government organizations	Total increase	%
Hotels	2.6	70.3	72.9	(2.4)
Hairdressing	15.0	24.8	39.8	(1.3)
Other personal services	7.3	91.3	98.6	(3.3)
Information services	0.1	48,.0	48.1	(1.6)
Advertising	0.7	10.6	11.3	(0.4)
Legal services	50.4	0.2	50.6	(1.7)
Services to buildings	2.1	102.9	105.0	(3.5)
Other services to establishments	13.2	104.1	117.3	(3.9)
Entertainment services	0.1	–9.5	–9.4	(–0.3)
Medical services	191.6	154.9	346.5	(11.5)
Educational services	–4.1	99.2	95.1	(3.2)
Other public services	0.8	210.9	211.7	(7.0)
Total services	279.8	907.7	1187.5	(39.5)
Wholesale commerce	–27.0	291.6	264.6	(8.8)
Retail commerce	205.7	716.6	922.3	(30.7)
Eating & drinking establishments	372.3	261.9	634.2	(21.1)
Total commerce	551.0	1270.1	1821.1	(60.5)
Total services and commerce	830.8	2177.8	3008.6	(100.0)

Source: RH 1980, Appx 113, 115 based on the Establishment Census

into private and government services – an increase of 3.4 per cent in their share of employment – without, however, any increase in their share in the national product: the reverse, in fact; their share fell by 2 per cent. Commerce, too, absorbed a good deal of additional employment without a comparable increase over the decade in output share – in fact, output share has stagnated since 1973, the period in which the bulk of the increase has taken place. Finance, insurance and real estate are the only branches of the tertiary sector which have increased their share of output faster (considerably faster) than their share of employment which is in any case small.

Unemployment on a scale which has plagued other industrial economies has been avoided in Japan, but at the cost of crowding more people – albeit a large proportion of them women, secondary earners with relatively low income expectations in the first place – into relatively low-income service and commercial occupations. However, as is shown in the previous table (derived from a different source and obviously non-matching, though the different periods used preclude one from knowing how much), if not all of this tertiary expansion is in the famous information industries, etc., neither is it all in the proliferating bars and fast-food shops. Medical and educational and other professional services also claim a respectable share of the employment growth.

The structure of manufacturing production

The decade of the 1970s saw a considerable shift in the inter-industry pattern of production, as is evident at the simplest level from table 2.5.

Table 2.5   Manufacturing and mining production indices (1975 = 100)

	1970	1973	1975	1980	1983
Final consumption goods (total)	94.3	123.4	100.0	148.0	(157.3)
capital equipment	91.0	120.1	100.0	150.7	(160.8)
construction materials	101.3	130.5	100.0	120.6	(108.1)
consumer durables	83.3	109.2	100.0	225.1	(264.5)
consumer perishables	90.2	102.7	100.0	122.8	(134.7)
Production materials (total)	—	120.1	100.0	134.6	(138.6)
mining products	—	112.5	100.0	102.9	(99.0)
steel products	93.8	117.7	100.0	122.8	(109.5)
non-ferrous metals	92.9	127.7	100.0	143.4	(138.4)
chemical products	—	120.6	100.0	127.2	(126.2)
oil and coal products	—	108.1	100.0	90.2	(64.7)
textile products	—	120.6	100.0	107.7	(103.4)
Total	92.5	117.0	100.0	142.4	(149.4)

Source: KY 1981, pp. 116–17; 1984, pp. 100–01. (The 1983 figures are in brackets because they are a hybrid of the old index based on 1975 price weightings and the new index based on 1980 price weightings.)

The general pattern is easily summarized. The strong sectors which most effectively recovered their growth dynamism after the 1975 recession are consumer durables and to a lesser extent capital equipment – both, but especially the former, buoyed up by export demand – and the non-ferrous metals which feed into them. Consumer perishables also show relatively healthy and continuing growth, as did chemicals for the latter part of the 1970s, but it has begun to suffer the general fate of the basic materials industries since. The decline of oil and coal products is a measure of the substitution and energy-conservation policies with which Japanese industry responded to the rise in oil prices. Steel, in the teeth of world over-production, did actually recover 1973 production levels in 1979, but has suffered from the general decline in demand (thinner, stronger and more refined substitutes for large lumps of crude steel) as well as from the competition, in export markets, but also in domestic markets, of developing country producers. Such competition has been a major force determining the relative stagnation of the textile industry, of course, and has had some effect, too, (fertilizer exports) on chemical products.

Looking in more detail at differential growth between industries, Table 2.6 lists some 43 industries representing some 40 per cent of total manufacturing production, chosen because they were the industries for which it was possible to match the categories of the industrial census (the 2- to 4-digit categories listed in the table) with the categories used in MITI's summations of business indicators for manufacturing enterprises (for a purpose to be discussed below.)

Perhaps the most striking thing is that only eight industries actually experienced a decline in real value added (if one uses the *general* wholesale price index as the deflator (1970/79 equals 100/175) a procedure with obvious disadvantages, *vide* the way in which the much larger increase in oil prices inflates the increase in value added for oil refining). Those eight absolutely declining industries were (i) the industries affected by Japan's declining competitiveness in textiles, cotton and wool spinning, textile machinery and chemical fibres; (ii) industries badly hit by energy or naphtha prices – aluminium refining and, again, chemical fibres, and (iii) capital goods industries of former export strength badly hit by world recession – machine tools, ball bearings and above all ship-building. Those that experienced 50 per cent real growth or more (163 per cent nominal) numbered 15. Some owe

Table 2.6   Changes in capital, employment and value added by industry

	Classification and name of industry		Value added per worker 1970 Ym	Percentage increase 1970–9 inc.		
				Fixed capital equip- ment	Value added	Employ- ment
1	(2711)	Oil refining	10.10	+142	+369	+30
2	(264)	Chemical fibres	6.10	+19	−38	−43
3	(3021)	Cement	5.95	+102	+151	−32
4	(3216)	Aluminium refining	5.57	+106	+35	−43
5	(3611)	Automobile	5.46	+94	+151	+13
6	(263)	Resins, organic compounds	5.40	+76	+138	−17
7	(2652)	Detergents	5.36	+150	+186	−9
8	(2697)	Films	4.23	+207	+116	−8
9	(2654)	Paint	3.32	+112	+252	−9
10	(311)	Blast furnace iron-making	3.85	+180	+280	−14
11	(325)	Wires and cables	3.63	+50	+85	−20
12	(261)	Chemical fertilizer	3.58	−6	+101	−37
13	(2811)	Tyres	3.28	+92	+163	0
14	(262)	Soda/inorganic chemicals	3.41	+55	+197	−34
15	(3123)	Ferro-alloys, ferro-nickel	3.36	+88	+98	−43
16	(301)	Glass	3.19	+80	+123	−9
17	(352)	Domestic appliances	2.81	+172	+246	+12
18	(354)	Communications equipment	2.72	+76	+85	−10
19	(3441)	Machine tools	2.68	+19	+62	−35
20	(3494)	Ball bearings	2.65	+78	+67	−19
21	(3641)	Ship-building	2.62	+126	−8	−41
22	(3233)	Aluminium products	2.57	+185	+376	+29
23	(346, 347)	Industrial machinery	2.55	+71	+95	−17
24	(2481)	Office machinery	2.48	+195	+137	−12
25	(25)	Printing	2.27	+131	+215	+9
26	(316)	Castings steel alloys	2.24	+48	+76	−30
27	(24)	Paper pulp	2.22	+127	+136	−12
28	(356)	Electrical metering equipment	2.19	+66	+119	−17
29	(345)	Textile machinery	2.04	+27	+31	−47
30	(351)	Heavy electrical equipment	1.99	+95	+153	−2
31	(3612, 3613)	Automobile bodies, components	1.88	+125	+247	+12
32	(222–2224)	Building materials	1.88	+85	+139	−17
33	(3022, 23, 29)	Cement products	1.80	+169	+273	+7
34	(3752)	Cameras	1.63	+174	+166	+15
35	(2223)	Prefabricated buildings	1.63	+350	+469	+50

Table 2.6 *contd.*

Classification and name of industry			Value added per worker 1970 *Ym*	Percentage increase 1970–9 inc.		
				Fixed capital equipment	Value added	Employment
36	(357)	Electronic components	1.59	+102	+139	−16
37	(377)	Watches	1.53	+189	+230	+13
38	(28–2811)	Rubber products other than tyres	1.50	+107	+170	−14
39	(304–309)	Ceramic products	1.47	+81	+146	+12
40	(3482)	Sewing machines	1.44	+29	+104	−24
41	(2023)	Wool and worsted spinning	1.34	+8	+22	−56
42	(204, 205)	Knitting and other textiles	1.11	+37	+105	−28
43	(2021)	Cotton spinning	1.11	+17	+71	−48

Sources: Tsūsanshō Waga Kuni Kigyō no Keiei-bunseki gyōshu-betsu, 1970, or Kōygō tōkeihyō, 1970 and 1979.

much of that growth to export strength – cameras, watches, automobile parts, tyres, domestic appliances; some are growth industries as a result of the evolution of domestic consumer tastes – printing, aluminium products, paint, prefabricated buildings, and perhaps detergents and rubber products. The remainder, oil refining, inorganic chemicals, iron-making and cement, are probably spuriously represented in this category because their prices have been forced by energy costs well above the average wholesale-price increase.

Using these 43 industry categories the attempt was made to discern some overall pattern in the time trends. Is there any tendency for growth in value added between 1970 and 1979, or growth in fixed capital equipment, to be greater in those industries which, in 1970, had:

A higher ratio of fixed capital equipment per worker.
A higher value added per worker.
A higher return on capital employed (in major firms).
A higher profit margin on sales (ditto).
A lower proportion of value added paid to labour (ditto).
A higher proportion of value added spent on purchasing patents (ditto).

Table 2.7 Distribution of planned investments 1980–81

Industry		Capacity expansion	Rationalization & labour-saving	Research development	Repair replacement	Anti-pollution	Energy saving	Other
				Purpose of investment				
Printing and publishing	*	76.6	15.8	1.6	1.9	1.8	0.0	2.2
Beer and wines		62.4	13.2	1.0	8.9	2.9	1.6	10.0
Milling	**	55.8	15.7	4.4	16.3	2.7	0.4	4.6
Aircraft	**	50.3	5.9	10.8	7.4	1.7	0.3	23.5
Rubber products	*	47.6	24.2	9.2	8.4	1.8	3.2	5.6
Precision instruments	**	46.2	23.2	13.0	11.8	8.5	8.2	16.1
Plastics, soap, paint	**	43.7	19.8	9.0	11.4	4.0	1.9	10.2
Pharmaceuticals	*	42.6	7.8	27.9	13.3	1.3	0.8	6.5
Non-ferrous metals		41.9	17.6	5.1	12.6	4.5	5.1	13.2
Glass	*	40.7	12.3	3.6	16.2	3.9	8.5	14.7
Electrical machinery	**	39.9	28.2	17.6	4.9	0.7	0.5	8.2
Inorganic chemicals		39.7	10.7	4.0	13.9	5.0	8.0	8.9
Oil refining, oil products		39.5	10.3	1.1	14.1	14.6	7.8	12.6

Foods not elsewhere specified *	39.3	14.7	5.5	22.9	6.1	1.6	9.8
Organic chemicals	37.3	18.6	8.3	13.9	5.0	8.0	8.9
Livestock products **	35.8	17.9	6.6	16.5	4.4	2.8	16.0
Edible oils	34.5	19.5	4.3	22.5	4.1	8.7	6.4
General machinery	25.8	33.2	11.2	13.1	2.0	1.0	13.7
Automobiles *	23.2	22.0	11.5	5.6	4.1	1.0	32.6
Wood products	22.5	34.5	5.3	23.7	4.4	5.0	4.7
Paper and pulp	19.0	32.7	1.1	24.0	5.5	6.5	11.3
Ship-building	18.1	34.0	4.0	33.9	2.4	0.8	7.0
Railway equipment	18.1	43.9	1.6	23.9	3.5	1.7	7.2
Sugar refining *	17.0	22.7	3.7	15.6	9.0	2.3	29.6
Cement **	16.0	14.6	2.6	11.7	8.7	33.5	12.9
Textiles	15.8	37.4	7.0	23.7	2.8	6.7	6.6
Steel	13.0	31.7	4.3	22.0	5.3	15.4	8.4
Fertilizers	6.5	26.7	7.7	33.0	3.5	17.1	5.5

* 19–25 per-cent increase
** 25–43 per-cent increase
Source: Nihon Kaihatsu Ginhō (Japan Development Bank), *Chōsa* No. 47 (Bessatsu) September 1981.

A higher proportion of value added spent on depreciation
(ditto).
A higher proportion of profits retained with the firm (ditto).
A higher (or lower) debt-equity ratio (ditto)?

The answer is that any systematic tendencies discernible are
faint. There *is* a slight tendency ($r = 0.3$) for capital investment to
increase more in the industries already least labour intensive, and
also in the industries where there is a higher return on capital
employed ($r = 0.5$). The increase in value-added has a small
correlation with gross value added per worker in 1970, but this
may well be the spurious effect of the fact that the high value-
added-per-worker process industries had the biggest increases in
nominal value-added due to energy-price increases. If these
industries are excluded the correlation disappears.

Investment levels at the end of the decade were lower than at
the beginning. The 1970 Manufacturing Establishment Survey
showed the year's total investment in buildings and equipment
to be equal to 31 per cent of the capital stock (again of buildings
and equipment) at the beginning of the year. In 1979 that figure
was down to 18 per cent. The above-average sectors are starred in
table 2.7: two stars for the seven most heavily investing industries
ranging from aircraft with a 43 per cent increase in capital (from a
tiny base, however) to electrical machinery with a 25 per cent
increase, and one star for the seven whose capital stock grew by
19–25 per cent.

High levels of investment can, however, be a function of a
variety of considerations: intensified competition in declining
markets, de-manning investment to reduce costs, rapid obsolesc-
ence of equipment through technological change, investment to
adjust to changes in cost structures (especially changing weight
of energy costs, but also of labour costs) as well as competition for
expanding shares in expanding markets. Certainly, as the rest of
table 2.7 shows (it is based on a sample of 2,800 leading firms),
there is no correlation between the total volume of investment (as
a proportion of capital stock) as indicated by the stars, and the
proportion of that investment primarily devoted to capacity
expansion which is reflected by the rank order of industries in
that table.

Clearly the categories of the table must be to some extent
overlapping – some investment for the repair and refurbishing of
existing capacity may well have had some labour-saving implica-

tions; some energy-saving investment may have replaced equipment which would soon have had to be replaced anyway, etc. And without an indication of the relative volumes of investment which are difficult to measure meaningfully given the problems of the sample which forms the data base for this table, the figures are difficult to interpret with any sensitivity. Nevertheless, the difference between the industries at the top of the table which are facing expanding markets, and those facing shrinking or declining markets and tougher price competition at the bottom, is clear. The former put a large proportion of their investment into the expansion of capacity and rather less into repair and replacement; the latter vice versa. But, even that latter group of industries, declining or, in the Japanese phrase 'structurally depressed' though they might be, are still 'progressive' industries in the sense that they are putting a fair proportion of their investment into rationalizing – labour-saving and cost-cutting – as well as into replacement investment, and some of those industries, like cement, are still among the heaviest investors.

The changes in the structure of manufacturing production revealed in the tables given above are only partly the result of deliberate structural adjustment – as we shall see in the next chapter. They are only in part, that is to say, a consequence of the fact that there was a consensus prevailing in Japan from the early 1970s to the effect that Japan *ought* to expand production in the 'knowledge-intensive' industries and reduce the importance of energy-intensive, pollution-prone, labour-intensive industries, and of the fact that certain policies to encourage the growth of the former and encourage exit from the latter industries were adopted. But they are also in part a consequence of the fact that the consensus *also* formed business firms' expectations of where future profits were likely to lie, and those expectations, confirmed by initial experience, had a powerful effect in directing investment behaviour.

A precondition for both of these mechanisms having a marked effect on the industrial structure was the high rate of investment. With business firms' fixed capital investment running at 15–17 per cent of GDP, an industrial structure can change fast.

That the policies deriving from the consensus were successful – or at least that the consensus 'ought' has been translated, partly through policy, into 'is' may be granted. Such success is certainly claimed for the economy in a recent MITI document which compares the growth rates of those industries singled out in the early

Table 2.8 Annual growth rates 1970–78 quantities and/or values

	Growth rate p.a.		Whether faster before or after 1975
	Quantities	Value	
All manufacturing (quantities: value-added weights)	3.7		After
" (value)		11.5	Before
R & D intensive industries			
fine chemicals (value)		13.4	After
computers and related equipment (value)		14.4	After
nuclear power equipment (value)		35.0	Before
semi-conductor, I.C. (quantity)	31.8		After
" " (value)		23.1	After
aircraft (value)		9.9	Before
industrial robots (value)		22.4	After
Sophisticated assembly industries			
plant engineering (value) (1975–8 only)		13.1	

pollution-control equipment (value)	21.7		Before
electrostatic reproducers (quantity)		15.4	After
" " (value)		28.8	Equal
desk calculators (quantity)	52.8		Before
" (value)		4.2	Before
NC machine tools (quantity)	22.5		After
" " (value)		20.4	After
prefabricated housing	1.3		Before
Fashion-type industries			
Apparel industry (value added) (1970–75 only)		16.5	After
stereo sets, etc. (value)		13.3	Before
electronic organs (quantity)	9.7		Before
" (value)		19.6	Before
Knowledge-intensive industries			
Information-processing/software (value)		35.3	Before

Source: MITI, 1980a, p. 341.

1970s forecasting documents as the ones which ought to expand, with the average. The categories used in table 2.8 are MITI's own.

Some of these industries behave 'conventionally' in the sense that demand increases at a period of high growth and falls during low growth – electronic organs, for example, where growth before 1975 was greater than afterwards. Others are at an advanced stage of the product cycle with a slowing rate of growth of demand – like desk calculators where the astonishing rate of cost and price reduction is reflected in the discrepancy between the 53 per cent increase in the quantity sold and the 4 per cent increase in value. One industry, at least, faces an inelastic demand – pollution equipment for which a once-for-all change in standards led to a once-for-all rush to equip – largely before 1975. But there remain others – semi-conductors, computer numerically controlled machine tools, computers, fine chemicals, industrial robots – which are at an early stage in the product cycle with an accelerating rate of growth, where the growth rate has been greater after 1975 than before. These are the frontier industries where the capacity to innovate and to absorb innovations rapidly is a prime determinant of international competitive strength, and where Japan's possession of precisely that capacity has enabled exports as well as domestic demand to contribute substantially to rapid growth at a time when the overall growth rate had fallen to a lower level. Note that the aircraft industry does not come into this category. It is an industry held, as it were, in reserve. Japanese manufacturers are modestly extending their capacity in this field, but not yet making a big push – as they are in the whole range of electronics – to challenge the world leaders.

Trade patterns

The composition of Japan's foreign trade shows a quite rapid evolution corresponding to (and as just mentioned, often as a precondition for) the evolution of the structure of production. Tables 2.9 and 2.10 give the figures for major categories.

The very strong growth in total exports, more than a doubling during the decade and a nearly 60 per cent increase in the six years following the oil crisis, has matched – and was encouraged (if only by exhortation) in order to match – the serious rise in import bills after 1973 in a country whose dependence on imported oil (82 per cent of all primary energy in 1978) was greater than that of any other industrial nation. One telling statistic may

Table 2.9   Exports and imports – volume indices 1965–82 – principal items

	1965	1970	1973	1975	1982	Growth 1975–82 (%)
EXPORTS						
Total exports	100	202	273	323	541	67.5
foodstuffs	100	139	116	93	105	13.6
yarn	100	268	284	292	290	–0.6
cloth	100	128	119	155	171	10.4
garments	100	121	69	52	52	0.1
chemical products	100	280	364	383	420	9.4
non-ferrous metal products	100	114	107	111	192	71.2
metal products	100	184	205	215	328	52.3
machinery	100	263	423	529	1070	102.0
IMPORTS						
Total imports	100	222	320	268	353	22.5
textile raw materials	100	126	148	103	113	9.4
metal ores	100	244	324	279	294	5.6
oil seeds	100	171	192	171	231	35.1
timber	100	255	308	231	222	–4.0
Total materials (excl. fuel, food)	100	107	244	198	221	11.1
Food	100	162	244	217	306	41.5
Fossil fuels	100	243	313	296	285	–3.6
chemical products	100	239	429	267	716	168.6
machinery	100	342	463	495	699	41.6
metal or metal products	100	216	305	190	405	113.2
Total manufactures	100	269	461	372	687	85.1

Source: KY 1981, 1982, pp. 276–7, 1984, pp. 260–61.

be taken as a measure of the intensity of the export drive. Japan had to double her exports in real terms between 1973 and 1982 in order – because of the relative price changes – to import 7 per cent more in real terms. Price shifts cost 8 per cent of 1975 GNP (see table 2.19b on page 57).

As for the pattern of growth there has been a steady trend towards a heavier proportion of high-value-added products. The highest growth rates of exports are in machinery and non-ferrous metal products. The growth of car exports from 1.1m units to 4.7m units between 1970 and 1979 is an example: so is the eight-fold increase in exports of scientific and optical machinery

($0.5bn – $3.9bn) over the same period. At the same time there remains continuing strength in the 'heavy and chemical industries', the growth of which was the dominant feature of the 1960s. Steel exports reached 34m tons in 1977, nearly double the 17.5m of 1970, and were still not much below 30m tons five years later in spite of the world recession – the growth of the Chinese market which took 40 per cent of exports being one major factor.

Ships declined with the world recession, but with only a modest loss of market share. Others of the leading export growth items of the 1960s – radio receivers (38m sets in 1970, 37m in 1979) and synthetic-fibre fabrics (1.3bn m² in 1970, 1.6bn in 1979) were marking time (by dint of quality improvements). Of the items in which the NICs are most directly competing with Japan in third markets, as well as at home, garments is the only one of those separately listed in that table, exports of which have fallen below the 1965 level; the other textile categories are declining more slowly for reasons which will be discussed in chapter 4.

The *volume* indices for imports show that, while raw material imports have increased to feed the growing volume of industrial production, a much greater growth of imports has occurred in machinery and chemical products. Manufactured imports as a whole have increased at nearly double the rate of total imports. That price changes reverse these weightings when values, not volumes, are considered is clear from table 2.10. Raw materials made up 61 per cent of the value of imports in 1979, compared with 56 per cent in 1970, though one additional element in this is the increasing tendency to import semi-processed rather than unprocessed raw materials – zinc or nickel or lead ingots rather

Table 2.10   Exports and imports: major categories by value 1970–82

	Exports		Imports	
	1970	1982	1970	1982
Food	3.4	1.0	13.6	11.0
Raw materials	1.0	0.7	56.0	64.1
Light industry products	22.4	12.1	5.5	6.6
Heavy and chemical industry products	72.4	85.1	24.3	16.3
Other	0.8	1.1	0.5	2.0
	100.0	100.0	100.0	100.0

Source: KY 1982: pp. 262–3; 1984, pp. 246–7.

than ore, etc. Non-ferrous ore imports increased in value by 2.7 times between 1970 and 1979; imports of metals by 3.6 times. This is partly a response to rising energy costs and rising perception of pollution costs – with some Japanese firms relocating their smelting and refining facilities abroad – partly a response to the fact that Third World producers have installed their own downstream processing facilities and insist on selling semi-processed rather than raw materials. The involvement of policy in this process of adjustment will be considered apropos of the aluminium industry in a later chapter.

The growth of manufactured imports since 1965 is a somewhat complex story. In the initial period there was a continuing surge in the import of sophisticated equipment which could not be made in Japan, or not made to the same quality in Japan. That category has diminished with Japan's increasing industrial capability – though aircraft remain an obvious example of a broad category where Japan is non-competitive and there is an increasingly complex pattern of intra-industry specialization in trade with industrial country producers of capital equipment or of consumer durables. Table 2.11 shows the changing pattern of trade specialization between Japan and West Germany in a number of items between 1970 and 1980.

Table 2.11   Machinery trade with West Germany 1970–78 ($m)

	Japanese exports to W. Germany (X)		Japanese imports from W. Germany (M)		$\dfrac{X-M}{X+M}$	
	1970	1978	1970	1978	1970	1978
Machinery total	267.0	2716.5	333.9	1001.9	−11.1	46.1
General machinery	93.8	405.6	238.0	435.0	−43.4	−3.5
Electrical machinery	105.9	1143.2	33.4	153.8	52.1	83.2
Transport machinery	20.9	642.9	41.8	295.4	−33.3	37.0
Precision machinery	46.4	524.8	20.7	117.7	38.3	62.7
Domestic appliances	10.8	21.4	8.5	14.8	11.9	18.2
refrigerators	0.2	0.4	0.4	0.9	−36.8	−41.0
vacuum cleaners	1.2	1.4	0.0	0.0	100.0	100.0
electric razors	0.2	1.7	4.7	9.7	−91.4	−70.7
electric space-heaters	0.0	0.0	0.5	1.8	−100.0	−100.0
micro-ovens	5.3	16.2	0.0	0.0	100.0	100.0

Source: MITI, 1980a, pp. 233–4.

A second strand in the growth of manufactured imports is the increasing consumption of luxury consumer items; fashion goods, fancy foods and drink, etc. The third is the increased substitution of domestic production by imports of light-industry products (garments were already cited) from Third World countries with a lower standard of living and lower wage costs than Japan. In table 2.10 this third trend is made manifest in the shift in the proportion of manufactured imports – an increase in 'light-industry' products and a decline of 'heavy- and chemical-industry products'.

Korea stands out among the other NICs as a source of such imported manufactures. According to a recent study, intra-industry specialization (taking a fairly narrow definition of what constitutes an industry, i.e., at the 3-digit level in the Standard International Trade classification) was almost absent as between Japan and Korea in 1964; 62 categories were exclusively imports from Japan, 11 exclusively exports from Korea to Japan, and for only 12 was there any kind of two-way trade. By 1977, there were no fewer than 96 3-digit categories of two-way trade; in 21 of them exports were at least half imports or vice versa (source as for table 2.12). Nevertheless, the pattern of trade still remains sharply dissimilar. Capital goods and intermediates (SITC 5–7) make up 88 per cent of Japan's exports to Korea and only 34 per cent of the trade the other way. The classification in table 2.12 from a recent Japanese study differentiates manufactures into five categories and shows a striking contrast which remains in spite of the

Table 2.12   Korean–Japanese trade by labour/capital intensivity 1964, 1977

Category of manufacture	Exports Japan to Korea		Exports Korea to Japan	
	1964	1977	1964	1977
Labour-intensive materials	10.8	6.1	0.0	11.2
Labour-intensive finished goods	5.7	13.3	63.8	59.1
Capital-intensive materials	23.0	27.4	0.0	0.0
Capital-intensive finished goods	30.6	9.0	22.6	11.3
Technology-intensive high value-added goods	29.9	44.2	13.6	17.5
	100.0	100.0	100.0	100.0

Source: NIRA, 1979, p. 12.

change between 1964 and 1977. But these imbalances are over-shadowed by the overall imbalance in trade. Japan's exports to Korea were three times imports from Korea in 1970, a little less than double – with a far larger volume each way – by 1979. The gap in visible trade was nearly $3bn. per annum. Thereafter the Koreans became more resistant to Japanese exports while imports from Korea remained fairly stable, thus reducing the gap to half that figure by 1982. But there was little amelioration of the imbalance with the other Asian NICS – a $4bn. export surplus with Hong Kong in 1982, $2bn. with Taiwan, $2.5bn with Singapore. The four Asian NICS together, with some $26bn. of trade with Japan in 1982, bore as large a share of the deficit in trade with Japan as Europe with some $32bn. worth of trade. (The area which has a surplus in trade with Japan, of course – $20bn. in 1982 – is the Middle East, but the export momentum of the early 1980s was rapidly building up an overall Japanese trade surplus expected to reach $40bn. in 1984.)

Altogether, the extent to which structural change in the Japanese economy has helped to create space for the expansion of the NICS – or to put it another way, the extent to which Japanese consumers have profited from the opportunity to import cheap manufactures from the NICS – is strictly limited.

There has, as already noted, been increasing import of semi-processed rather than raw materials, and there has been some cession of export markets, especially in the USA in textiles and clothing, ceramics, flatware and consumer electronics to the Asian NICS. But imports of such products into the Japanese home market itself have been extremely limited. At the same time, Japanese exporters have been quick to take advantage of the rapid expansion in the NIC demand for capital goods. As a consequence, in 1979 Japan supplied 65 per cent of Korea's manufactured imports but took only 19 per cent of her exports compared with 36 per cent of Korea's exports taken by the USA. For the other East Asian NICS, the figures were 31 per cent, 12 per cent and 31 per cent, respectively. The overall picture of trade in manufactures between Japan and the NICS (divided into Brazil and Mexico and the four Asian countries) is shown in table 2.13.

One econometric study, using input–output tables to calculate the impact of trade with South Korea on Japanese manufacturing in general and on small and medium firms in particular, concludes that for all the four years between 1965 and 1980 selected for study, and in spite of Korean specialization in more labour-intensive

Table 2.13 Trade in manufactures between Japan and selected markets ($bn.)

| | Brazil and Mexico | | Korea, Taiwan, Hong Kong, Singapore | |
	M from Japan	X to Japan	M from Japan	X to Japan
1970	0.3	—	2.3	0.2
1973	0.8	0.1	4.8	1.5
1975	1.2	0.1	6.2	1.4
1979	1.9	0.2	13.7	3.1

Source: EPA, 1981, p. 528.

goods production, exports to Korea gave rise to more production and more employment in Japan, than imports from Korea could have displaced (on the assumption that domestic substitution for these imports *was* possible). The margin is considerable, being calculated to be a gain in employment, in enterprises with fewer than 300 workers alone, of between 15,000 and 30,000 jobs depending on the year. (Suzuki 1984).

Enterprise structures

Japan's 'dual structure' is well known, if less commonly re-marked upon in Japan now than it was in the 1960s. Until the mid-1970s, the general view of the evolution of that structure saw two tendencies. One was for a narrowing of the differentials in productivity, earnings and job security between the large enter-prises and the smaller ones. The other was for the large-scale sector steadily to expand in both employment and output at the expense of the small-scale.

The first trend has not necessarily been reversed, though perhaps the range of differentiation in productivity and levels of capitalization etc., within the small-scale sector has grown. But the second trend has been very clearly reversed. Since 1973 the growth of productivity in the large-scale sector has been accom-panied by declining employment. Table 2.14 is drawn from the Establishment Census.

A different survey (the industrial census – also establishment-based) gives the following comparisons of employment, output and productivity (table 2.15) which show that the larger firms, while losing in share of employment, are nevertheless gaining a further productivity edge over the smaller firms. The value-added per worker in establishments with fewer than 10 workers

Table 2.14   Changes in employment by the size of establishment, manufacturing 1972–8

Size of Establishment	Employment/(thousands)						Change	
	1972		1978		1981		1972–8 %	1978–81 %
1–4	965	(7.3)	1,036	(8.2)	1,090	(8.5)	+7.4	+5.2
5–9	1,138	(8.6)	1,246	(10.0)	1,296	(10.1)	+9.5	+4.0
10–29	2,308	(17.4)	2,414	(19.3)	2,506	(19.5)	+4.6	+3.8
30–49	1,160	(8.7)	1,172	(9.4)	2,718	(21.1)	+1.0	+3.9
50–99	1,508	(11.3)	1,442	(11.5)			−4.4	
100–299	2,130	(16.0)	1,887	(15.1)	5,253	(40.8)	−11.4	+1.0
300–	4,089	(30.7)	3,314	(26.5)			−19.0	
	13,298	(100.0)	12,509	(100.0)	12,863	(100.0)		

Source: RH, 1981, Appx. p. 18 and KY p. 152, the triennial Establishment Census

was 30.5 per cent of that for workers in establishments with more than 300 – compared with 33.8 per cent in 1972. Wage differentials, however, have changed less: 37.8 to 37.4 per cent. (Only in the 20–99 workers range was there a noticeable loss – from 68 per cent of the big firm figure to 63 per cent.)

These averages conceal considerable differences, however. The smallest size category includes, on the one hand, low-technology family workshops in the textile and garment trades; on the other, highly specialized venture businesses or highly skilled independent jig and toolmakers. Clearly, however, the former predominate. Small business is concentrated in the

Table 2.15   Changing shares in employment, output and value-added by size of establishment: 1972–9

Size	Employment A		Output B		Value added C		C/A	
	1972	1979	1972	1979	1972	1979	1972	1979
1–9	17.4	19.9	6.6	7.0	8.9	9.9	0.51	0.50
10–19	11.2	10.6	7.0	6.5	8.0	7.6	0.71	0.71
20–99	25.0	15.3	20.5	22.6	20.3	22.7	0.81	0.82
100–299	15.9	15.3	17.1	17.1	16.6	16.6	1.04	1.08
300–999	14.5	13.1	21.3	22.0	20.0	19.6	1.38	1.50
1000–	16.0	13.3	27.5	24.8	26.1	23.5	1.63	1.77

Source: MITI, 1981, Tables pp. 7–9.

low-productivity areas. It is the large firms, not surprisingly, which are dominant in exports. Table 2.16 shows the proportion of value-added produced by firms with fewer than 300 employees by manufacturing branch, together with an analysis of the structure of final demand derived from the 1978 input–output table. It will be seen that the small firms play an above average role in those sectors where exports are of below average importance.

One further aspect of enterprise structure is the degree of oligopoly. Here the picture seems to be one of remarkable stability. Uekusa's calculations of overall concentration ratios (share of top three and top ten firms) for 163 industries showed no very great increase between 1965 and 1974, and more partial calculations for individual industries show no significant movement since then (Uekusa, 1982, pp. 29, 196). As for Japan's mysterious *zaibatsu* – the loose groupings of firms deriving from the pre-war conglomerates – the situation hardly changed, at least between 1975 and 1979. The 22 major Mitsui firms had 17.9 per cent of their shares held internally by other firms of the group in 1979 and took 20.6 per cent of their loan finance from the group bank. In 1975 the figures had been 17.5 and 21.2 per cent respectively (Uekusa, p. 268). Much the same story applies to the other similar groups. There is no reason to suppose, either, that there has been any change in the profitability of the conglomerate firms which Caves and Uekusa showed to be lower than for comparable firms, most notably when profits on equity were measured, but even, if to a lesser degree, when the measure was profits plus interest against capital employed. (Caves and Uekusa, 1976, p. 506.)

Possibly of greater and expanding significance in the economy are the agglomerations of satellite firms clustered around major manufacturers such as Hitachi, Toyota, Matsushita, etc. These are much less well measured, however, and the significance of the growth of such groups for the economy more a matter for speculation.

Overseas relocation

The total overseas investment of Japanese firms reached $36bn. by the end of 1980 compared with $2–3 bn. at the beginning of the decade – a much smaller share in relation to GNP than the USA or UK, but now beginning to push ahead of West Germany. This represents, however, only about 1½ per cent of the capital stock of Japanese companies and is consequently not a massive structural change.

Table 2.16 Structures of final demand by industry and proportion of value-added from firms with fewer than 300 employees. 1978 input–output table (above average figures in boxes).

	Household consumption	Government capital formation	Private capital formation	Exports	Other	Value added of smaller firms (% of total)
Manufacturing total	38.1	9.0	25.8	22.3	4.8	58.0
Food and tobacco	91.0	0.4	1.1	1.8	5.7	78.7
Textiles	61.4	2.4	7.6	18.6	10.0	92.0
Garments	74.6	2.4	6.6	11.0	5.4	97.5
Timber: wood products	21.6	13.5	54.9	5.8	4.2	94.0
Furniture	26.1	11.7	43.7	5.5	13.0	91.6
Pulp, paper	51.9	6.0	16.9	13.7	11.5	70.8
Printing, publishing	60.4	4.0	10.2	7.5	17.9	65.6
Leather and leather goods	72.8	1.9	5.5	18.8	1.0	90.9
Rubber products	39.1	6.3	16.5	33.2	4.9	43.0
Chemicals	56.5	3.9	10.2	21.5	7.9	41.5
Oil, coal	43.9	10.6	20.0	20.0	5.5	20.4
Ceramics, glass, cement	14.7	28.7	42.9	10.1	3.6	75.3
Steel	12.6	14.7	34.5	38.0	0.2	30.9
Non-ferrous metals	17.8	16.4	30.7	33.6	1.5	40.4
Metal products	21.7	15.3	44.1	14.1	4.8	81.5
General machinery	8.9	9.0	51.4	28.2	2.5	57.3
Electrical machinery	17.1	9.1	40.5	30.2	3.1	35.8
Transport machinery	25.8	10.0	22.4	38.4	3.4	25.0
Precision machinery	30.4	7.3	19.1	40.1	3.1	54.3
Other	45.0	7.7	22.8	16.8	7.7	80.8

Source: RH, 1981, Appx. 104.

Table 2.17 Currently operating overseas ventures in textiles and clothing by starting date and country

	1964 or before	1965–69	1970–74	1975–79	1980–81
Korea	–	2	35	4	1
Taiwan	2	24	15	1	–
Hong Kong	2	3	7	2	–
Singapore	2	3	3	1	–
Thailand	8	7	12	1	–
Malaysia	1	1	4	7	1
Indonesia	–	–	16	10	–
India	1	–	–	–	–
Sri Lanka	1	2	1	2	1
Philippines	1	–	8	2	–

Source: Tōyō-Keizai, 1982, pp. 10–11.

Several happenings of the 1970s have prompted Japanese firms to invest more abroad. They have done so in adjustment to:

1 Anxiety about raw material supplies. Some 20 per cent of the investment is in mining, two-thirds of it in developing countries and the bulk of the rest in Canada and Australia. The Japanese Government has been instrumental in putting together large consortia of firms (for aluminium development projects, for example) with the help of loans from the Overseas Economic Co-operation Fund.
2 Rising energy and pollution costs have made the location of smelting and refining facilities in developing countries more attractive.
3 The threat or actuality of restrictions on Japanese exports has provided the stimulus for local production within markets first penetrated by exports. The third of the manufacturing invest-ment (itself one-third of total investment) which is located in industrial countries is largely of this kind, particularly that of recent vintage, while much of the earlier investment in develop-ing countries was a response, similarly, to those countries' im-port substitution industrialization policies.
4 A lesser part of this manufacturing investment, however, is also the result of an attempt to capture the advantages of cheaper labour in developing countries. This was a strong motive for overseas investment (especially in textiles and consumer electro-nics) in Korea and Taiwan in the late 1960s and early 1970s. Now

that the wage-cost advantage has diminished in those countries, however, the volume of such investment has declined. None of the other Asian countries where wages are still low is thought to have the necessary cultural or political preconditions for success-ful investment which the other post-Confucian countries (or those like Malaysia and Thailand with post-Confucian enclaves) had. The figures of table 2.17 show the declining number of overseas ventures in the textile industry and the following table 2.18 shows the declared intentions of the investors concerning the current purpose of their operation, by region. (The figures relate to 6,865 firms. It is not clear how full a coverage this is of the firms still currently operating overseas out of the nearly 24,000 investments authorized by the Japanese Government up to 1981.) The proportions which say that they are producing directly for exports to Japan correlate with the proportions concerned with exploiting minerals, suggesting that the number of overseas manufacturing ventures designed to produce for the Japanese market is small. They would in any case be confined to Asia where, as will be seen, only 17 per cent of all firms said that they were primarily producing for the Japanese market.

Growth investment and consumption

Table 2.19a reflects the gearing-down of the Japanese economy from growth rates averaging 10 per cent to growth rates averag-ing 5 per cent. Consumption has increased, investment dimi-nished, the shift being in both respects greater in the private than in the public sector, the crucial parameter for growth rates being the investment of private sector enterprises which went from 18 to 15 per cent of GNP. The 1975 recession and the low levels of profitability attained in the mid-1970s have been partly responsi-ble for this shift, though it is noteworthy that private industry's investment never fell below 14.1 per cent (the 1977 figure: the peak having been 20.9 per cent in 1970) and was still 16.0 per cent in 1975 at the depth of the recession.

Conclusion

Various kinds of structural change have been charted in this chapter – in the structure of output and employment by industry, in the structure of trade, in various aspects of industrial organization, and in major macroeconomic parameters. Various

Table 2.18 Main purpose of investment and main market for overseas ventures, by region

	Asia	Middle East	Central South America	Africa	North America	Oceania	Europe
Main purpose of investment							
To secure materials supplies	5.5	6.1	10.8	19.8	8.7	27.0	1.6
Cheaper labour cost advantage	27.1	8.2	10.2	17.3	1.7	1.8	1.6
Taking advantage of local protectionist policies	15.7	15.3	16.6	17.9	1.5	5.6	3.4
To sell in local or third markets	36.7	40.8	39.4	27.8	53.8	40.2	64.9
Information gathering	7.3	15.3	9.3	3.7	25.9	12.3	23.0
Other	7.7	14.2	13.6	13.5	8.5	13.2	6.6
	100.0	100.0	100.0	100.0	100.0	100.0	100.0
Main market							
Japan	16.6	5.1	12.8	28.6	16.1	26.2	10.8
Country of manufacture	57.9	79.5	67.0	63.3	75.7	61.7	59.4
Third countries	25.5	15.4	20.2	8.2	8.4	12.0	29.8

Source: Tōyō-Keizai, 1982.

Table 2.19a   Composition of gross national expenditure, current prices 1971–82

		1971–3 average		1981–2 average
Household consumption		53.3		57.9
Non-commercial non-governmental services to households		0.5		0.4
Government final consumption		8.2		10.2
Fixed Capital investment		35.1		30.2
of private firms	18.4		15.2	
private housing	7.3		5.8	
public enterprise	3.5		2.9	
public housing	0.5		0.3	
other government	5.4		6.0	
Changes in stocks		1.6		0.4
Exports		11.5		16.7
Imports		–10.2		–15.9
		100.0		100.0

Source: KY, 1982, pp. 62–5; 1984, pp. 46–9.

Table 2.19b   Composition of gross national expenditure, 1971–82, revalued at 1975 prices

		1971–3 average		1981–2 average
Household consumption		55.3 (100)		51.9 (139)
Non-commercial non-governmental services to households		0.5 (100)		0.5 (118)
Government final consumption		9.4 (100)		9.5 (150)
Fixed capital investment		35.3 (100)		31.7 (133)
of private firms	18.0 (100)		17.2 (142)	
private housing	7.5 (100)		5.3 (105)	
public enterprise	3.7 (100)		3.1 (122)	
public housing	0.5 (100)		0.3 (90)	
other government	5.6 (100)		5.7 (151)	
Changes in stocks		1.6 (100)		0.6 (53)
Exports		11.2 (100)		19.9 (263)
Imports		–13.5 (100)		–13.9 (133)
		100.0 (100)		100.0 (148)

Source: KY, 1982, pp. 62–5, 1984, pp. 46–9.

proximate causes for these individual changes have been noted in the course of that descriptive exposition. In the following chapter we shall look at some of the mechanisms which facilitated those changes – both those facilitating the micro-adjustment behaviour of individual economic factors which cumulate to create structural change, and those which represent conscious structural adjustment.

II The agents of adjustment

3
The enterprise

The last chapter has measured *what* happened. Now we consider why – how these changes came about as a result of changed behaviour by Japanese firms, Japanese workers or unions or the Japanese government; what those changes were in response to, and how far they were conditioned by the special character of Japanese values or institutions. Let us begin with the enterprise.

Enterprises

The changes in the composition of manufacturing output have been achieved partly by the relative decline of enterprises in relatively declining industries and the growth of enterprises in the growth industries, partly by diversification of production within enterprises.

Thus of the 50 largest firms (measured by turnover, excluding trading companies) in 1971, 38 were still in the top 50 of 1981. Eight of the 12 newcomers were oil and electricity supply companies put there simply by price changes, two were electronics firms (Sony and Fujitsū), and two were supermarket chains. Of the 12 displaced from the top 50, five were textile firms, most of which had slipped badly below the élite threshold, one ship-building and one shipping firm, the two leading non-ferrous metal electrical firms, one pharmaceutical firm and two makers of agricultural and construction machinery (TKTG, July 1971, August 1981).

It is, in other words, a fluid situation with considerable movement in the fortunes of individual firms. About the pattern of such movement a few generalizations are possible.

The first is that intra-industry diversification is relatively easy: diversifying in a totally different industry, though more frequent of late, is more difficult. Most firms have a tenacious sense of 'belonging' to a particular industry, and the assumption that it is in that industry that the bulk of its activities must lie is usually accepted by its decision-makers. An aluminium-smelting company may shift the weight of its operations to the manufacture of window frames. A Fuji Denki Seizō starts making electrical machinery in 1923, moves into communications equipment and spawns a new firm, Fuji Tsū, in 1935; its battery business grows and Fuji Denki Kagaku is hived off in 1950, later to become a major silicon-chip maker, and then the two oldest firms come together in 1972 to create Fujitsū-Fanuc which comes to dominate the NC machines and robot market. But still the whole family is firmly in the electrical and electronics industry. It does not diversify into food or chemicals.

A major reason is that diversification rarely takes place through acquisition. Companies are not bought and sold with the same ease as they are in other countries. It is partly a matter of the absence of easy mechanisms for acquiring a controlling interest through the stock market, which is itself a function of the low position occupied by the shareholder in the scheme of things (of which more later). But that this is not the only reason is shown by the example of some very few companies which *do* try to grow by acquisition. Japan Miniature Ball-bearings is one such. The fact that this is a slightly maverick firm, run by a strong-minded managing director who is contemptuous of traditional business practices and is seeking to establish a genuine multi-national, giving *full* managerial status to foreign managers in the firm's Singapore and US plants, points up the more important reason for the rarity of take-overs. Japanese firms with their 'lifetime commitment' are quasi-communities which find it hard to assimilate colonies of 'foreigners'. Where, for example, there have been mergers (of firms in the same industry) the welding together of two disparate elements into a single enterprise community, and the development of a new enterprise culture, can take a very long time: in Japan Steel everyone is said to be still aware of who is a Yawata man and who a Fuji man more than a decade after the merger took place. The integral absorption of a firm from a very different line of business whose employees have a very different kind of expertise would be even more troublesome. Nor does the alternative of acquiring a company to be run as a separate subsidiary much appeal to Japanese manufacturing firms. Only the boards of trading companies easily accept the role of financiers in a conglomerate sitting at the centre of a web of activities which they cannot pretend to control except by very broad performance criteria. The boards of manufacturing concerns are specialists. The directors of a Japanese steel company form the top echelon of a steel bureaucracy, men who have worked all their lives in the company and been selected as the best of their generation (generally all at about the same age, in their early fifties) to become its guiding spirits. They are steelmen, whose whole expertise is in steel. They are apt, too, to believe that running a company actually requires substantive expertise in the products and markets with which the company is involved. They are not easily attracted, therefore, to the idea of acquiring a company in another field.

Hence, when diversification takes place, it is usually not through take-over but through the company setting up an internal project team and developing a new activity from within, gradually accumulating expertise within its 'own' workforce. The direction of diversification is most often determined by technological expertise – as when a fibre firm moves into brake linings or polyester VTR tape film. Sometimes a firm follows the logic of its marketing expertise – as with Kanebō's 'quality of elegant living' strategy, moving from textiles through cosmetics to accessories, interior design, etc. Much more rarely is there – by the same strategy of internal development – a real leap, as in the case of one firm from spinning to electronic components (FT, 16 December 1982).

Along whatever path, a large number of Japanese firms in industries with poor long-range market prospects have been taking these new initiatives. Whereas, in 1963, the proportion of the output of a hundred-plus leading firms which was classified (in a two-digit classification) in an industry other than that of their main product was 17 per cent; by 1975, the proportion was 27 per cent (Gotō, 1981) and it is doubtless a good deal higher today. Some of the diversification of textile firms will be described in a later chapter. Ship-building firms over the last ten years have turned their skills in fabricating large steel objects to a variety of fields, especially plant engineering, prefabricated housing, and large-scale environmental modification schemes. An agricultural implements firm, apart from redoubling its efforts to export to Third World markets as the home market declines, has moved to an emphasis on general electric motors and taken up fire pumps. The corporate bureaucracies of firms in these industries have shown a certain degree of enterprise and risk-taking initiative.

Business confidence

What are the factors which have enabled them to do so and, even more important, enabled firms in the industries with growth potential to seize that potential? The first, and arguably the most important, is the prevailing mood of confidence. The performance of the Japanese economy over the last twenty years has bred a general buoyancy and confidence and sense of purpose which is a powerful stimulus to investment. The strength of that prevailing mood owes a lot to the cultural homogeneity of the business-official community – a good deal greater even than in European countries, *a fortiori* than in the USA. That cultural homogeneity and the power of the consensus mean that dominant moods tend to be very dominant which also makes possible slightly manic-depressive swings – as in the near-panic gloom of the reaction to the first oil crisis. But the underlying confidence bred in the previous fifteen years of growth reasserted itself, and in the late 1970s the confidence came to be based on something more than the past experience of growth; it came to rest increasingly on a belief in Japan's technological capacity. Japan began to have more new contracts for the export than for the import of technology in 1973. Her share of US patents registered by foreigners has exceeded that of the European countries since 1979. The mood was well captured by a foremost economics monthly in December 1981 with its lead article entitled 'The Japanese century has begun'. The burden of the argument was that since Prometheus the geographical centre of innovation has tended to move around. Now it was shifting for a while to Japan. The evidence for this view is considerable, if by no means, yet, conclusive. There is little doubt that in the key field of electronics the race is now between Japan and the USA, but whether either will emerge with a clear supremacy must remain in doubt. (Okimoto et al., 1984). Certainly the speed of Japan's emergence as industrial innovator is a good augury of future success, as, also, is its accumulation of scientific manpower. Japan produced 20,000 first-degree electrical and electronic engineering graduates in 1980 compared with the 14,000 of the USA (Okimoto et al., p. 30). All engineering graduates combined numbered 74,000 in Japan with another 43,000 graduates from other natural science fields – whereas the much larger population of the USA produced 53,000 engineers and 180,000 with other science degrees. (Kagaku Gijutsuchō, 1981, p. 15)

Veblen wrote in 1918 of 'Japan's opportunity' – the opportunity for military imperialism presented by the optimal conjunction between the rising curve of industrial power and the declining curve of feudal obedience which individualistic capitalism was eroding. Her present 'technological opportunity' is at the point of intersection between the rising curve of scientific capability and the declining curve of diligence which affluence is only slowly eroding. Japan has some of the best electronics engineers in the world *and* they are prepared to stay at their lab benches into the small hours when they are engaged on an urgent project to put their firm ahead of the competition. The prevailing mood of confidence which is the first factor facilitating bold planning in Japanese firms would seem to rest on sound foundations.

Education

A second factor is the high level of education and literacy, the high level of consumption of written material particularly of a technical kind (textiles are served by at least three newspapers appearing daily or two to three times a week), and the general belief in information-gathering and ratiocination as a way of life. The enrolment figures are impressive; well over 90 per cent of each age group continue full-time education to the age of 18 – the three years beyond the end of compulsory schooling – and nearly 40 per cent proceed to some form of college or university education. It is an intensely competitive merit-based system (the object being to gain admission to a university as high up the prestige hierarchy as possible), but clearly whatever the highly competitive educational system does to the souls of those who pass through it, it stocks and sharpens their minds – and stocks a high proportion of them with scientific, technical, legal and other industrially relevant matter. At the same time, simply as a set of selection filters, the educational system is highly efficient at putting top brains into top companies and ministries – that is to say, putting them in charge of a disproportionately large share of the nation's resources.

Financing

Thirdly, Japan's high rate of household (and family enterprise) savings has already been mentioned – some 12 per cent of GNP in 1970 and again in 1982, having gone as high as 16 per cent in 1974–5. These funds provide a ready supply of new capital to supplement corporate savings, and Japan has banking institutions which have developed considerable expertise in making those savings available for long-term investment.

To describe those institutions is not easy since their informal structure is important as well as their formal structure (See Prindl, 1981, on which much of what follows is based.) It is, to begin with, a highly differentiated structure; in the private sector there are 13 general-purpose city banks, the foreign-exchange-specializing Bank of Tokyo, the three long-term credit banks and seven trust banks, as well as a number of co-operative institutions. The long-term credit banks and trust banks are founded to take long-term deposits and give long-term loans to industry, but that function is not confined to them, nor are they in practice confined to it. In the public sector are the Export-Import Bank and the Japan Development Bank and a number of financing institutions for small business, housing, regional development, etc. And above them all towers the Bank of Japan which has, together with the Ministry of Finance, developed a credit policy designed to promote industrial investment.

The key to the system is the network of mutual confidence which enables the banks to be in a more or less permanent state of 'over loan' and consequently dependent on 'over borrowing' from the Bank of Japan. Reserve ratios are set low and their adjustment is not used as a macroeconomic regulator. The adjustment of the Bank of Japan's interest rate is a potent instrument however, for its direct effect on the over-borrowed city banks' prime rate, but not one which much affects the *demand* for credit which is relatively inelastic: corporations dependent on bank loans (see below) cannot hold off borrowing, and can, because of their dependence on the banks, be dissuaded from doing anything so unfriendly as to pay back loans when the economy is slack or the interest rate has been raised to cool it down. Quantity controls on credit are exercised directly, however, by informally allocating the banks' quarterly ceilings for credit expansion. There is also, informally, guidance concerning the allocation of credit towards sectors whose expansion is considered desirable in the national interest. More of this later when we come to consider the Government's industrial structure policy in greater detail. Suffice it to say for the moment that, with a plentiful supply of savings available for recycling, the policy has generally been such as to create a good investment climate. Real interest rates have been kept low in comparison with other industrial countries. The annual average base lending rate for Japanese banks fell steadily from 9.0 per cent in 1955 to 7.0 per cent in 1972, in spite of a slow growth in inflation rates. After a jump to over 9 per cent in (the 21 per cent-inflation year of) 1974, it resumed its fall to 6.3 per cent in 1979, then went up again with the new inflationary spurt of the second oil price rise and back down to 7 per cent in 1983.

Effective borrowing rates for companies are often raised 1 or 2 per cent (by minimum deposit requirements, for instance) – more so for smaller companies than for larger ones – and, of course, the fall in inflation during the 1980s has meant that real interest rates have been rising since 1980. This, together with the long-term prospects of exchange-rate gains and changes in American pension fund laws, has attracted a good deal of foreign capital to Japan – enough to provide more than half the new equity and debenture capital absorbed by Japanese companies in 1983.

This availability of bank credit has been of great importance for Japanese industry because such a high proportion of the capital employed in industry comes through the banking system rather than through the share market. For manufacturing enterprises in 1979, the Ministry of Finance estimate that their net worth amounted to 19 per cent of total liabilities; long-term borrowings were 15 per cent, corporate debentures 2 per cent, short-term borrowings 16 per cent and suppliers' credit 27 per cent. (Okurashō, 1979). By 1982, after another three years of careful management, net worth was up to 23 per cent and suppliers' credit down to 24, but the other figures remained unchanged.

Ownership and control

This high gearing pattern is not as dangerous as it would be thought to be in Europe or North America. Between the banks and their corporate customers there are relations of trust and mutual obligations of a kind which will be discussed in more detail later apropos of trade in intermediates. It is understood that a borrower will keep a proportion of its loan on deposit with its creditor – at lower interest rates than it is itself paying, thus effectively raising the borrowing cost. (When the proportion to be kept thus banked is made formal, the Fair Trade Commission deplores the practice and carries out an annual survey to see how widespread it remains (Kōsei, 1980, pp. 183–7)). In return the banks may hold a token proportion of the shares of the company. It will be understood that short-term loans will normally be rolled over, and that when a firm is in severe difficulties the bank will be co-operative – and may even take a leading role – in the reconstructuring of the firm. So important are these ties of inter-corporate obligations seen to be that the banks have recently adopted the practice of 'relationship management'; instead of firms dealing separately with the foreign exchange department, short-term loan department, securities department, etc., a special liaison group is established for each major firm and, as in German banks, these groups do very much make it their business to acquire expert knowledge of the firm they deal with. The relationships are not exclusive; polygamous ties are normal. Even within the major groupings such as those of the Mitsui or Mitsubishi enterprises (of which more later) the main group bank rarely supplies more than 20–30 per cent of any firm's credit. In 1978 among the 20 top firms in the Mitsui group, the average proportion of borrowings derived from the group's two banks (the Mitsui Bank and the Mitsui Trust Bank) was 21 per cent – with the maximum being the 63 per cent of the Hokkaidō Mining and Steam Ship Company (Uekusa, 1982, p.269).

Nevertheless, the role of the lead bank is important as a most illuminating account of the rescue and turnaround of a leading automobile manufacturer, Tōyō Kōgyō, makes clear. (Pascale and Rohlen, 1983.) There are, indeed, those who argue that the whole capital procurement system confers a competitive advantage on Japanese companies as important as the relatively low price of capital – the advantage that the complex system of control and guarantee creates a pattern of mutual insurance which diffuses risk and consequently encourages possibly risky investment. Nakagawa and Ohta describe the system as a 'multi-umbrella system' (1981). Only a relatively small share of capital comes through an impersonal capital market on a purely contractual basis. Most of it is channelled from investors through mediating agencies which let them in under their umbrella – supplying not merely money, but also confidence-inspiring endorsement, advice and information. High gearing, in this view, has many positive advantages. And, of course, although the commercial banks play the leading role they are not the only agencies which provide these credit 'packages'. There are also the government banks such as the Japan Development Bank which mobilize funds through the special account called the Fiscal Investment and Loan Plan from sources such as the Post Office savings, and thirdly there are the trading companies which sometimes supply, or help to negotiate or guarantee, investment as well as trading credit.

But the ownership of equity capital is equally distinctive. Table 3.1 compares the distribution of share ownership for companies quoted on the London Stock Exchange, and on the major Japanese exchanges. Neither set of figures is wholly accurate

Table 3.1   Distribution of equity ownership: Britain and Japan

	UK 1981	Japan 1982
Persons and charities	30	28
Stockbroking companies	—	2
Unit trusts	4	} 1
Investment trusts	} 7	
Other financial companies		
Banks	0	} 38
Insurance companies	21	
Industrial and commercial companies	5	26
Pension funds	27	—
Foreigners	4	5
Public sector	3	—
	100	100

Sources: Stock Exchange, *Stock Exchange survey of shareownership, 1983*. Okumura, 1984, p. 55 (originally data from the National Association of Stock Exchanges, Japan). Both are nominal value-based figures. The British distribution by current values changes the figures by 1 or 2 per cent only.

because of nominee problems, but they do not much affect the differences between the two countries which are very real.

The most widely remarked trend in shareholding in the modern capitalist West is the substitution of institutional for individual share-ownership. In this the two countries are not very different. What is distinctive about Japan, however, is a number of differences in the pattern of *institutional* holdings which add up to a substantial difference in the significance of share-ownership and the constraints on management.

(a)   The pension funds responsible for such a large segment of share-ownership in many other countries are absent. In Japan's life-time employment system these funds are disaggregated into separate reserve funds *within* the financial structure of the companies with whom the prospective pensioners do their life-time service.
(b)   Banks hold equity shares in considerable quantity in Japan: shares and debentures made up 11 per cent of bank assets in 1980 (KY, 1982, p.240). The Fair Trade Act, reflecting American theories about the dangers of a concentration of financial power, limited the proportion of any firm's equity which a bank could own, and in 1980 that limit was lowered (with several years' grace

period before conformity was mandatory) to 5 per cent. In fact, within the Mitsui group, for instance, the Mitsui Bank held more than that in only eight firms: between 6 and 7 per cent in 6 and nearly 10 per cent in Mitsui Petrochemicals (Uekusa, 1982, p.268).

(c)   Insurance companies are very substantial investors in equity in Japan as elsewhere. But the Japanese pattern of mutually obligated trading relationships imposes a distinctive character here too. Insurance companies hold those shares not solely – or even primarily – to maximize the returns to their policyholders. They are equally concerned to secure a tight hold on the insurance business of the companies whose shares they hold. It is not a matter of 'control' in the sense of implicit threats of unseating directors by shareholder voting power, but of the managers of the insurance company establishing a moral claim on preferential access to the insurance business of an industrial company *vis-à-vis* that company's managers.

(d)   The same pattern of 'mutual-obligation-cementing' explains a large part of the last, equally large segment of shareholding – the quarter owned by industrial and commercial companies. Only a small part of its represents *controlling* interests in subordinate firms in the *keiretsu* hierarchy of a giant parent, because those firms are generally not quoted on the stock exchange. For the most part these are holdings of a firm's shares by the suppliers and customers of the firm or the providers of services to it. And the holdings are often reciprocal. This pattern was deliberately promoted in the late 1960s, as what was called a 'shareholding stabilization strategy'. The objective was primarily to protect firms again the possible consequences of capital liberalization: attempts at contested takeover might well result, it was feared, if American firms brought their predatory habits to Tokyo. After a period of wide-spread popular interest in shareholding in the late 1950s, the low level of dividend yield (typically 1–2 per cent) had disillusioned many people who were simply seeking an investment, and they were very happy to unload their holdings and take their profit from growth – particularly since the rise in the share index, already made steep by the low-dividend:high-profit-retention policy, was accelerated by the demand for shares from the companies seeking these mutually protective shareholding arrangements (Okumura, 1984, p.80).

All of this adds up to the following picture. Let us divide shareholders into those whose motive is to maximize returns on their investment and those with other motives – mainly to establish some claim to consideration from the firm's managers. The former rationally seek to take their money out of firms likely to get into trouble; the latter stick loyally with their shareholding through troubled times. In Hirschman's categories (1970), the former are implicit threateners of exit; the latter are exercisers of voice. On the rough assumptions that (a) half the individual share-ownership represents equally loyal, residual family ownership and employee share-owner schemes; (b) that banks' and insurance companies' motives split 50/50, the voice-exercisers make up a 60:40 majority over the exit-threateners. It should be added, too, that many of the remaining individually-owned shares are in the hands of full-time speculators. The Stock Exchange consequently has a somewhat unsavoury reputation, and movements in prices of individual shares are more easily shrugged off by managers as of little concern. The share price, in other words, is less likely to be seen as an index of the 'consensual judgement by the most informed and judicious observers of the health and prospects of the firm'. As such it carries less moral clout.

The combined effect of (a) the relatively small importance of the shareholder in the corporate finance manager's scheme of things and (b) the fact that the shareholders are dominated by corporate owners more interested in long-term growth and the stability of their trading partners and customers than in dividend revenue, is very much to reduce the pressure from shareholders on corporate managers – to reduce it to a degree not easily imagined by those used to thinking of the British or American economic system as a 'normal' and universal form of capitalism. This very much reduces the importance of short-term profits among corporate objectives and permits the development of a managerial culture which makes market shares rather than profits the index through the contemplation of which managers can massage or flagellate their egos. It is also important that it is primarily their egos and not their personal bank balances which are in question. The common American system whereby managers' bonuses depend on the half-yearly performance of their individually accounted profit-centre is practically unknown in Japan.

The 'ability to wait', to take low profits over a fairly extended period as long as one has one's bankers' confidence in the long-run future, is, of course, a factor which helps the expansion of new firms in new industries, as well as the diversification efforts of established firms wanting to spread their risks by entering a new field. It has a considerable importance for the development of international competitiveness in the innovative frontier industries where aggressive pricing, low profits but high volumes can take firms more rapidly along the learning curve to a low-cost, high returns position – a strategy which Magaziner and Hout have well analysed (1980, pp.10–28). American companies engaged in the mass production of the 16K and 64K chip and the race for the 256K chip are apt to complain of the Japanese ability to accept low profits as a quasi-unfair trading practice.

Lifetime commitment

What is often remarked on as a disability under which Japanese companies labour – the lifetime commitment and the fact that the wage bill thereby becomes a quasi-fixed cost – can paradoxically be seen as an advantageous stimulus to diversification. Where workers can be dismissed at will, a firm faced with shrinkage in its traditional markets can be tempted to solve its problems in the short-term by cutting costs to get back to profitability. Where that option is not available – or involves heavy once-for-all payments as inducements to early retirement – there is likely to be a stronger incentive to diversify into some new product line in order to get the best out of workers who have to be employed anyway. Likewise, the decision-taking managers themselves cannot improve their personal future by quitting and moving on into an upswing industry. They can only collectively decide to try to move *their firm* on to an upswing product line. They have to get their firm on track to long-term profitability because it is the only firm they have got.

Markets, concentration and relational contracting

A final factor is a little difficult to evaluate – the high propensity to cartelization in Japanese industry. Economists and politicians and business school gurus of a 'marketist' (more commonly, if less aptly, called 'monetarist') persuasion are apt to hold up Japan as a shining example of the virtues of intense competition. Not everything they say is wrong by any means. The sense of corporate unity does give an extra edge to the zeal with which the men of Toyota do battle with the men of Nissan which is rare in other countries. (Toyota could no more think of employing an ex-Nissan executive, for instance, than the wartime British army would have inducted a captured German officer into its ranks.) But this arena of real competition is limited to (a) consumer markets which (b) are expanding. Elsewhere trading patterns seem somewhat different from the textbook model of competition.

The various forms of co-operative effort between competing producers within the textile industry will be described in a later chapter. They show a tendency for the balance between perception of competing interests and the perception of a common interest between rival producers of the same commodity to tilt further towards the latter than in most other countries, in spite of the business zeal which Japanese companies otherwise show. The laqueur workers of Kyoto showed this tendency when Hideyoshi settled them there in the middle of the sixteenth century. Their descendants in regional markets still do so today. To give one example recently encountered near the town of Fukuoka: industrial estates in most countries are the creations of local governments or speculative developers. The one outside Fukuoka was created (taking advantage of a very small government subsidy) by 16 rival timber merchants operating within Fukuoka city. Faced with increasing neighbourhood pressure because of what their saw-noise and wood-smoke were doing to environmental amenities, they jointly organized the purchase of a block of land and its development as an industrial estate which they could divide up into individual plots. In all probability (as an traditional guilds almost anywhere) these timber merchants had at the minimum a gentleman's agreement not deliberately to try to seduce any of a fellow dealer's regular customers. There may well have been formal or informal understandings about prices too, though it is equally likely that they were partially undermined by secret discounts.

Similar understandings, at the national level, become more serious as constraints on trade and conspiracies against the public. There is a Fair Trade Commission whose job it is to put a stop to such things. As an example of its operations it may be worth summarizing Uekusa's description of the Commission's discoveries about the comfortable arrangements established by Japan's six producers of ethyl acetate. They got together to form the Japan Ethyl Acetate Association in October 1966. They began, modestly, with an agreement to keep market shares stable – itself no mean achievement since three had shares of 20 per cent plus, two of 13–14 per cent and one of only 7 per cent. (Moreover, being some naphtha-based and some carbide-based they had rather different cost structures.) In 1970 somewhat more teeth were put into the agreement by a system of 'adjustment purchases'. Where two or more firms were selling to a single customer, they agreed to freeze their respective shares. If the customer insisted on buying more from one company than its frozen share, that company was obliged to buy an amount equivalent to the excess from the companies which took the balancing losses. In addition to this 'micro-adjustment system' as they called it, there was also a 'macro-adjustment' agreement after each year-end accounting. Companies whose overall sales had exceeded their allotted shares bought balancing amounts from the under-achievers. This naturally entailed a price agreement. The price of ethyl acetate which had shown a slightly falling tendency since early 1969, going from 7.2 to some 6.7 yen a kilogram over a couple of years, fluctuated around that 6.7 mark thereafter (until naphtha prices sent it shooting up in 1973). A further twist was an agreement that all dealings should be through the Mitsubishi Trading Company. This was to eliminate the secret discounts which might result from direct dealing – Mitsubishi having every incentive not to collude in any such practice since it could easily be punished by the Association by being deprived of the trade.

The Fair Trade Commission moved in on the Association in 1971 and at the end of its hearings, in December of that year, ordered the cartel arrangements dissolved, and a renunciation of the Association's misdemeanours published. The renunciation was indeed published, in the form of newspaper advertisements, on 11 February 1972 – ten days after the Association's executive had taken a secret but minuted decision to continue the arrangements, with a few extra twists to preserve appearances. When the Fair Trade Commission got evidence of this and launched a second enquiry, it decided this time (by then it was September 1973) to order the dissolution of the Association and the closure of its offices – a somewhat unusual ruling. It remains, however, something of a puzzle why the Commission did not exercise its option to take the Association to the High Court where a fine for malfeasance could have been levied (Uekusa, 1982, pp.190–3).

As will be obvious, the teeth of the Fair Trade Commission are somewhat wobbly. It does have powers to make dawn raids and thereby acquire evidence of conspiracies which conspirators are unwise enough to minute. Since an amendment of 1977 it has had powers to levy a fine to exact from cartel members the excess profits gained by their anti-social behaviour. Altogether, between 1947 and 1975, it ordered the dissolution of some 447 cartels, about a half of them being in manufacturing for, presumably, the national market; many of the rest being agreements of wholesalers in regional markets. Over 60 per cent were cartels arranged within formal industry associations (Uekusa, pp.199–200).

Cartels are strongest, of course, where concentration ratios are high, in producer rather than in consumer goods industries, and in industries with high levels of fixed costs. They form in depressions and are apt to break in boom periods. In these respects Japanese industry behaves no differently from other industries. The distinctively Japanese characteristics are that the 'groupishness' of Japanese cultural traditions seems to make them form more easily, and, secondly, for a variety of what MITI officials consider to be good 'public interest' reasons, their formation is, sometimes officially in accordance with explicit laws, sometimes covertly, condoned by the responsible department of MITI, in consultation with the ex-MITI officials on the Fair Trade Commission. By and large it is a negotiated, not a judicial process. It has been asserted that Japan has only about 30 lawyers well versed in anti-monopoly legislation; the USA has about 15,000. Even allowing for the enormous general differences in the litigiousness of the two societies (the USA has thirty times Japan's number of lawyers), this is a substantial difference – 0.2 per cent and 3.3. per cent of the cadre respectively specializing in monopoly laws (Nakagawa and Ohta, 1981, p.29).

More will be said of this later when we come to consider the role of government and its structural adjustment policies. Here our concern is with the question: what difference does the propensity easily to form cartels in recessions – and even to have them officially condoned by government – make to the corporate behaviour of Japanese firms, in particular to their ability to undertake the diversifying initiatives which help them to run down activities in which, for example, they are no longer competitive with the NICs, and take up activities in which they still have comparative advantage?

Caves and Uekusa are stern:

Japan's anti-monopoly policy has been a hobbled and limited copy of that long used in the United States. The enforcement has fallen far short of the U.S. model, which itself hardly enjoys total adherence. The Japanese economy has borne significant costs in the forms of allocative inefficiency and diversion of rivalry into costly non-price forms. We can detect no corresponding gains. (Caves and Uekusa, 1976, p.522)

Their evidence for the last statement was a statistical study which showed significantly higher profit rates in industries with higher concentration (and it was assumed greater proneness to cartelization) – the relationship being stronger when gross profits on capital employed were measured rather than profits net of interest charges. As for 'costly non-price rivalry' advertising showed some relation to concentration ratios, but less than in similar studies of Western societies (Caves and Uekusa, p.507).

Analysis obsessed with (static) allocative efficiency does not provide full answers to the questions posed above. In any case the recession cartel is not a device which is confined to the high-concentration-ratio industries, and its effects need separate analysis. Uekusa in his more recent work suggests that their main effect is to encourage over-investment (Uekusa, 1982, p.188). The prospect of being able to weather a recession by agreed production cutbacks provides the confidence needed for investment. Moreover, the fact that agreed shares at cartel time will be based on immediate past performance gives a strong incentive to expand capacity when the going is good and the competitive jostling is going on.

All of this, one might argue, contributes to a strong investment climate which favours, also, investment in *new* diversifying lines of activity as well as in capacity expansion in traditional lines. Perhaps the more relevant connection to changes in the industrial structure, however, is to the run-down of industries in decline. There, cartel-proneness cuts both ways. On the one hand the stimulus to investment in the earlier boom periods worsened the over-capacity problem in industries like cardboard, plywood, aluminium, steel, etc., in the late 1970s. On the other, the cartel habit could easily be taken a stage further. Because there was an established tradition of recession cartels with production quotas it was relatively easy to move on to the next stage of agreed quotas for permanent reduction of capacity by the scrapping of plant – as we shall see apropos of ship-building and aluminium later in chapter 5.

One other distinctive, and not often properly appreciated, feature of the Japanese economy deserves mention, though, like cartelization, its implications for dynamic efficiency and structural change are ambiguous. It is (again like cartelization) a matter of the substitution of administration for markets, but in the context this time of vertical relations between tied suppliers of intermediates and their customers rather than in horizontal relations between competing producers.

The advantages and disadvantages of vertical integration have been discussed by economists such as Williamson (1975) in terms of the choice between markets and hierarchies. Does an automobile firm buy its lubricating pumps in the market, with all the problems of getting the information necessary to assess alternatives, the difficulties of security of supply, etc., or does it integrate and take the alternative problems of possibly sub-optimal scales, difficulties of management control, increase in sunken capital, etc.? What the literature does not fully take aboard is the possibility of an intermediate alternative – 'relational contracting' (Goldberg, 1981) between the user of an intermediate and a 'tied' – sometimes more, sometimes less tightly tied – supplier; relations, in Hirschman's terms, of 'voice and loyalty' rather than of 'exit and entry'.

Such relationships ramify widely throughout the Japanese economy – relationships involving a degree of trust and moral obligation going well beyond the minimal requirements of honesty (non-adulteration and false description, no short-weighting, etc.) which apply to spot transactions in the market. The Japanese-style employment contract is the form of such relationships most well known in the West. Managers accept an obligation not to dismiss their regular workers, and workers feel, though are not bound by, an obligation not to desert; managers trust workers to work with reasonable conscientiousness to make the firm a success, and workers trust managers not to play ducks and drakes with their interests.

Similar patterns hold between suppliers and purchasers of other commodities besides labour. A lot of these relationships are 'vertical', not only in the upstream/downstream sense but as between superiors and inferiors in market power. The 64 firms which belong to the Association of Co-operators with Toyota – suppliers of wheels and electrical assemblies and generators, etc., who do little business with any other firm but Toyota – *may* be in a slightly stronger bargaining position by virtue of the Association's ability to represent them collectively – but not much. When there is a recession and Toyota starts suggesting that they should be paid in 90-day bills instead of 60-day bills, or that it might begin to take into the home factory much of the work which it is sub-contracting out, etc., the only thing they can rely on is the relation of trust they have, partly with Toyota's purchasing manager as an individual, but more importantly in a corporate and impersonal way with the purchasing department. This may be partly a matter of institutional connections – whether the parent firm holds any of the dependent's share capital (or vice versa since selling shares to a dependent supplier is one way of exploiting its dependency), and whether there are any 'old boys' from the parent firm transferred into management positions in the sub-contractor. But most importantly it is the reports which a succession of purchasing agents have filed and the casual remarks they have made to their subordinates about a sub-contractor's co-operativeness, reliability and quality performance which determine the nature of that relationship and determine whether Toyota sees it as a firm which can be easily dispensed with, one that can be squeezed hard when Toyota is in difficulties, or one whose representations about its own difficulties have to be listened to sympathetically at price-fixing time, and which one would not put in risk of bankruptcy unless Toyota itself were in grave danger. It is significant that a number of large firms have been encouraging their dependent firms to diversify their markets. They want to make them less dependent precisely in order to reduce the moral obligation of being depended on (Okumura, 1982, p.37).

But trust/obligation relations are not confined to these situations of dependent inequality. The fact that the ethyl acetate producers whose cartel is described above *were* able to run a cartel of that kind is entirely because the users of ethyl acetate were accustomed to having 'relational' contracts with just one or two or three suppliers whereby they bought a steady 25 per cent of their requirements from one and 47 per cent from another, with the price to be adjusted from time to time whenever one party could convince the other that 'fairness' required it. And the big trading companies are there as intermediaries, one of their major functions being to provide the information, and sometimes mediation, which allow criteria of fairness to be established. The world's biggest steel-maker, New Japan Steel, sells its 35 million tons of steel to a mere dozen customers – the trading companies which also provide the ore it uses and sell the ships that its customers make with its steel. It is also in many fields the 'bargaining champion' of the steel industry. For example, the automobile companies buy their steel in relatively stable proportions each from two or three producers. The prices paid follow the price established between the two 'champions', New Japan Steel and Toyota Motors (Okumura, 1982).

Such relations are at their densest within the large enterprise groups. This is to be expected in the vertically organized groups – all the firms belonging to what is called the *keiretsu* of a Hitachi or a Toyota or a Mitsui Ship-building, some of them wholly or partially-owned subsidiaries, some of them suppliers or assemblers or distributors tied in by 'relational contracts'.

But similar ties, on a basis of greater mutuality and equality of bargaining strength, are also the prime source of cohesion for the major enterprise groups which are not hierarchically organized like the keiretsu and for which the only common collective name is *gurūpu*, i.e. 'group' (though the word *keiretsu* is, confusingly, sometimes used for them too). These comprise the three major ones deriving from the once centrally directed zaibatsu conglomerates, Mitsui, Mitsubishi and Sumitomo, and the three newer ones clustered around major banks (Fuyō, Sanwa, Daiichi Kangin). Between them the six have a quarter of the capital and 16 per cent of the sales of Japanese companies, 6 per cent of the employees and 27 per cent of the profits (all figures for 1977; Kōsei, 1980, p.140). They do have interlocking directorships to a small degree – that is to say 29 per cent of the firms in these groups have at least one director from another firm in the same group, though that accounts for less than 3 per cent of all directorships. The average group firm has 23 per cent of its equity in the hands of other firms in its group, and gets 21 per cent of its loan capital from the group's bank(s). But there is no central direction; instead, there are associations of company presidents which, to quote the Fair Trade Commission's recent summary:

. . . range (July 1979) from 21 to 45 in membership and meet monthly (in one case every three months). The substance of these meetings consists chiefly of reports by individual members on the general economic situation or the financial situation, or lectures by outsiders – means of exchanging information and increasing mutual intimacy. The presidents of the old zaibatsu groups also discuss joint charitable donations, trade marks and names, and on occasion new ventures which one or two members might take up jointly, or the plight of member firms in serious difficulties. (Kōsei, 1980)

Add to that description the fact that many firms in the three old zaibatsu groups still share the same (Mitsui, etc.) name and logo, and sometimes capitalize on that fact to do joint advertising and one has pretty well fully described the formal overt functions of these groupings. Their informal significance is perhaps greater: they are networks of preferential trading relations. Group 'kinship' reinforces the relations of obligation and trust, sustained and symbolized in the company presidents' meetings, and mirrored in numerous Mitsui, Sumitomo, etc. Friendly Societies in numerous foreign capitals which organize golf tournaments and New Year parties, and, yes, lectures by local experts, for the representatives of the group's firms. Dropping an established and loyal supplier of ethyl acetate for a small price differential is difficult enough. But the manager dropping a supplier within the same group needs a tougher skin. He can imagine only too well his president sitting there at next month's meeting, pouring a friendly cup of *sake* for Ethyl Acetate's president and getting a frosty stare in return. He can imagine *his* president coming back discomforted and wanting to know what this nonsense is all about. So he is very careful.

To repeat, these stable patterns of 'relational contracting' both within the groups and in the economy in general, are found both in interdependency relationships between parties of equal power, and in dependency relationships of unequal power. Overall, however – though it would be difficult to give quantitative evidence – the unequal dependency relationships, as between final manufacturer and parts sub-contractor, predominate. That is to say that a large proportion of such relationships represent a *substitute* for vertical integration. Whereas a European or American firm finding short-term market relations an unsatisfactory way of securing its supplies is forced to the alternative of hierarchy – incorporation in a pattern of vertical integration – the Japanese cultural context makes 'relational contracting' a *viable alternative*.

That doubtless explains the overall *frequency* of such relations in Japan, which is suggested by a very illuminating statistic. The volume of wholesale trade in Japan is four times the volume of retail trade, compared with a multiple of 1.2 in France and 1.6–1.9 in the USA, UK, and West Germany (Okumura, 1982). This statistic is usually quoted as an indication of the 'unrationalized complications of the Japanese distributional system' – see, for example, the latest MITI 'vision' (MITI, 1980(a), pp.141, 351), but Okumura is surely right in suggesting that it has more to do with the fact that the ease of forging 'relational contracts' makes into 'wholesale trade' a myriad of transactions which in other economies would be internal transfers from department to department *within* firms.

This means that when one comes to ask about the social costs and benefits of the predominance of relational contracting in Japan, the alternative with which a *lot* of these trading relations have to be compared is, indeed, not a free cut-throat market, but intra-firm transfers. Clearly this is not the whole story, however. (Compare the steel/automobile transactions described above.) Much of this relational contracting does substitute for what, in Western economies, are likely to be more open 'spot-contracting' markets – or markets closer to the spot-contracting pole.

What difference does it make? What difference does the prevalence of these features in the Japanese economy make to the economy's adjustive adaptability? Here, surely is a source of rigidities which must lead to allocative inefficiencies of considerable proportions. That is undoubtedly the case. There is, however – as with the other cognate rigidity of the life-time employment system – more than one side to the question.

First, take the matter of the cost in putting up barriers to entry and preventing healthy competition among domestic suppliers. It might be, for example, that if the six producers of ethyl acetate did not have the safety net of their established trading relationships – if there was free market competition between them – prices would be driven down, the least efficient firms might go under and fewer, more efficient firms would survive. Alternatively, other chemical firms with a new and more efficient process technology might move into this market and be encouraged to use their superior techniques by the prospect of capturing a good market share. On the other hand,

1   The security of the 'relational contract' is not absolute. A supplier or sub-contractor which was unable to meet the prices and quality standards which other suppliers were providing to their customers (and the trading company intermediaries may be a powerful information source for judging this) would in the end be dropped – perhaps after a grace period allowed for 'reform'. So there *are* market mechanisms at work, albeit 'lagged' market mechanisms.

2   At the same time, the security of prospects which a reasonably

efficient supplier can feel assured of makes it more willing to invest in new processes or to undertake production of new products than it might otherwise be – a factor of some importance in, for example, the automobile industry where a new model may require new investment in the parts suppliers as well as in the parent assembling firm.

3   A customer firm, if it is likely to find it difficult to ditch a supplier, has a stronger interest in making sure that the supplier is efficient. Schonberger, in his excellent book on Japanese manufacturing techniques, records his puzzlement at finding the testing and quality-control operations in Japanese factories always set up for easy display to visitors – if necessary with glassed walls when, say, destruction testing required a sealed-off environment. The reason was that factories were constantly being inspected by engineers from purchaser firms concerned to exercise 'voice' to improve or maintain the quality of the products they bought (Schonberger, 1982). Large firms with high level technical capacity may be willing to give technical guidance to its suppliers to that end, thus accelerating the diffusion of technology. It is common in the engineering industries for large firms to 'second' engineers or technicians or skilled workers 'on posting' to their suppliers for this purpose. We shall see in a later chapter that the chemical fibre firms which produce new fibres requiring special treatment from weavers and finishers likewise provide a good deal of guidance. All of these last three factors may play a part in explaining the high level of investment in Japan's small and medium firms. The level of robotization in such firms, for instance, is surprisingly high.

4   One of the by-products of the system is a general emphasis on product quality. The obligatedness which is the central feature of the system is, after all, a moral sentiment. Hence delinquency, a lapse from sincerity, in the other partner to the relation can release one from the obligation. It may not be easy to ditch a supplier because he is not, for the moment, giving you the best buy. It is much easier to ditch him if he is not giving you the best buy and is not even *seen to be trying* to match the best buy. The single most obvious indicator of sincerity of effort is product quality. A supplier who consistently fails to meet quality requirements is in danger of losing even an established relational contract. One manager of a part-producing firm spoke of the quality weapon as the way that parent companies squeeze the last ounce out of their suppliers. It was not uncommon for him to be rung up

at one in the morning to be told that the last batch of components was proving to have an unacceptable proportion of defects. Could he send someone over (60 miles away) to check through the consignment? Otherwise, they were sorry, but they would have to return the whole batch. And he would then have to find some loyal senior worker whom he could turn out of his bed and send off into the night. (Compare this with the manager of a British pump factory who cheerfully suggested that his castings supplier kept a little pile of defective castings in the corner of his factory ready to throw in one or two when he had a batch of sufficient overall quality to bear a few blemishes without too much complaint.) The superior quality and precision of parts produced by NC machines and robots may be another reason for the speed with which small and medium firms have invested in such machinery.

The capacity for rapid innovation and the emphasis on quality have been important features in Japan's success in international competition. They can be attributed to a variety of features of Japan's cultural legacy and structural situation, and can hardly be seen as the consequence solely of the system of trading relationships based on trust and mutual obligation. But that system does act as a very powerful reinforcer of the innovation/quality syndrome and these benign consequences of the system have to be set against any losses of allocative efficiency it may entail – and might, indeed, outweigh them.

5   Finally, one cannot stress too strongly that all the examples of relational contracting discussed here, *and* the cartelization of the ethyl acetate producers, concern producers' intermediates, not consumer goods production. In consumer markets competition is extremely keen. Even in industries of high concentration with relatively unchanging products like beer and dairy products with three and two major producers respectively, competition seems to be real, if muted; in the field of consumer durables where product innovation is at the heart of the competitive process, it is intense. And that helps to preserve dynamism in the whole system; as long as Toyota and Nissan are locked in desperate rivalry the pressure to improve quality and cut costs can transmit itself all the way down through the relational contracts which make up the sub-stratum of their production systems.

So far we have been considering the effects of the system in dampening competition among domestic suppliers. One needs to look, as a separate issue, at the way it dampens competition, also, between domestic and foreign suppliers, constituting an important element of the non-tariff barriers of such potent political consequence.

One clear effect is to reduce the *need* for adjustment. Other countries may need tariffs and quotas to keep out low-cost imports from developing countries: Japan has a kind of 'natural immunity' requiring no government mediation. Brazilian and Korean steel-makers can land steel in Japan with a clear price advantage against domestic steel, but for a long time they made very little headway. The major trading companies might have been willing to handle it and risk offending their powerful clients, the domestic steel-makers, if those steel-makers had not been suffering severely from recession and capacity under-utilization. As matters stood, the offence would be too great to risk. So only small importers would handle it. (Some were small Korean-owned steel stockholders selling to Japanese firms with temporary shortages; others might, on investigation, prove to be, if not actually dummy companies of, at least not unconnected with, the major trading companies.) Some of them would insist on the tainted steel being landed at a dock from which no domestic steel was moving out. If a loyal employee of a domestic steel company were to see it coming in, a guard might be posted and any trucks which came to fetch a consignment might be followed to their destination so that the disloyal firm could be identified. Even so, in the end the fingers in the dike cannot stop the import trickle from getting larger if the price differential is large enough. Imports of steel were up to 2.5 per cent of Japan's domestic consumption by the end of 1983, and in some lines were over 20 per cent, with decisive effects on domestic prices.

As a form of protectionism the appeal to solidarity and customer loyalty, apart from its long-term unreliability, has slightly different consequences from the more overt forms such as tariffs and quotas. First, it causes worse political problems. It leads foreigners to suspect some secret conspiracy plotted in the subterranean GHQ of Japan Incorporated. And, indeed, no overt action of the government, no tariff reduction or renewal of quota restrictions, can remedy the matter. It can only lean in secret on the steel industry, offering administrative guidance that free trade is best. And when there is disagreement within MITI between the free traders of its international bureau and the steel-protectors of its basic industries' bureau, the leaning is not likely to be very hard, and the temptation to deny all knowledge of such practices, when challenged in international forums, is strong.

Economically, however, as a form of protectionism against low-cost foreigner-producers with a long-term structural comparative advantage, it is probably slightly less unfortunate in its consequences than overt protection – unless that overt protection is clearly degressive, a mere cushioning schedule of tariffs to provide a fixed-term declining advantage to the home industry while it sorts itself out. It *is*, in the long run, unreliable. However long-standing the relational contract, if the price differential between domestic and equal-quality imports is too great, and seems to be *not* the consequence of temporary exchange rate fluctuations, but of a lasting difference of cost structures, then purchasers will switch. Even if nothing comparable has happened yet with steel, the big growth in imports of aluminium in the late 1970s is a case in point. In short, the system has the effect of delaying adjustment – its part in delaying adjustment in the textile industry will be considered in the next chapter – but it does not delay it for ever. Moreover, the removal of the barrier happens gradually and covertly as the result of the one-by-one defection of major purchasers. It does not require an overt tariff-reducing or quota-removing act of government against which the threatened industry can mobilize all its political forces. When 'natural immunity' wears off, the threatened industry has no recourse but *then* to begin to demand formal protection – as the steel industry has recently begun to do, asking for an anti-dumping duty on the one hand and trying to bring Posco, the Korean steel firm, into its price cartel on the other (*Economist*, 10 March 1984). By then it may be too late. Installing a new protectionist measure is always a harder political task than defending an existing one.

The conditions of efficiency

We have reviewed six factors relevant to the 'adjustment capacity' of Japanese firms – the general atmosphere of confidence, the high levels of education and effective information-gathering, cheap and available credit, the reliance on bank loan rather than equity capital, the life-time commitment, and (if ambiguously) the tendency to substitute administration for markets; oligopoly and a strong propensity to cartelization on the one hand, and a preference for long-term 'relational' contracts for sub-contracting and the sale of intermediates on the other. All seem to add something to an explanation of why Japanese firms have been quick to react to a down-turn, or the looming prospect of a down-turn, if their market fortunes decline (whether it be from taste changes, or a loss of competitiveness because of changing energy prices or the developing technological capacity of the NICS) by diversifying into new and more promising fields – and also why new entrants in those fields had been able quite rapidly to grow.

The seventh, and major factor, is the government policy framework. Before we come to assess its importance, however, let us look at the other actors in the 'private' sector, besides the corporate decision-makers, namely the workers and their union leaders.

4
The workers and their unions: Their response to and influence on firms' adjustment strategies

Overall, the 1970s showed a considerable increase in employment in Japan, by some 11 per cent between 1970 and 1982, or 5.4 million extra jobs (defined, however, as providing gainful employment for at least one hour a week). There was at the same time, as the figures of table 4.1 show, a doubling of unemployment – from 0.6 to 1.4 million (more about definitions later), though this still left Japan with what counts in the modern industrial world as a remarkably low unemployment rate below 3 per cent. There were various changes in structure over those 12 years too. The long-standing trend towards waged and away from self-employment or family employment continued and affected women more than men – an increase of 21 per cent in male wage-and-salary employees, and of 29 per cent for women, though this addition of 3.2 million extra waged jobs for women was accompanied by the increase to some 2.5 million of the number employed as 'part-timers', working, usually though not necessarily, for shorter hours, but nearly always for lower hourly wages, much lower bonuses and with less security than 'regular' or 'permanent' employees. The other major shift in structure which most concerns us here was in the industrial distribution of employment already charted in chapter 2. Some industrial firms have expanded; others contracted.

Some of these changes happen through the labour market processes of retirement, entry into the labour force, and voluntary movement of individuals seeking to better themselves. Yet it seems implausible that in an economy in which a large segment of the labour force sees itself, and is seen by its employer, as having entered into a 'lifetime contract', shifts of the magnitude involved could have happened by those processes alone. Sharp decline in the output of some firms and industries at the expense of others has generally, in other industrial economies, involved dismissals of redundant workers. What happened in Japan?

Traditionally, the unions – and the larger enterprises at least almost uniformly have to deal with unions – had maintained a posture of 'absolute opposition' to any kind of employment reduction affecting their numbers. In earlier post-war years, strikes against 'rationalization' were widespread and often violent. The run-down of the coal industry in the 1960s, even at a time of strong aggregate excess demand for labour, was not accomplished easily. Only after the bloody prelude of the Mitsui mine strike did the unions finally come to admit the need for some kind of compromise and the government the need to provide generous compensation to buy that compromise.

Memories of that history are very much alive in the minds of managers and employees in the 1970s, and the desire to avoid conflict was strong. Most large firms had developed procedures for consultation with their unions which involved regular discussion of the outlines of annual budget plans – including manpower budgets. Usually there were firm understandings that any changes which the pressure of events might impose on manpower budgets would be discussed with unions first. And there was a

Table 4.1   Selected indices of the Japanese labour economy, 1970–80

Year	Real GNP	Manufacturing output	Labour force	Wage/salary employment	Unemployment %
1970	100	100	100	100	1.2
1971	104.7	102.7	100.6	103.2	1.2
1972	114.1	110.2	100.8	104.7	1.4
1973	124.1	126.9	103.4	109.3	1.3
1974	122.6	122.0	103.0	110.0	1.4
1975	125.6	108.4	103.3	110.3	1.9
1976	132.2	120.6	104.4	112.3	2.0
1977	139.2	125.6	105.8	114.0	2.0
1978	146.4	133.7	107.4	114.9	2.2
1979	154.0	143.6	108.6	117.2	2.1
1980	161.4	150.4	109.6	120.1	2.0
1981	167.9	151.8	110.8	122.1	2.2
1982	173.4	152.5	112.1	124.0	2.4

Sources: KY; RH; Rōdōshō, Yearbook; KR, 1984. Figures are for calendar years. GNP and manufacturing output are valued and weighted at 1980 prices. The labour productivity figure is based on quantity measures of output and man-day measures of labour input. Working hours, wages and work stoppages are for enterprises with 30 or more employees. Labour force data derive from monthly household-based sample surveys.

general belief among management that, both on pragmatic and on moral grounds, it is worth spending a lot of money not just 'to buy industrial peace' as it might be put in other cultural contexts, but also to avoid the damage to morale in the enterprise inevitably caused by expelling some of its members 'simply' because they had become unnecessary through no fault of their own. There were some local upheavals, but by and large adjustments were carried out without damage to established employment practices – as the strike figures in table 4.1 testify.

As chapter 2 showed, the major reductions of waged labour forces were in manufacturing firms (the 'generation shift' out of agriculture did not involve paid employees, of course). Three distinguishable causes can be isolated.

The first was the continuation of the long-run process of substituting capital for labour in manufacturing – a rational response to changes in relative prices. If one takes the wholesale price of 'general and precision machinery' as an index of the cost of capital, between 1960 and 1973 it rose by 20 per cent while average wages in manufacturing rose by 420 per cent. Between

| | Monthly working hours in | Labour productivity in | Real monthly compensation in | Work stoppages | |
Year	manufacturing	manufacturing	manufacturing	½ day or longer	less than ½ day
1970	100	100	100	100	100
1971	98.4	104.3	107.6	111.8	197.5
1972	97.8	115.9	119.0	110.5	149.9
1973	97.1	136.4	131.3	147.2	283.0
1974	92.5	135.6	133.2	230.6	270.7
1975	89.8	130.3	132.8	150.0	232.4
1976	92.9	146.3	136.4	120.3	242.7
1977	93.2	153.7	137.1	75.8	191.9
1978	93.9	166.9	139.8	67.1	165.0
1979	94.9	185.2	145.0	51.0	116.4
1980	95.1	196.9	145.1	50.3	128.9
1981	94.7	201.6	144.9	42.1	273.3
1982	94.5	203.5	147.9	41.7	261.9

1973 and 1980 the difference, though less, was still wide enough – 43 per cent and 107 per cent respectively (KY, 1982, pp.9, 183).

The second element was, of course, the changes in the structure of demand and international competition which created what came to be called, towards the end of the decade, the 'structurally depressed industries' – those which faced restricted markets or unbeatable competition and could only cut back production.

And the third element was the OPEC Shock, the inflation which followed it and the severe deflation by which it was countered, leading to a 14½ per cent fall in manufacturing output, and a 12½ per cent fall in shipments (KY, 82, p.5).

The combined effect of these factors, particularly the acceleration of the cut-backs in the crisis years 1974–5, is clear in the index of employment in manufacturing in table 4.2. The B figure is derived from a household-based labour force sample survey and relates to all wage and salary employees, though the index does not change very much if the self-employed are included. (It is anchored in the five-yearly population census, and the fit proves good at each five-year check.) A is based on the triennial establishment survey (with updates for intermediate years) and covers only establishments with thirty or more 'regular' workers – those hired on open-ended contracts, including part-timers, but not daily workers or seasonal or fixed contract workers – and counts only such workers. The discrepant trends confirm the shift in manufacturing employment to firms of smaller size noted in chapter 2.

In both indexes the sharp cut-back comes in 1975, but whereas the larger firms covered by A (with their developing automation programmes) continue the momentum of manpower reduction,

Table 4.2   Indices of manufacturing employment

	A	B		A	B
1970	100.0	100.0	1976	91.6	99.0
1971	100.7		1977	90.7	98.4
1972	98.8		1978	88.8	96.2
1973	99.0	105.2	1979	88.3	96.8
1974	98.7	105.0	1980	89.2	99.2
1975	93.5	98.8	1981	90.2	100.7
			1982	90.8	100.6

Source: KY 1982, pp. 196, 198; 1984, pp. 180, 182.

the more comprehensive figure reaches something of a plateau thereafter.

For the purposes of our present discussion, series A is the more important. Not all the workers counted in it as 'regular' would be those who are institutionally defined as 'regular' or 'permanent' members of the work-force within the firm – i.e. members of the union favoured by an implicit 'life-time employment' guarantee – since many workers classified as 'part-time' or 'temporary' for purposes of union membership, welfare benefits or job security would still be on open-ended contracts and so counted as 'regular' by the survey. But it is clearly the index most relevant to our question about the larger firms: how was trimming of the labour force achieved in spite of the 'life-time guarantee'?

Let us concentrate on the crisis years of 1974–5 when the problem was most acute. The manager's prime concern when he has to cut back output is to get a corresponding reduction in labour costs which can be done by:

(a) cutting wages.
(b) cutting paid hours of work (chiefly overtime), or
(c) cutting employment.

Of these the easiest institutionally to cut is paid employment in the form of overtime, and fortunately there was a lot of it to cut. Table 4.1 shows the index for manufacturing working hours per worker for the decade. The fall was sharp between 1973 and 1975 – from 182 hours a month to 168 hours a month, well beyond the 1 per cent a year long-run trend (KY, 1982, p.202.) This represents the combined effect of four factors.

First there was an acceleration of the long-run transition to the 5-day week, usually accomplished by a steady increase in holiday Saturdays. Days worked per month in manufacturing fell from 22.6 to 20.8 between 1970 and 1975, but this also included some short-time working – the second factor – as well as the longer-run trend, since the figure was back to, and stable at, 21.2–21.3 between 1978 and 1982 (KR, 1984, p.132). Thirdly, there must have been some effect from the continuing substitution of middle-aged housewife part-timers for full-time younger girls or men. And finally, probably the biggest element was the reduction in overtime – for the manufacturing average from 19 hours in 1970 to 9 in 1975 (KR, 1984, p.132).

The reduction in work hours accounted, in fact, for more than a half of the reduction in labour inputs between those two years. Hours worked fell by 7½ per cent, and employment by 5½ – leaving less than 2 per cent of the 14½ per cent reduction in output to a decline in labour productivity. (These, remember, are figures for enterprises with 30 or more workers. The employment cut revealed by the second index in table 4.2 is half a per cent greater.)

According to an American study (Neef and Capdevielle, 1980) a similar 12 per cent reduction in labour inputs in the United States in the same years was accounted for by a 9 per cent reduction of employment and a 3 per cent reduction in hours per worker – the sort of difference one would expect between a 'hire and fire' economy and a 'life-time guarantee' economy. Nevertheless, the 'life-time guarantee' sector of the life-time guarantee economy did shed 5½ per cent of its labour force in two years. How was this done?

First a point should be made about the urgency and speed with which it had to be done. Cutting labour costs is not the only concern of a manager faced with a production cut-back. He also has a problem of dealing either with the conspicuous and probably disruptive idleness of a few individuals with nothing to do, or, if he shares the work around, of establishing relaxed work routines which can later be retightened only with difficulty.

In Japan this is a problem of much smaller dimensions than in societies where workers are hired in their occupational capacity, for their occupational skills. The Japanese worker hired into a large firm defines himself primarily as a member of that firm, not as a member of an occupation group. Occupational consciousness is low, therefore. A skilled fitter would consider it entirely reasonable that if there is no fitting to be done he should temporarily be asked to weed the flower beds beside the factory gates, or be sent off for two or three months to augment the external sales force. The flexibility takes up the slack for a while: factories get a new coat of paint, old machines are rehabilitated and disposed of on the second-hand market, quality circles have extra meetings. But still these are only postponements of a labour-surplus problem, no solution to the problem of unnecessary labour costs.

In aggregate terms there was no problem at all in cutting the labour force by 5½ per cent. Natural wastage by voluntary quits, even in firms with more than 500 workers, was running at 15 per cent per year in 1973, and although that rate has come down after the mid-1970s crisis made jobs more precious, it was still around 10 per cent for the last half of the decade.

Add to that another 1–1½ per cent for death and retirement, and a slightly higher percentage for temporary workers whose contracts come to an end.

This leaves straightforward sackings and other departures at managers' initiative with a very small role to play. But their miniscule proportions of total movement out of firms did become very slightly less miniscule in 1975, especially in smaller firms, less likely to be unionized.

The 3 per cent figure shown in table 4.3 for firms of between 30 and 100 employees represents about 75,000 redundancies, and if the rate were similar in firms of even smaller size (rather than bigger, which is more probable) that would represent another 95,000. The sum total for all industries (including the fall-out from bankruptcies) was estimated at 400,000, or less than 1 per cent of the labour force in 1975, double the figure of, for example, 1979. (RH, 1981, Appx. 115) It must be remembered, however, that these are redundancies so defined by the employer, for this is an establishment-based survey.

All these statistical averages conceal the severity of impact on particular firms and industries. Textile firms, for example, were particularly badly hit, suffering simultaneously from recession, an import surge and a big price increase in the naphtha base of chemical fibres. As a later chapter describes, many of them were

Table 4.3   Involuntary quits: manufacturing (as percentage of employees at start of period): annual

	Disciplinary dismissals		Departures at the employer's initiative (including formal voluntary early retirement schemes)	
	30–99 employees	500+ employees	30–99 employees	500+ employees
1970	1.2	0.5	1.7	0.8
1973	1.1	0.4	1.1	0.3
1974	1.0	0.3	2.2	1.0
1975	0.9	0.4	3.0	1.3
1979	1.0	0.2	1.3	0.6
1982	1.1	0.2	1.2	0.4

Source: RH, 1976, 1983 Appendices. (For 1975 to 1982 the calculation is based on the assumption that the distribution of quits by reasons was the same in establishments of more than 500 and enterprises of more than 1000 workers.)

forced into big reductions in their workforce, made somewhat easier by the fact that a large proportion of their workers were women, and the 'life-time' for which work is guaranteed to women is short – basically until marriage and first childbirth. Many firms caught between severe cash-flow difficulties and social constraints – in the case of a larger firm a union determined to defend its members' employment; in the case of an owner-managed smaller firm, the social stigma of throwing his workers on the scrap heap – admitted defeat and went into formal bankruptcy. The number of firms declared bankrupt which had fluctuated between 6 and 10 thousand since the mid-1960s rose to 11 and 12 thousand in 1974 and 1975 and was between 15 and 18 thousand for the last half of the decade. Many more firms stopped short of catastrophe and adopted plans of emergency reconstruction. The following newspaper report – first repercussions of the sudden contraction of the hi-fi market in 1981–2 – is typical of many which have appeared in the last decade.

It was announced yesterday (1 November 1982) that the leading audio firm Akai is about to undertake a company reconstruction which will involve large-scale voluntary redundancies. Because of the serious contraction of the audio market, the firm's recent results have worsened to the point at which urgent action was required. It is expected that the number of volunteers for retirement called for will exceed 200, including managerial staff, and the whole male workforce of one thousand plus will be eligible. The plan is to be put to the employees today. Most of the audio firms have sought a way out of the crisis by 'making work' – bringing in-house work formerly given to sub-contractors – by putting production workers on to sales and other rationalization measures, but this is the first firm to embark on a programme of cutting employment by voluntary redundancies.

Other parts of the programme include stopping the recruitment of female employees next year and relying on the natural wastage rate of 300 a year to reduce the female labour-force. The wage/salary structure (the best or second-best in the whole industry) will be adjusted. All managers above section chief level will take a five per cent cut and directors' salaries will also be cut – 25 per cent for ordinary directors, 10 to 20 per cent for executive directors. Since Akai has no union, the plan will be put to the employees today and applications for voluntary retirement will be accepted from November 15 . . .

The cause of all this is the contraction of the export markets, particularly the European markets, on which Akai depended. For over a year production of tape decks has been 30 per cent down on the previous year. Until last year it was possible to cover the gap with sales of video recorders, but, although sales continued to forge ahead, the firm has got caught up in the fierce competition among Japanese makers, and margins have been so squeezed that six of its seven 100 per cent-owned overseas sales subsidiaries have made losses – totalling some Y4–500m. (*Nihon Keizai*, 2 November 1982)

One of the Ministry of Labour's quarterly surveys since 1974 has been concerned with the extent to which, and the means by which, manufacturing firms have been pursuing policies of deliberate 'employment adjustment' – i.e. reduction – of labour inputs if not of employment (Rōdōshō: Yearbook). At the peak – the first quarter of 1975 – three-quarters of the firms surveyed said that they had employment adjustment policies, a figure which thereafter steadily fell to around 15 per cent in 1980. Reduction in overtime was easily the most common method reported. Some of the other headings in the classification are worth further comment.

Cut-backs in recruitment, if prolonged, are generally seen as a real and undesirable threat to the long-term vitality of a firm, as well as the source of the long-term structural problems of a top-heavy workforce – high average wages and too many senior managers and foremen pretending to manage too few junior managers and workers. Hence, firms tended to keep on with their plans for the annual March recruitment of school and university leavers. Over a million vacancies were offered by manufacturing firms alone for middle and high-school leavers in March 1975, the trough of the depression, compared with nearly a million and a half the year before – though optimism faltered rather more the next year when the figure fell to half a million. (Actual recruitments for the three years were 270, 210 and 168 thousand respectively. RH, 1979, Appx. 27.) What many firms did do, however (and this was the second most commonly reported expedient), was to freeze all recruitment of workers other than virgin career employees straight from school or university. In 1973 manufacturing had been offering 300,000 such vacancies open to experienced workers. In 1975 that figure fell to one-third of its 1973 level (RH, 1979, Appx. 25).

The hiring of *temporary and seasonal workers* and their dismissal at times of recession are often spoken of as a crucial source of flexibility for Japanese firms – the insecurity of the temporary workers being seen as the price they pay for the security which the permanent workers enjoy. The fact that only 21 per cent of firms said they had recourse to dismissal of temporary workers at the peak of the crisis in the first quarter of 1975 – the same proportion as resorted to temporary lay-offs – suggests that the importance of this feature may be more limited than is often supposed. The monthly (household-based) labour-force survey does count the proportions of 'regular', 'temporary' and 'daily' workers (the last category being mostly in forestry, construction and – 15 per cent of them – in public relief work for the aged; altogether they make up some 3 per cent of the labour-force). According to this series, temporary workers made up about 5 per cent of the labour-force for the decade preceding 1973, rising to a monthly average of 5.5 per cent in that year. In 1974 it fell to 5.0 and the next year to 4.7. Thereafter it rose steadily to a level of 6.4 per cent in 1980 – higher than it has been for nearly two decades. Many firms, clearly, their confidence in the permanence of growth shaken, are securing themselves against another down-turn by recruiting more temporary workers – and the slacker labour market has increased the supply of workers willing to accept precarious employments. Another similar trend is the replacement of unmarried girl 'regular' employees (union members if there is a union, not easily sackable even if there is not; see the quotation about Akai which even in a crisis situation had to wait for natural wastage to take its course) by older married women employed as 'paato'. The proportion of the total female workforce aged 30–50 went up from 35 to 45 per cent between 1970 and 1980 (KR, 1984, p. 126). 'Paato' is short for the English 'part-timer', but it is not so much their time input as their status which distinguishes these workers – estimated at 2 million by 1980. In a 1982 survey in manufacturing they were found to work on average seven hours a day, for an hourly wage 82 per cent and bonuses of only 28 per cent of those of regular female employees. In larger firms they are generally on a fixed-term (if renewable) contract and thus are counted in the figure for 'temporary workers' quoted above. They are often given paid holidays and insurance rights and there may well be genuine differences in skill and experience between them and the younger 'permanent' women employees. In many smaller manufacturing firms – and especially in the hotel and catering and service trades – they are on open-ended contracts like any other 'regular' worker, but are simply worse paid and treated (sometimes, even, paid less than the legal minimum wage), often not even insured for workmen's compensation or unemployment, and are easily dismissable. There is a sufficient supply of housewives looking for a secondary income in most areas to make these conditions acceptable (Gyōsei, 1982 and RK, 1984, pp. 191–4).

Reassignments and transfers include not only the flexibility of movement between jobs within a plant already discussed, but also transfers from plant to plant within the firm, and assignments to subsidiaries or to 'co-operating firms' – sub-contractors – as technical advisers or quality-control experts. Also in this category are the loans of workers from one firm to another – as when, in the mid-1970s, Japan Steel lent some of its surplus workers on rotation to Isuzu Motors – several thousands for a year at a time. (They kept their Japan Steel wage and status and Isuzu paid Japan Steel a lump sum for their services.)

Another 'Japanese-type' expedient – resorted to by a fifth of the firms surveyed in 1975 – was the *temporary lay-off*. This involves payment of a retainer to employees told to stay at home which was always greater than 75 per cent, and sometimes over 90 per cent of their wages. The government provided a subsidy for this purpose which will be described later. Apparently, the pleasure the workers took in their almost fully paid holidays was not complete, or wore off after some time. There was, at any rate, much concern expressed at problems of 'deterioration in morale and skill' during these lay-off periods (Japan Institute of Labour, 1979, p.21).

In most firms with regular consultation practices all of these measures would be discussed with the unions before implementation, even a cut back in recruitment. The penultimate measure, the one which the company would suggest most reluctantly because of the union opposition it would anticipate, is a *voluntary resignation/early retirement* scheme – the ultimate horror, of course, being *dismissal*.

The reasons why unions could be expected to object very strongly even to voluntary schemes are:

(a) Because of doubts about the voluntariness of the proceedings among loyal employees very susceptible to hints about the nobility of sacrifice,

(b)   Because of the divisiveness and damage to morale which such hinting would bring, and

(c)   Because the tougher the opposition, the higher the inducement premium over and above the severance pay entitlement of the formal pension scheme by which the opposition could hope to be bought off.

Some examples of the working of such schemes are given in chapter 7 and the Appendix. Very often the scheme would begin among the swollen ranks of upper management. Usually the number of persons desired for resignation and the eligible age brackets would be announced. If a sufficient number came forward by the deadline, that finished the business for the time being. If there were not enough volunteers, another round of solicitation was made. If this still did not produce enough volunteers, specific individuals might be 'tapped on the shoulder' and asked if they would consider volunteering for resignation. Given the atmosphere which prevails in Japanese firms, there is little real difference between that and actually being fired, though the compensation level may be made more especially generous. Taira quotes a sample survey of workers who had lost their jobs, conducted by a trade union organization. The sample included 700 workers who had accepted voluntary early retirement (Dore and Taira, 1984, ch.4). Of these – all men aged 40 plus, two-thirds of them with only nine years' education – 36 per cent said that they were attracted to volunteer by the severance pay. (The amount they received was not clear, but it can be inferred that the average was a little over 40 months' salary.) Twenty-four per cent, however, said that they feared they might be singled out for dismissal or an explicit invitation to volunteer – humiliating even if resisted. Other replies (some gave several reasons) included the thought offered by half of the sample of volunteers that 'the employer of his industry had very poor prospects' – which might have been sour grapes or might refer to premonitions of bankruptcy or the conviction that they could better themselves by moving on – 12 per cent said they had been thinking of changing their jobs anyway. Seven per cent had been offered 'reassignment' alternatives which did not appeal to them.

The final expedient – nearly always resorted to only after attempts to find volunteers had failed – was what was known as 'designated dismissal'. There were some spectacular cases of prolonged industrial conflict arising from such action by managers. It seems that they were more common in 1978 than in the first impact of the recession in 1975. Many firms which had managed to absorb losses for one or two years found themselves, when there came another downturn after the partial recovery of 1976–7, pushed towards more desperate measures. The figures for involuntary separations (table 4.3), for total unemployment and for the proportions of the unemployed dismissed from a previous job (table 4.7) all peak in this year.

An example of a firm which took the 'designated dismissal' option is Oki Electrical whose managers decided by the middle of 1978 that they had to reduce their 12,000 staff by 1,500. There had been continuous discussions about the dire plight of the company and the possible need for redundancies since the beginning of the year, and figures of one to two thousand were being mentioned to the union. In March, the union offered the company a list of 10 ways in which it could save money and improve efficiency without cutting wages or employment. (They did not include bringing in work presently put out to sub-contractors, though expenditure on sub-contracting as a proportion of sales did fall in 1978 to 7.2 per cent, having been around 9 per cent in 1975–6 and 10 per cent in 1973–4.) But finally the crunch came in a formal memo to the union and a simultaneous letter to all employees in October. The relevant section of the formal notification to the union may be worth translating. It runs as follows.

Voluntary retirement

1   Number of volunteers called for: 1,500 union members.
It is hoped that the number of volunteers will reach that figure, but if by any chance it should not, management will proceed to designated dismissal. (It may be added that as far as managerial staff are concerned [i.e. non-union members: managers above the age of 30–35, plus, probably, even younger university graduates in the personnel department], we have so far been pressing a policy of 'encouraged retirements', but now intend to pursue this more vigorously.)

Who is eligible?

All permanent employees may volunteer, but those in the following categories are particularly encouraged to do so.

1   Those whose work performance is not good.
2   Those with problems in their work record, e.g.
    (i) a poor record for absenteeism, late arrival, early leaving.

      (ii) health or ability problems in keeping up with the work.

     (iii) lacking in the will to work.

     (iv) a record of disciplinary offences.

3   Those who have not shown a very high degree of co-operativeness with measures taken by the company, e.g.

       (i) not obeying instructions or orders.

      (ii) not reacting co-operatively with supervisors or colleagues, and disturbing personal relations on the shop-floor.

     (iii) breaking shop-floor disciplinary rules.

     (iv) showing a non-co-operative attitude to company policies.

4   Those who have a source of relative income security after retirement, e.g.

       (i) a private income.

      (ii) a working spouse with a considerable income (including cases where married couples both work for the firm).

     (iii) a private business.

     (iv) where children have left home and demands on family income are reduced.

5   Those who will be hard put to it to conform to the tough measures the company may have to take in future, e.g. those who would not be able to respond to transfer orders which involve changing skills or changing home.

6   Any others who, in ways similar to the above, are not able to make a great contribution to the company.

The document went on to list the enhancements of normal retirement provisions on offer. The union had already, a week earlier, had a ballot to establish the right of its leaders to call a strike to prevent the company from issuing a redundancy plan. The majority was 87 per cent (12 per cent against, 1 per cent abstentions). This was taken as adequate authorization for protest strikes after the vote had failed to prevent the issue of the plan. A series of one-hour, half-day and full-day strikes was held over the two weeks of the volunteer period. The company's only concession was to reduce the numbers target from 1,500 to 1,350. At the end of the two weeks 1,060 had volunteered. The company sent dismissal notices to 286 others the following day, giving them a week to transform themselves to volunteers with the pecuniary advantages attaching to that status. It offered a list of the 286 to the union which refused to accept it and called for a ballot to renew its strike mandate. The ballot was organized in four days, and the proposition was lost by a 7 to 3 majority. All but 78 of the designated became volunteers. The union shifted to negotiation about the changes in work practice and production reorganization which had formed the rest of the company's package, and secured a number of concessions. Within two-and-a-half months the affair was over (Shokugyō 1980, pp. 22–117).

Wage levels

So much for the way the conventions of the Japanese employment system and the strategies and priorities of unions constrained the process of workforce reduction in the larger Japanese enterprises. Trimming employment, of course, is only one means to the end of cutting labour costs. The other means is to cut wages.

This – certainly in the immediate aftermath of the oil crisis – Japanese companies notably failed to do. The annual level of wage increase settlement had been steadily rising in the early 1970s. Settlements for the previous four years had allowed for increases averaging 12, 15, 16 and 21 per cent respectively, giving real wage increases of something like 10, 8, 11 and 9 per cent. In spite of, or perhaps because of, the intense sense of economic crisis of the early months of 1974 (what Rosovsky once called something close to a national nervous breakdown), the unions were not to be persuaded out of their determination to extrapolate the trend, and in the face of a monthly inflation rate just approaching its peak level of 27 per cent per annum, they demanded increases around 40 per cent for the March–April 1974 Spring Offensive. Whether through an increase in militant determination of the unions or a strengthening of employer resistance, the number of strikes reached levels unknown for many years (see table 4.1). The outcome was a private industry (weighted) average settlement rate of 33 per cent, with the public sector following close behind in the way that had by then become fully institutionalized. The actual surveyed increase in monthly pay (given the drop in hours, etc.) was 27 per cent, and the inflation out-turn for the corresponding period (fiscal 1974–5) was 22 per cent on consumer prices.

The result – coming at a time when the disruption of the oil and commodity price rises and the efforts to control inflation were putting heavy brakes on the growth in output – was not only to fuel inflation but also to maintain and even increase real wages in spite of reduced average working hours, thus effecting a sizeable shift in the proportion of national income going to wages at the expense of profits. This once-and-for-all shift has never been fully undone, but with some slight recovery of profits the system has stabilized. Gradually the processes of propaganda and discussion built up a consensus around the view that the crisis was not just a temporary hiccup, that the good days of double-figure growth were over, that the national economy's health was precarious. All this, and perhaps other subtler changes on the union side, helped to moderate union pressures with the results shown in table 4.1: a steadily – even dramatically – declining rate of major work stoppages, a total growth in real wages in the years 1975–80 of only 10 per cent, while labour productivity was growing by 35 per cent in volume terms and profits slowly creeping back up. Restiveness increased in the 1980–82 downturn as wage settlements were held at or below expected levels of inflation. It was muted, defensive restiveness, however: the increase in stoppages (see table 4.1) was of the 'less than half a day' variety. The sense of confidence in the future as cornucopia which prevailed in the early 1970s is no longer there and the edge of militancy is consequently blunted. And as table 4.5 shows, it is not profits which have been increased by the holding down of wages. (Much less dividends. The figures in the table are, of course, for returns on nominal capital. At current stock values which have tripled over the period – latterly much sustained by the demand of foreign purchasers – dividend yields ranged from under 5 per cent in 1970 to about 1.2 per cent in 1982.) The key has been the movement of the terms of trade against Japan noted in chapter 2. Corporate earnings (both dividends and retained) rather than wages have borne the brunt of the burden of increased import prices. It is not surprising that, as the export drive swung past the target of covering imports, and began to build up large surpluses again in 1983–4, a union think-tank should have based its argument for higher wages in the 1984 Spring Offensive precisely on those surpluses. Wages should be allowed to run parallel to productivity gains in manufacturing even at the expense of a bit of inflation. That way internal demand could be boosted, export cost advantages reduced, and the dependence of the economy not just on exports but on export expansion in a hostilely protectionist world, would be reduced (Keizai 1984). The 1984 outcome, however, was once again a modest settlement about one percen-

Table 4.5 Share of employee income and operating surplus of firms

	Share of employee income in GDP	Ditto as an index, corrected for the increase in the proportion of employees in the labour force*	Trading profit: margin on sales	Dividend return on capital %
1970	43.3	100.0	4.7	11.6
1973	48.1	105.3	5.2	12.8
1974	51.9	112.9	4.4	11.6
1975	53.9	117.1	3.0	9.3
1976	54.2	116.2	3.2	9.4
1977	54.5	116.0	3.0	8.8
1978	53.4	116.0	3.1	8.9
1979	54.0	115.5	3.6	9.2
1980	54.2	114.3	3.5	9.7
1981	55.1	115.5	3.1	9.5
1982	55.8	116.6	2.8	8.6

* i.e. $\left(\dfrac{\text{employee share}}{\text{GNP}} \div \dfrac{\text{employees}}{\text{labour force}} \right) \div (\text{ditto } 1970) \times 100$

Source: KY, 1981–3, p. 56, 1984, p. 40, 194 Okurashō (Yearly) (a).

tage point above the expected level of inflation.

So, flexibility in wage costs was indeed achieved and has been a factor favouring adjustment. How far was this due to the famous bonus system – the wage-payment pattern whereby as much as a third of the annual wage is paid out in mid-summer and year-end bonuses, rather than in monthly wage packets? To a limited degree, is the answer. Bonuses are separately negotiated with the unions – commonly in an Autumn Offensive which sets the rate for December and the following June – and their level is supposed to be more directly related to the firm's profitability than monthly wages. However, the degree of flexibility of the bonus payment should not be exaggerated. Bonuses *are* sticky downwards, especially in the big firms with unions, for these payments are fully incorporated into workers' income expectations; they are not just a marginal extra. Cutting them, therefore, while not quite so difficult as cutting the monthly wage, is not easy. It will be seen from the table that, even in 1975, the average large firm paid higher bonuses in nominal cash terms than the year before, even if they slipped back (but only to 1972–3 levels) in terms of the proportion of the annual wage. In the smaller firms flexibility was greater, but not all *that* much greater.

Table 4.6   Bonuses: increase and proportion of annual wage.
Manufacturing average. Summer and winter bonus combined

| | Percentage increase over previous year | | 'Months' worth' of regular pay paid as bonus | |
	firms with 500+ workers	firms with 30–99 workers	firms with 500+ workers	firms with 30–99 workers
1967	14.8	18.6	3.67	2.38
1968	19.6	28.0	3.91	2.68
1969	22.5	24.3	4.21	2.90
1970	20.9	22.2	4.40	3.04
1971	13.0	11.9	4.38	2.97
1972	13.5	17.8	4.29	3.05
1973	35.0	43.9	4.82	3.67
1974	30.2	28.8	5.06	3.80
1975	7.4	7.3	4.73	3.11
1976	10.1	11.7	4.53	3.11
1977	6.1	5.5	4.37	3.04
1978	4.6	6.4	4.26	3.03
1979	11.1	12.2	4.39	3.17
1980	9.3	10.0	4.48	3.29
1981	7.4	4.2	4.55	3.24
1982	4.3	1.9	4.52	3.15

Source: RH, 1980, 1983, Appx 40–1.

A more important institutional factor than the bonus-payment method for understanding the restrained behaviour of wage levels is the Spring Offensive method of wage determination itself. It achieves what many other countries seek to achieve by an incomes policy – the establishment of an authoritative norm for wage increases. The difference is that the Japanese norm is not set by government or by tripartite council. It is an emergent norm, a little like the wage leadership of IG Metall, but of slightly wider application. The synchronization of the pay round and the co-ordination of strategies, both by unions and managers, means that before any particular firm or industry gets to serious negotiation about, or even formulation of, a particular pay claim, there has been a preceding period of intense public discussion (in the press and in seminars at prestigious research institutes) concerning what the economy can afford as an *average* increase in wages. And out of that discussion there does emerge a consensus as to the 2–3 percentage-point span within which the norm will be established. That consensus has a powerful influence on the

wage leaders when they sit down to bargain and, within a week
or two of serious bargaining (starting with a schedule of weekly
one-day or two-day strikes established beforehand) establishes a
'norm' – i.e. the figure for 'the average percentage increase in
settlements so far this year' which thereafter changes very little
because it has such a persuasive influence on subsequent settlements.

Among the reasons why this system works and the consensus
gets established are, first, that neither Japan's political and social
history nor the structure of management and authority in
Japanese enterprises gives Japanese trade-union leaders grounds
for that underlying sense of diffuse class resentment which so
often complicates British industrial relations (most manifestly, in
the 1980s, in the nationalized industries which are not even
within the sphere of private capitalism). Secondly, and not
unrelatedly, trade-union leaders in Japan tend to share with
managers a belief in the desirability of careful macroeconomic
management of the economy, a belief that there *are* criteria of
truth and reasonableness and not just political expediency which
can and ought to be applied to all assertions about the effect of a
given level of wage increase on GNP growth (even, sometimes, a
belief that there are determinate answers to such questions).
They share, also, the economic sophistication and the data to
make arguments on these lines meaningful. The Japanese have
been practising for 20 years the kind of detailed calculating
trialogue about macroeconomy which was tried briefly in Britain
in the last year of the Heath government, and all the parties
engaged have got rather good at it.

The publication cited in this book as KR is a fine example of the
quality of the data available for such discussion, a compilation of
statistics which would make any TUC official – if he ever *were*
required to make some reasoned statement about the overall level
of wage increase the economy could afford and to rely on *Economic Trends* for his arguments – green with envy. It is published,
every January in time for the run-up to the Spring Offensive, by
the Japan Productivity Centre, a body with a tripartite governing
structure. The 1984 edition starts off with several pages of 'quick
reference guides' from which one can read off the percentage
growth, from any year to any other year, among the years 1955,
1960, 1965, 1970 and 1973–82, in nominal GNP, real GNP, numbers
employed, numbers employed for wages and salaries, nominal
GNP per person employed, and the same in real terms, consumer

prices, mining and manufacturing output, wholesale prices, average wages, real and nominal from wage statistics and average remuneration per employee from national income statistics, and labour productivity – the last five being shown separately for both fiscal and calendar years. A parallel set shows the same variables for the same year-spans but in terms of annual percentage increases. It is set up so that one can instantly read off the fact that, say, from calendar 1978 to calendar 1982 productivity went up 22 per cent, nominal wages 28 per cent, but real wages 6 per cent; or that if one takes fiscal years the figures are 19, 26 and 6 per cent, or that annualized these are growth rates of 4.2, 6.3 and 1.3 per cent respectively – and so on. There follow detailed sections on national income, wages (36 tables drawing on the widest range of sources; Ministry of Labour, MITI, EPA, Personnel Agency, Chambers of Commerce, Central Arbitration Board, and the Spring Offensive Trade Union Struggle Co-ordination Committee), productivity (15 different tables of varying provenance), employment, work hours, prices and family budgets, unions and disputes, international comparisons, and medium- and long-term forecasts – with, in 1984, a special summary of data on part-time workers. The notes to the tables, and the appendixes on statistical sources on national income accounting and the concept definitions used in employment statistics, or wage and price statistics are models of high vulgarization. The spirit of the publication is revealed in the punchy colloquial preface to the 1965 edition, reprinted in every subsequent year. It starts by reflecting on the fact that Tokugawa Japan had only static statistics of land area and forests and population. After 1870, the first word for statistics translated the German etymologically – 'government tables'. Now they are at the heart of all planning and rational discourse in business as well as government.

And how is it with unions and industrial relations? Compared with not so long back the use of statistics has made great strides. Concrete figures have increasingly replaced 'somewhat', 'considerably', 'extremely' in argument. You don't often now hear the charge that 'government statistics are a device for oppressing the people'. There is greater consensus as to how one can objectively use statistics on wages, prices, productivity . . .

Existing statistics have problems. First, they are scattered in the obscure annual reports of various Ministries and public bodies. . . .

Secondly, raw figures often need processing. . . .
You can be given figures for total sales, value-added and wage
bill, but until you turn them into labour share of value-added
ratios you can't do much with them.
Productivity figures need to be put together with wage figures.
And one needs not only the volume productivity figures
produced by the Japan Productivity Centre but also national
productivity – GNP per capita per worker. . . . The third problem is that people are far too tolerant of statistics being mis-
used only to make a short-term political point by people who
know perfectly well how shaky their figures are but pretend
they don't and count on other people's statistical ignor-
ance. . . . As Lord Disraeli said: there are three kinds of lies;
knowing uttered lies, lying silences and statistics . . .

Having thus improved on Disraeli the author goes on to
explain how the compilation will improve on that situation in all
three respects, not least, in the third respect, by the detailed
annotations, warnings and background information. Recently
the compilation has sold 140,000 copies a year.

Supply of new skills

One final question arises concerning worker and union response
as constraints on enterprise adjustment policies. How well – to
put it in Western terms – did the labour market respond to the
expanded demand for the skills needed in the expanding
technology-frontier industries?

The answer is, of course, that one should *not* put it in Western
terms. Response to market signals did doubtless:

(a) have some effect on career choices among children choosing
different paths through the educational system,
(b) provide some stimulus to entrepreneurial effort in running
private vocational training schools for scarce skills – though
according to the Education Ministry's statistics, the number of
pupils in such schools declined by 6 per cent from 1972–8 – from
1.3 to 1.2 million – and the bulk of them, anyway, were in driving
and cooking and dressmaking and bookkeeping schools.

But a far larger role in the provision of new skills for new
technologies was played —

(a) by larger firms doing their own training (of people with an adequate schooling or experience base to receive it), and
(b) by the decisions of public authorities to expand the courses of study which provide that necessary theoretical base for in-firm training.

As for the first, life-time employment practices eliminate Becker's distinction between enterprise-specific skill-training which it is sensible for the firm to pay for, and training in general skills which it may justly hesitate to pay for because those skills may be taken elsewhere by their possessor, and they may be available, without investment, in the market anyway. Life-time employment provides incentives to invest in every kind of training as well as reducing the availability of general skills in the market.

As for the public provision of the basic intellectual training necessary for the acquisition of high-level industrial skills, Japan had 311 students on tertiary-level engineering courses for every 100,000 of the population in 1970, and 337 in 1978. To give an idea of the scale of this effort, Britain had 47 and 46 respectively in those years, though for pure science did rather better than Japan – 70 per 100,000 in 1970 compared with Japan's 44, and 74 in 1978 compared with Japan's 47 (Mombushō, 1979, p.15). Outputs of electrical engineers are notably higher, proportionate to population, in Japan than in any other country. 'NTT, the country's telecommunications giant (the Japanese British Telecom) recruits 3,000 electronics graduates a year – more than the entire output of the UK.' (*The Times*, 12 June 1984).

Workers and their unions: who bore the brunt of adjustment?

Clearly, all these processes of adjustment were not painless. Workers were paid as a whole in lower rates of wage increase than they had come to expect. Many of those who remained with their firms suffered the disruption of transfer to unfamiliar jobs and often unfamiliar places. But those who suffered most were clearly those who lost their jobs and did not immediately find new ones.

The most obvious index of the extent of this suffering is the unemployment rate. Official definitions of unemployment are more restricted in Japan than in most countries, and some adjustments are needed for cross-national comparability. One adjustment exercise shows how the application of American criteria –

including those laid off on near full pay and school leavers waiting to take up a promised job – would in some months of some years considerably more than double the unemployment rate (Taira, 1983). Such an adjustment might well give a truer index of under-utilization of the economy's labour capacity. Here, however, we are looking at unemployment not as a problem of sub-optimal utilization of available resources (in which sense it is probably, in most economies, wholly trivial in comparison with the under-utilization of the abilities of those who are actually employed), but as a 'misery index'. Hence a different adjustment would be in order. The figures in table 4.7 add to the standard official figures (for the average monthly employment rate) those who, though counted as not in the labour-force because they neither had a job nor looked for one in the previous week, say that they would like a job in principle and are currently available to take one. Column C counts all such people, column B only those among them who said they had made some moves to find a

Table 4.7   Some unemployment statistics

	As percentage of the labour force			Officially counted unemployed	
	Officially counted unemployed (seeking work in previous week)	Adding job-seekers during previous month who are currently available	Adding others who say they would like a job and are available	Percentage who are heads of families	Percentage who left previous job involuntarily
	A	B	C	D	E
1970	1.1			34	
1973	1.3			32	14
1974	1.4			33	
1975	1.9			36	33
1976	2.0			39	
1977	2.0	3.3	4.2	35	
1978	2.2	3.6	4.7	36	35
1979	2.1	3.3	4.9	36	30
1980	2.0	3.0	4.0	33	28
1981	2.2			35	24
1982	2.4			34	28
1983	2.6				

Source: KR 1984, p. 118; Rōdōshō, Yearbook, mimeo. Columns A and D are annual averages from the monthly labour-force surveys; B, C and E derive from the more detailed March survey. The relevant questions for B and C have not been asked since 1980.

job in the previous month. (It is assumed that the average monthly adjustment would not be greatly different from the adjustment indicated by the March special survey, the only month when information about the preferences of those not in the labour-force is collected.)

The record becomes less impressive when these adjustments are made – the increased rate raising the unemployment rate of women in particular, it being generally women who are on the fringes between the categories 'not in the labour-force' and 'unemployed work-seekers'. Nevertheless, by the standards of European and North American economies these are enviably low rates – sustained with only a half per cent increase on the official rate to the end of 1983 at a time when even West Germany was following the rest of Europe on the road to double-figure unemployment.

The leap in unemployment of 0.6 per cent – or at most 1 per cent – between 1973 and 1975 may be taken as a fairly accurate measure of the overall impact of the mid-1970s recession – there is no interruption of the smooth long-run trends in the labour-force/non-labour-force figures to suggest that any other adjustments should be made. Nor were there any untoward kinks in the self-employment/family workers trends *except* that the trend for family workers in non-agriculture to decline was reversed after 1977. But that is of ambiguous import – it was also increasing in the late 1960s and the number of non-agricultural self-employed (nearly 7m or 8 per cent of the labour-force) has been steadily increasing all the time.

So, most of those who lost jobs as a result of recession and adjustment in the structurally depressed industries moved into other wage employment, a good many of them shifting from the manufacturing to the service sector. How difficult was their transition? A number of field studies of redundancy cases suggest that new jobs were found fairly rapidly for most of the unionized firms. In the Oki case quoted earlier, the firm claimed that 520 of the 1350 people who left or were pushed, took up the personnel department's offer to find alternative jobs, and 280 were actually placed – simultaneously the firm was offered over a thousand job places by companies keen to employ former Oki workers (Shokugyō, 1980, p.52).

But clearly smaller firms cannot lean on their suppliers to offer jobs to their left-over workers as firms like Oki can, and it is probable that the redundant included considerable numbers in poor mental or physical health who were only on the verge of employability, and had to resort to dependence on relatives and friends when the protection of the life-time employment system was withdrawn. The numbers shown by the March special surveys to have been unemployed for over a year reached its highest point for men – 190,000 or 21 per cent of the unemployed – in 1978 and thereafter declined (130,000 and 14 per cent in 1982). The peak for women (70,000) was reached in 1979 and the figure has moved irregularly since (and within the range of sampling error).

A somewhat more representative picture than the Oki case is presented by a wider union survey of redundant workers. Of those contacted (by unions) a fifth had been found jobs by their previous employer, and 4 per cent by their former union – though only after an average interval of three months. Another third were still unemployed and looking for work (Dore and Taira, 1986).

What made their situation slightly easier was their severance pay, the median size of which was equal to 37 times the median worker's monthly pay. The apparent generosity, by European or American standards, is diminished when one considers that this represents a combination of redundancy compensation *and* pension fund entitlements. Also, their new jobs were giving them lower wages – one quarter less for the median worker – and they would have had to earn 8 per cent on their severance pay (very difficult with Japan's low interest rates) to make up the difference.

Of the unemployed, also, 20 per cent were still in touch with their former firm in the hope of getting a job through its good offices, but it was clear that the majority were looking for jobs through the public employment agency and newspapers – methods which had provided jobs for only a fifth of those who were re-employed. In 'dual labour market' language, these are workers who have left the primary- and joined the secondary-job sector – the world of unstable low-wage unemployment. And this, indeed, is the fate of most 'permanent' workers after retirement from their primary careers.

An overall picture of the pattern of job loss and gain is given in table 4.8. One or two points incidentally arise from these figures. First, the overall quit rates for the four years 1974–7 range between 19.6 and 24.0 per cent and totalled 85.5 per cent. If there was no lapse of memory in this survey, only one quarter of the

Table 4.8   Job-leavers, voluntary and involuntary, and their subsequent careers. Position in March 1978 of all those who had left wage/salary jobs since March 1974, by the voluntariness of their last leaving (10,000s).

	Male	Female	Total
Involuntary job-leavers	280	124	404
now employed	200	73	273
unemployed (sought jobs in last week)	40	8	48
no job search in last week but would like job	21	27	48
no expressed wish for job	19	17	36
Voluntary job-leavers	392	603	995
now employed	273	213	486
unemployed (sought job in last week)	24	16	40
no job search in last week but would like job	39	196	235
no expressed wish for job	56	178	234
Percentages			
job-leavers/total labour-force	19.7	34.2	25.3
involuntary leavers/total leavers	41.7	17.1	28.9
still wanting job/involuntary leavers	21.7	28.2	23.8
still wanting job/voluntary leavers	16.1	35.2	27.6
active job-seekers/total wanting job	51.7	9.7	23.7

Source: RH, 1979, Appx. 116.

labour-force (20 per cent of the men and 35 per cent of the women) had been involved in producing that 86 per cent of quits. In those years, in other words, 75 per cent of the labour-force stayed where they were and the other quarter changed jobs more than three times each on average.

Another calculation which confirms that general picture suggests that among male production workers in firms with ten or more employees, those with five or more years' service in 1978 made up 64 per cent of the number employed five years previously. A similar study showed that stability rate to have been slightly lower at 60 per cent in 1972. Interestingly, however, that slight increase in stability masks different trends in firms of different size. In the biggest firms with more than 1,000 workers the rate went from 77 to 70 per cent. The trend was the other way in smaller firms. For those with 10 to 99 employees, for instance, the rate was 45 per cent for 1967–72, 57 per cent for 1973–8 (RH, 1979, Appendix p.114). The same applied to wholesale and retail commerce – an indication, perhaps, that the process of diffusion of large firm 'life-time employment' practices to smaller firms was still continuing in spite of – or because of – the mid-1970s' recession.

A second incidental point to be made about the table is that the proportion of involuntary job quits, as measured in this survey of the *quitter*'s perception of the reasons for leaving (29 per cent overall, 32 per cent for men) is about five percentage points higher than the proportions which emerge from the standard annual survey of *firms*' recorded reasons for their employees' departure. Perhaps, given the nature of the surveys and their potential for revealing embarrassing gaps between theory and practice, one ought to say *only* about five points higher.

As for the main point to be made about the table – the patterns of job turnover – the table reveals several things about differences between men and women. Far more women than men have had the experience of leaving jobs and a much higher proportion of them (83 per cent as against 58 per cent) have done so voluntarily. Of those who left involuntarily the proportion still looking for a job was not too different, but a much higher proportion of the men in that category (38 per cent to be precise) are shown by the breakdowns in the original table from which this table was drawn to be men whose involuntary quit was due to retirement. Of those who still want a job, a far higher proportion of men than of women are actively looking for one – i.e. made some move to get one in the survey week. As one would expect, a much higher proportion of women are secondary earners who can afford to wait until the right kind of work comes along. In fact, the breakdowns show that of the 600,000 men who say they would like a job but were not actually seeking one in the survey week, 150,000 were men whose involuntary leaving of their job was due to retirement and another 280,000 were men who voluntarily withdrew from their job for health or domestic reasons – the majority of them, probably, from among the 980,000 (out of the 6.7 million total of job leavers) who were not employees, but self-employed or family workers (RH 1979, Appendix 119).

Who bears the brunt: older workers

The retired workers just mentioned – those on the edge of the labour-force, many not very actively seeking work but hoping that something will turn up – were very much at the centre of concerns about unemployment in Japan in the 1970s, and should play a key role in any assessment of 'who bore the brunt' of structural adjustment.

The 'life-time employment' of Japanese large companies has never meant employment up to the moment of withdrawal from the labour-force. It has traditionally meant employment until the age of 55; the firm can automatically discharge its employees after maximum use of their most productive years. The mitigating factors have been, first, the retirement bonus, usually amounting to the equivalent of 3–4 years' salary after thirty years' service; secondly, the possibility of re-employment in the firm for a few further years, particularly for those who have reached the higher ranks of their particular promotion scale – nearly always at a diminished salary, and often on a gradual disengagement basis; and thirdly, the possibility for employees of large firms of being 'placed' in employment, with another smaller company in some way (as supplier or customer) dependent on it – a transition which may take place before 55 in order to get established early enough to make the second career a meaningful one. Not every-body did get so placed, however. Labour-force-by-age statistics show that in every industry Japan has a lower proportion of workers aged 55–64 than in the USA, Sweden, UK or West Ger-many (6 per cent of the labour-force overall, as compared with 9–11 per cent), but *also* a higher proportion over 65 – again 6 as opposed to 1–3 per cent (RH 1980, Appendix p.190). More older workers *need* to work after the retirement bonus runs out and before the pension (currently running at about 5 per cent of the average industrial wage) begins at the age of 70.

Two long-term changes brought this system increasingly into question. On the one hand the great decline in mortality (male expectation of life at birth had reached 73 by the mid-1970s) lengthened the period of retirement well beyond what a normal retirement bonus could take care of, while the decline in fertility increased the proportion of old people who *could* not, and the increase in individualistic ideas increased the proportion who felt that they *should* not, depend on their children. Secondly, this individual welfare problem was matched on a national account-ing scale by the prospect of a rapidly rising dependency ratio. Because of the suddenness of the falls, first of mortality then of fertility, the proportion of the population aged 55 and over was expected to leap from 15 per cent in 1980 to 24 per cent in 2000, a faster change than in any other nation's history and a rate in 2000 fully five points higher than the present relatively stable high rates of UK or Sweden.

In the early 1970s, no one had any doubt that something had to be done. One common response to the welfare problem was the pension scheme, partially supplementing, partially replacing the lump-sum retirement bonus. Two-thirds of the firms quoted on the stock exchange had such schemes by 1979 (RH, 1980, Appendix p.206), but the pensions were still – like that state old-age pensions paid from age 70 – seen to be only of 'pocket money' proportions. The preferred solution – tackling also the overall dependency of ratio problem – was to raise the retirement age.

Everyone agreed in principle, but most senior managers balked at doing anything in practice. One can imagine that boards of directors would cast a particularly cold eye on such proposals. Few get to be a director until their early fifties, and not having to retire at 55 is a key element of their privileges. Likewise, even if below director rank, the more senior the manager, the more likely he is to be re-employed at part pay after retirement. And it is natural for senior people to believe that the justification for their privilege lies in the fact that they are the brightest and the best who *do* go on maturing in wisdom and experience more than they decline in vigour and imagination, and that for lesser mortals for whom the reverse is the case the firm needs to have the option of hurrying them on out, in order to make way for younger men. The seniority wage curves of Japanese firms – rising, as they do, more steeply at the beginning and then flattening out, with the deceleration starting, usually, for manual workers in the late thirties and for managerial workers in the early forties – are generally seen as combining two principles. One is correspondence with current 'contribution' seen to be steadily enhanced by experience (more so with managers than with men: hence the later onset of deceleration in their seniority increments). The other is need arising from family responsibilities. In the 'model wage curves' abstracted by the Central Arbitration Board from various company practices, the 'typical worker' is expected to have one dependant at 25, two at 30, three at 35, four between 40 and 50 (a widowed mother joins the wife and two children) and then three again, when he is 55, as the eldest child becomes independent. The second principle leads to people being 'underpaid' by the criterion of the first principle during their early years and 'overpaid' during their later ones. And while this was quite acceptable, managers were likely to feel that the first principle would be too far lost sight of if retirement ages were raised. The firm needs to have the chance gently to ease out dead-beats. Transition to a later retirement age would pose promotion blockages. And so on.

The unions, however, were dominated by the older manual workers, including those who were least likely to be sure of re-employment after 55. They pressed for change in the early 1970s. Growth rates were still good. There was no surplus of labour. 'The consensus' – the constant alarmist magazine articles about the 'ageing problem' – added strength to the unions' case. A large number of firms made agreements with their unions providing for a progressive raising of the retirement age over a period of years. Then came the recession, the disappearance of a generalized state of labour shortage, a spate of emergency measures by firms in trouble to urge *early* retirement on their workers, and a growing realization that the future was probably one offering less work to be done rather than more. The movement towards later retiring ages continues as table 4.9 shows.

But the conviction has gone out of it, as the survey of managerial opinion reported in table 4.10 suggests. Far fewer of those who responded could think of more than one reason in 1981 as compared with 1974. And the most common answer was not, as it had been, in terms of benefit to the firm itself, but in terms of obedience to 'a consensus'. That consensus about social responsibility was reinforced in 1978 by a law requiring all firms with more than 100 workers to employ workers over 55 to the extent of at least 6 per cent of their labour-force. By 1980, 52 per cent of firms had met their legal quota – in fact two percentage points less than the year before. Notably delinquent firms were sternly required by the local labour office to present plans for achieving conformity to the law at an early date (STN, 1980, p. 103). How much the law accounts for the forward movement in 1980–1 shown in table 3.9 is hard to say. A certain amount must be owing to the working

Table 4.9   Retirement ages in a sample of firms: 1974 and 1981

| | | *Percentage of firms with retirement age of* | | | |
		55	56–59	60	61 or more
Firms with 5,000 or more workers	1974	38	51	11	—
	1980	35	37	27	—
	1981	30	33	37	—
Firms with 30–99 workers	1974	52	6	37	4
	1980	37	18	40	4
	1981	36	15	44	3

Source: RH, 1981, Appendix p. 97.

Table 4.10   Reasons for postponing retirement age

1974		1981	
To make use of the abilities of experienced workers	47%	Because society expects it	41%
Because of union pressure	38%	Union pressure	28%
To improve work motivation	32%	Utilize abilities	27%
Because of labour shortages	28%	Improve work motivation	16%
Because later retirement is something society expects of business firms	24%	Labour shortage	11%
Because changes in production conditions make it easier to employ older workers	18%	Production changes: easier to employ elderly	4%
Average number of replies per firm	1.9		1.3

Source: RH, 1980, p. 137.

through of the earlier agreements for a progressive schedule of changes in the retirement age concluded with unions several years before.

Nevertheless, it remains true that, in spite too of special measures by the state, it is the older workers who have suffered most from the changes of the last decade. In 1975, when, according to labour market statistics there were still 2.8 jobs chasing every 15 to 19-year-old job seeker, there were eleven workers aged 55 or more chasing each job for which they were eligible. (The 1973 figures had been 7.4:1 and 1:2 respectively; by 1980 there were 2.6:1 and 1:6.) (STN, 1980, p.40). Men aged over 55 make up 20 per cent of officially counted male unemployment (only 9 per cent in 1955) (RH, 1979, p.138) and two-thirds of them have been unemployed for more than six months (compared with 20 per cent of the 35-year-olds) (RH, 1981, Appx. 96). Some care should be taken in interpreting these figures, however, since insured workers who retire from their jobs have to register as job-seekers at the local employment exchange if they are to draw their six months' insurance benefit entitlement. (And are likely to tell the same story about being job-seekers to labour-force surveyors.) The officials know they have no intention of taking jobs and never offer them one, but nevertheless they are counted in the applicant/vacancy statistics. In one office I visited the over-60s made up 15 per cent of the registrands, and 97 per cent of them were drawing insurance benefit – compared with 70 per cent of the under-45s, though the latter included a number of women who were stopping work to have a baby and likewise had registered to draw their insurance entitlements.

It should be remembered, too, that by no means all those who 'lose their job' in the late fifties and sixties are coming out of wage employment. Many are self-employed enterprisers and their family co-workers. The 'structurally depressed' cottage industry trades – notably textiles, clothing, leatherwork, ceramics, flatware – have a high proportion of such workers. Most of them are 'hanging on' – which explains why output levels are maintained in these industries even after import competition has driven prices down. Frequently they do so much longer than previous generations did. They do not have the chance to move on, as their fathers did, to the status of 'retired grandpa helping out at a pinch' because *their* children have all moved on into industries with better prospects. Some of them do give up, however, when they cannot work hard enough to get a living wage from their gross profit margins, and they may have a worse time even than former employees in finding an alternative job.

Japan seems regularly to produce a lot of fiction about old men, particularly their vapid sexual fantasies. The 1970s, however, saw a lot of fiction and documentaries about the traumas of retirement which had clearly captured public attention – the man who cannot stop himself from riding his commuter train with his packed lunch just to see if the factory is still there; the humiliations of all the formalities of registering to collect unemployment insurance, etc. The more workaholic a society, the greater, clearly, the pain of non-work or the cessation of work.

Who bears the brunt: unions

One final topic belongs to this section on 'who were the victims of adjustment'. How did the unions fare? Too often it is assumed that unions belong to their members and that no distinction need be made between the interests of workers and the interests of unions. But that is clearly a mistake. Unions have full-time staff with their constellations of interests. In societies where unions are market-based, not enterprise-based, with professional *union* staff independent of any firm in the industry – i.e. in most industrial societies other than Japan – workers in a declining industry can be offered the most generous terms – no redundancy, run-down of the workforce purely by natural wastage, large redundancy bonuses to tempt them into voluntary retirement, etc. – but *their* general satisfaction will not be matched by the comparable satisfaction of the union officials. The livelihood of the latter depends on the total *number* of workers in the industry, not on their identity, and stoppage of recruitment is just as bad news for them as dismissal of workers.

The enterprise union system in Japan by and large does not give union officials these extra, personal reasons for opposing rationalization adjustment in declining industries. Most full-time union officials are on leave from a job in the firm and expect to return to it in a few years' time anyway. Usually only a small number of federation officials whose salaries are a minute proportion of the union dues paid by their industry constituency have become union officials for life. The situation is slightly different in a small number of industries with large and very active industrial federations. It so happens that textiles, the subject of the case study in later chapters, is one of these and the story of that union's response to the threat of declining membership – diversification and the conquering of new fields – will be told there.

5
Government and employment

The role of government in facilitating and directing the adjustment process has many facets, but it would seem sensible to begin, following on the previous discussion, with its interventions in labour matters, starting particularly with the problems of the aged. A number of schemes have been devised:

1 A special counselling service for older workers was set up in 1974 and had about 250 centres by 1980 – in which year it succeeded in placing some 20,000 workers – 29 per cent of that year's applicants. There was also a special scheme for workers 'with particular difficulties' in which 'those over 45' were included along with the handicapped, ex-prisoners and homeless workers. They were eligible for special counselling and retraining as well as the special allowance for six months, but the meagre uptake (2,500 in 1980) suggests that few of the 'ordinary' aged were deemed, or wished to be deemed, eligible (STN, 1980, p.112).

2 A 'talent bank' system, chiefly designed to channel older men with professional skills who had retired from larger firms into small and medium firms. Again, on a small scale, with some 6,000 workers placed in 1980 (STN, 1980, p. 109).

3 A new departure in 1980 was the establishment of a hundred new 'Silver[-haired] Talent Centres'. These were an attempt to provide community-organized 'make-work' to supplement the incomes of older people – a modern equivalent of the Unemployment Relief Work Scheme which had been organized since 1949. The latter still provided some income and comfort to over 95,000 workers in 1980, two-thirds of them women whose average age was 63, and one-third men whose average age was 66. Like farm prices, and leather imports, unemployment relief work is a *no-go* area for public policy. Its *habitués* enjoy a convivial day of chat and tea-breaks punctuated by occasional road-mending or folding of paper flowers. They are, in effect, civil pensioners whose established rights to their modest daily allowance are sometimes reinforced by the vociferous demonstrations of their militant

unions. Their average length of service to the cause of unemployment relief was no less than 21 years 4 months in 1980, no new
admissions to their ranks having been permitted since 1971 (STN,
1980, pp.666–71, 424–63, 165–85). The Silver Talent Centres were
intended to break away from the air of 'appeasement of the
aggressive poor' which tends to surround these make-work
schemes, and to create more informal community-centred,
community-run operations. They are controlled by a community
council of local municipal officials, directors of old people's clubs
and community centres and they send their registered odd-
jobbers out on request for gardening, park tidying, household
repairs, envelope-stuffing, bicycle park supervision, etc. In 1980
each centre got a subsidy of $25,000 and provided 10 days' work
a month for some 500 people each (STN, 1980, pp. 117–25). My
own sampling of a single Silver Talent Centre found it quite
unable to think of a way of making contact with a retired white-
collar or managerial worker who could help with a survey; gar-
deners and helpers with house-removal they could find in plenty.
4   Other relatively inexpensive measures were those aimed at
firms about to release retirees on to the market. The 1978 law
requiring employment of a proportion of old people has already
been mentioned. A second measure was to try to universalize the
'best practice' of those firms which tried to provide for the
re-employment of their former workers in subsidiaries and suppliers' firms, or within the firm itself. This was done by requiring
those firms with a retirement age under 60 to appoint a 're-
employment manager' and to draw up a 're-employment plan'
for their retirees. There were also provisions for pre-retirement
retraining grants – to cover lost wages as well as training costs.
The take-up appears to have been slight. For firms which had
already raised the retirement age to 60 a subsidy was available
(about $1,000 a year for small and medium firms, $750 for large
firms – a little under a month's salary) for workers re-employed
up to the age of 65 (STN, 1980, pp.105–7).
5   Finally, from mid-1979, a special employment subsidy was
started for older workers – to operate in districts where the
unemployment rate was over 2 per cent and the overall vacancy/
applicant ratio worse than 0.7:1. Those who offered them a job
with the promise of keeping them in it after the end of the subsidy
period – and who by such hiring thereby raised either the number
or the proportion of old people on their books – could receive
three-fifths of their first year's wages and a half of their wage for

the next six months if they were over 55 – somewhat more for a small or medium firm (i.e. with less than 300 employees) and somewhat less, in either case, if the employee hired was between 45 and 54. Over 100,000 workers were accepted for subsidy under this scheme between July 1979 and June 1980, and it was extended for a further year (STN, 1980, p.87).

The two other major forms of labour market intervention, apart from these special measures for older workers, were:

(a)   those responding to what were perceived as cyclical difficulties in particular industries hit by recession,
(b)   those responding to what were perceived as the structural difficulties of declining industries.

It was, not surprisingly, the need for the first in the recession years of 1974–5 which prompted the institutionalization of this activity. After a certain amount of *ad hoc* experimentation the new system was inaugurated with a complete revision of the 1947 Employment Insurance Act. The new 1974 Act came into general operation in April 1975, certain provisions in January of that year. The contribution structure was changed to put a larger share of the burden on the employer – 8 permil of the payroll with 5 permil coming from the employee, compared with an equal 6.5 permil share previously. The compensating new departure was that the funds could be used not only for subsistence benefits to the unemployed (plus the usual training, job search and house removal allowances, etc.,) but also to subsidize firms to *prevent* unemployment. Eligible firms could claim one half (larger firms) or two-thirds (up to 300 workers) of money paid out as retainers to laid-off workers (but not more than normal unemployment benefit which was calculated in 1975 to be about 50 per cent of the average wage) (Sekiguchi, 1978, p.23.) The subsidy could be paid for 200 days per employed worker per year. Eligibility was a matter of being in an industry in which production had fallen by 10 per cent over the previous year, or being a sub-contractor to a larger firm which had gone bankrupt, or being in an industry subject to a recession cartel, and in any case being a firm currently working not more than a given maximum number of hours of overtime per worker. At the peak period of utilization of these provisions – between January and August 1975 – the scheme paid out a quarter of a billion dollars for 28 million man-days of lay-off. The numbers involved in any one month averaged 340,000 during this period (Sekiguchi, 1978, p.22.).

Grants were also made to encourage the 'loaning' of workers to other firms – two-thirds of whatever subsidization the original firm had to provide to maintain their wages, provided it was not more than half the wage paid by the firm to which they were loaned. The scheme was conditional on the arrangement lasting for at least six months (and on the recipient firm having been in existence for at least three months – and not being an *ad hoc* device for catching a subsidy!)

The distinction between a firm particularly hard-hit by a recession, but with eventual expectations of recovery, and a firm in a structurally depressed industry with little hope of recovery, is not easy to make. It was obvious from an early stage of the operation of the temporary lay-off subsidy scheme that some of the laid-off workers might never be re-employed. The first extension of the scheme to accommodate structural shifts in the economy was to make laid-off, or-about-to-be-laid-off workers eligible for an additional 'training grant preparatory to a move to a new industry'. But it soon became obvious that this was not enough. The shift in relative energy costs had decisively deprived certain industries (e.g. aluminium, electric arc furnaces), and the emergence of Asian competition had deprived others (e.g. plywood) of their comparative advantage. The Special Law for Particular Depressed Industries, which will be discussed later, was accompanied by a Law for Emergency Measures to deal with Workers leaving Particular Depressed Industries which came into force in January 1978. By March 1981, 39 industries were on the eligible list.

A firm in one of these industries which is proposing to contract and thereby shed a portion of its workforce (by either voluntary or compulsory retirement) must, having consulted with its union, present a plan to the local employment exchange which details the efforts it will make to find its workers alternative jobs. Those who do not get re-employed are issued with a pass-book which entitles them to special counselling and special benefits. Any employer who takes them on either for work or training as regular (permanent) workers will receive half (in small firms two-thirds) of their wages for six months. They can get a daily allowance somewhat greater than the unemployment benefit for up to one year for attending approved training courses, or for waiting for such courses to begin. (Or just for having been sacked, at the age of 35-plus, from a shipyard. The ship-building industry bargained the best terms, arguing the severity, scale and concentration of its redundancies.) The usual job-search, travel and house-removal grants are specially enhanced for these workers. They can claim the equivalent of a month's training allowance if they start their own private business within 18 months of losing their job. Up to March 1981 there had been nearly 6,000 firms declaring redundancies under these provisions, more than a half of them in ship-building and a quarter in textiles. Nearly 90,000 pass-books had been issued (STN, p.336).

Finally, among official measures for smoothing adjustment in the labour market, mention should be made of the Employment Promotion Agency, a well-established body dating from 1961, created as part of the scheme for running down the coal industry. It provides employment, in the first place, for a staff of nearly 5,000, the senior members of which are drawn from the Ministry of Labour. (It is, in other words, one of the organizations which allows the Ministry to set private firms a good example by 'looking after' its employees beyond retirement, though perhaps, quango-hunting members of the Administrative Reform Committee have suggested, on public funds this virtuous practice comes to the Ministry too easily and to the tax-payer too expensively.) It spends (1980) Y120bn. (half a billion dollars) provided from the employment insurance fund with a small supplement ultimately drawn from the Post Office savings. The Agency is given a number of delegated roles under particular legislation – the welfare of itinerant construction workers, special measures for former employees at American bases and for Okinawa, etc., – but it is primarily concerned with industrial training. It runs a university with a four-year degree course (as well as short courses) for industrial trainers, as well as three junior colleges with two-year courses, and some 86 training schools. All these training facilities are primarily for workers and would-be workers in small and medium firms which cannot easily provide training themselves. The more than 100,000 apartments which the Agency owns are provided for the same stratum of workers when they have to move away from their original homes in search of work.

One final institutional complex deserves mentioning – the national system of skill certification which serves to improve market information by giving employers certain minimum-performance guarantees for the skills which workers offer. Unlike societies where trade unions and professional bodies have established apprenticeship training and certification schemes or gained supervisory control over university and other institution-

al vocational courses as an integral part of their attempts to
monopolize the market for their skills – and did so long before
states took it upon themselves to be concerned about the skill
levels of their citizens – Japan is a typical 'late developer' in that
formal skill certification for the open market is almost wholly the
monopoly of the state (apart from seven 'approved certificates'
such as those issued by co-operatives in local areas which have
traditional skills of wood carving and the like). In 1980 there were
113 craft certificate examinations in operation – nearly all with
two grades and with average pass rates for the 150,000 who took
tests in that year of 43 per cent and 45 per cent for the lower and
higher levels respectively: the tests are no mere formality (STN,
1980, pp.303–13).

Again, however, these tests have traditionally been utilized
only for workers in the small- and medium-firm sector. The
65,000 who gained some qualification in 1980 have to be set
against the figure of over a million new entrants to the workforce
in that year. The reason is obvious. Employers who take on
workers under implicit life-time guarantees – and give them skill
training in the expectation of monopolizing the returns on their
investment – have no interest in encouraging their workers to
gain a certificate which might encourage them to leave and
chance their arm in the market which is the only place where the
certificate has meaning.

The traumas of the mid-1970s, however, did to a small degree
put this state of affairs in question. A report of the Minister of
Labour's Council for Medium-Term Labour Policy, asked in 1977
specifically to consider the retirement age and the problem of
older workers, recommended as one means of ameliorating their
situation a greater use of qualifications at both craft and professional levels. If a man, instead of simply being a manager with a
vast experience of the financial affairs of the Mitsubishi Widget
Company, acquires a qualification as a certified accountant, the
trauma of being 'tapped on the shoulder' and asked to accept
voluntary retirement, or the trauma of experiencing blocked
promotion in a top-heavy slow-growth firm and being given out
of kindness a nice title and a 'seat by the window', or even the
trauma of ordinary retirement at 55, would be less acute. His ego
could dress itself in a professional and not just an organizational
identity, *and* he would have better prospects of re-employment.
(See Sumiya 1978 and Tanaka 1979.)

Such arguments obviously appeal to the Ministry of Labour.

Labour markets (*external*) are its jurisdictional preserve and the
more they flourish the better. But these ideas seem not yet to have
made any notable headway. The most popular of the 113 craft
courses in 1980 were still predominantly the traditional self-
employment and small-industry skills. In order of popularity,
those tests which attracted more than 2,000 applicants were:
plumbing, carpentry, mechanical drawing, construction machinery repair, agricultural machinery repair, electronics assembly,
kimono   dressmaking,   window-sash-making,   plastering,
machine fitting, turning and house-painting (STN, 1980, pp.305–
10).

Electronics assembly is the only craft in the list which has any
obvious connection with the high-technology industries, and the
non-manual skills such as computer programming and so on are
not embraced within the system. The contribution of the system
remains primarily that of raising skill levels in the self-employed
and small firm sector and facilitating market mobility in that
sector. It does little to promote the transformation of the mix of
available skills made necessary by the shift in the industrial
structure towards a heavier bias on knowledge-intensive, high-
technology industry.

Government policies in the labour field: an assessment

The contribution of government labour policies to facilitating (i.e.
accelerating, minimizing the frictions and welfare problems
attendant on) structural adjustment of the Japanese economy
may then be summarized as follows:

1   In expanding the supply of the new skills required by expanding sectors, the general encouragement given by the Ministry of
Education to the growth of university-level engineering and
especially electronics engineering training, and the recognition
and enhancement of status given to a new category of vocational
training school (*senshū-gakkō*) doubtless had some impact, but
the role of government in craft skill development was small.
2   Schemes to deal with the welfare problem of joblessness
thrown up by both cyclical and structural difficulties were devised to operate 'with the grain' of the life-time employment
system – temporary lay-off subsidies, 'worker loan' subsidies,
and so on, and must have had some impact.
3   Schemes for 'compensation of the victims of adjustment' –

those in declining industries robbed of livelihoods which they had grown to assume they had a right to – also relied to some extent on utilizing a presumed-life-time employer's obligation to try to 'place' his redundant workers, but also involved more direct money compensation. They may well have contributed to the relative weakness in Japan of political demands for tariff or quota protection or subsidies to prevent declining industries from declining.

4 The long-term structural problem of an ageing labour-force and high dependency ratios is already treated (in this very long-term-future-oriented society) as a major current problem and piecemeal attempts to tackle it are already being made in spite of trends in the overall employment situation towards a reduction in the demand for labour.

5 But the best contribution of government in the labour field to the process of structural adjustment came from its overall management of the economy. Adjustment – cutting back on the 'loser' industries – caused less pain and suffering and gave rise to less political conflict than it would have done, had the economy not been following an expansionary course with unemployment held low. And the economy could follow that course because inflation was under control. And one important reason why inflation was under control was that wage-cost-push was held down by the moderate stance taken by unions in wage negotiations. This was not the achievement of a formal incomes policy, but the role of government in giving leadership, and in engineering policy consensus was of great importance to the outcome. It is to that role that we now turn.

6
Government and the business enterprise

Government's role in (a) charting the directions in which structural change could most desirably evolve – i.e. formulating a structural adjustment policy and (b) supplying incentives, both material and moral, for corporate decision-makers to move in those directions, has been very considerable.

The leverage available to the main ministry concerned, MITI (the Ministry of Transport looks after shipping, rail and road transport, Health and Welfare after pharmaceuticals, etc.), somewhat diminished at the beginning of the last decade with the easing of the foreign exchange shortage, hence of foreign exchange controls, hence of the rationale for the control over technology imports which had been an important mechanism for directing industrial investment. Under one legislative pretext or another, however, the formal licensing of major investment projects or their informal subjection to administrative guidance still continues – certainly in those producer-goods industries which are likely to need recourse to recession cartels and need, therefore, MITI's good will.

A number of influential Japanese are opposed in principle to the deployment of a strong industrial policy. Some argue that an industrial policy is something which only backward economies need. Now that Japan has grown up, a tough anti-trust competition policy would be more to the point. Secondly, the spread of Reaganomics across the Pacific has had its effect; 1981 saw the establishment of an Administrative Reform Commission dedicated to the 'small government' ideal, determined to root out inefficiency and the jungle of subsidization policies (but with a secretariat drawn from precisely that cadre of *dirigiste* officials who were the authors of those policies). Finally, there are a number of ardent internationalists who welcome anything which restricts the scope and impact of industrial policy, if only because a strong industrial policy reinforces the 'Japan Incorporated' image and with it all the foreigner-provoking mysteries of cultural impenetrability, intangible tariff barriers and the like which get Japan a bad name.

The bureaucratic and business establishment is largely un-moved by such considerations, however, and in one of its latest statements the Industrial Structure Council claims that there are certain reasons why an activist industrial policy is more than ever necessary. In two distinct ways there is now a greater divergence between a private and a social cost-benefit calculus. Rising ener-gy costs and the vulnerability of Japan's energy supplies create a national interest in developing new forms of energy which the price mechanism determining private rates of return cannot fully reflect. Secondly, consumer needs are turning towards more sophisticated quality-of-life concerns which call for industrial location patterns which run against the grain of profitability. Moreover, in general, as technology gets more sophisticated, lead times get longer, and investments in general get costlier, they also get riskier and more in need of the reinforcement of state insurance. MITI is not about to withdraw to a back seat (MITI 1980 (a), p.71; 1980 (b), pp.179–82).

There are, as has often been pointed out, very good reasons why it does not need to – reasons why the Japanese business world should be especially prone to co-operate effectively with government attempts to shape the industrial structure. They lie, in the accounts of most Western observers comparing Japan with their own society, in a strong sense of national purpose and the ability of the bureaucracy to mobilize a relatively disinterested consensus around a view of what is 'in the national interest'.

Cultural characteristics, specifically the value placed on soli-darity and cohesion, combine with the emotional deposits of a century of catching-up history – a long-haul struggle to carve out for Japan a respected place in an international community domin-ated by white-skinned countries of Mediterranean–Atlantic cul-ture – to create a deep-rooted sense of a cultural gulf which divides Japanese sensibilities from the sensibilities of other peo-ples (or perhaps of all except the other post-Confucian peoples), and gives every Japanese a basis for kinship with every fellow countryman.

Both of those features – the basic culture of inter-personal relations and the recent inculcation of patriotism – are important.

When the report of the Aluminium Sub-Committee of the Industrial Structure Council declares that it is in the nation's interest to sustain a certain loss-making aluminium smelting capacity for a few years, and seriously suggests that, formal state aid apart, the customers, bankers and electricity suppliers of the smelters should spontaneously offer sacrifices to help them stay in business, it does so partly because of those features of Japanese business relations described in an earlier section – the tendency to put more weight on trust, give and take, and loyalty to long-standing trade partners, and less on single-transaction profits and the legal protections of contract. But it also is partly because it assumes that the report's arguments as to why it is in *Japan's* interests to retain a 700,000-ton smelting capacity will be accepted as a reason for patriotic rallying-round.

So, also, when (as we shall see in a later chapter) importers of cotton yarn receive administrative guidance not to import with excessive zeal when a recession cartel has been declared in the spinning industry, the same sentiments are mobilized. There *is* some moral pressure on the importers – at least to the extent of prompting some of them to set up separate dummy companies so that the odium of doing business with foreigners to the detriment of fellow Japanese does not fall on them directly.

A second circumstance which favours the efficacy of Japan's industrial policy is the high prestige of the centrally important ministry, MITI, and its ability to recruit from the very brightest of the nation's talented graduates. Many of those recruited will have classmates in leading industrial firms, and career lines from the MITI bureaucracy can also run into leading positions in politics and public or private corporations, as Chalmers Johnson has recently documented in illuminating detail (Johnson, 1982).

One should add, perhaps, that many centuries' absorption of the Confucian tradition helps government officials to start off with something like a halo of authority, anyway. It is this which supports and makes *relatively* effective the 'guidance' which MITI offers with no particular statutory authority. (Only relatively: there are well-known cases of defiance, such as the automobile industry; see Magaziner and Hout, 1980). Consider, for example, the following routine newspaper report. It does seem a long way from a Britain where Mrs Thatcher prides herself on not having her government 'nanny' anybody.

> MITI is about to embark on an attempt to guide the makers of domestic appliances like colour TVs and refrigerators to establish their standard retail prices at a reasonable level. The reason is that the large discounts available at warehouse-stores have spread to the smaller retail shops, leading to a general discount war. Suspicions that standard retail prices are being

set in order to raise the discount rate are likely to bring consumer criticism on the whole standard retail price system, and to render a number of smaller retail businesses unviable . . . With VTRs and cameras, constant innovations make the discounting of older models inevitable. It is with mature products like refrigerators and colour TV, where every maker is more or less up to the same quality standard and there is not much chance to sell on the prestige of the brand name that the problem arises . . . The Fair Trade Commission has already drawn attention to the existence of problems with regard to standard retail prices, but with no effect. The discount war has continued. Hence MITI's decision to embark on guidance and when cases of firms unreasonably inflating their standard retail prices are found, to ask them to mend their ways. (*Nihon Keizai Shimbun*, 12 March 1984.)

A third factor facilitating a positive government role is the fact that Japan has a powerful set of industry associations which embrace the major firms in each industry, with few outsiders. The absence of multi-industry conglomerates and the way in which Japanese corporations firmly 'belong' within one industry or another has been already remarked on earlier in this chapter. So has the important role of trade associations in the formation of cartels. The general propensity to prefer co-operation to competition, when it can be clearly shown to be in one's long-term interest, often gives these associations considerable power to constrain individual firms in the interests of 'the industry' as a whole. This makes them ideal interlocutors for MITI officials' attempts to impose direction on particular industries; they can provide authoritative representatives of the industry on whom the acceptability of proposed measures can be tested, and they can be the channels for administrative guidance and for the organization of recession cartels, as well as safeguards against relations between officials and individual firms shading over into corruption – a means of guaranteeing even-handedness. Such 'opposite numbers' are so important that if they do not exist they have to be created. When MITI established a new bio-technology section in 1982, its first task was to be midwife to a new association. The relevant technical expertise was scattered – firms in the food industry, pharmaceuticals, fibre-making, petrochemicals, brewing, all had their own 'home' industry. No forum had until then existed to bring them together and such a forum was seen as urgently needed.

Fourthly, a sizeable part of Japan's household savings are channelled into the Post Office savings bank (thanks to tax inducements) and into national pension funds. These are recycled partly through various forms of public expenditure (nearly $40bn. by local governments and $50bn. by the central government in 1981–2) but also by lending through the various public development banks – to the tune of $60bn. in 1981–2 – under a variety of selected preferential loan schemes for special purposes.

So much for the facilitating conditions, present in Japan but not in most of the other industrial countries, which make easier the task of those who would seek to direct the evolution of the industrial structure. What, concretely, have they done with their opportunities to 'engineer' change? Concrete policies are best discussed under three heads: measures to create a national consensus around desirable objectives; measures to assist the emergence of infant industries; and measures to ease, accelerate or postpone the decline of industries in which Japan is losing comparative advantage.

Direction setting

In the matter of overall direction-setting for the economy, the Japanese government speaks with two voices – that of the Economic Planning Agency and that of the Ministry of International Trade and Industry. But although they are to some extent rival voices (the publications of the EPA make few references to – sometimes studiously avoid mention of – those of MITI and vice versa), they tend to speak in harmony.

The focus of the EPA's contribution to consensus building is two-fold. First there are the formal four-year, five-year, in 1979–80 seven-year, plans which are little more than exercises in econometric modelling, but the major public impact of which derives from their forecasted growth rates. These are important in influencing the optimism/pessimism balance in the long-term planning of the ordinary businessman. When the seven-year plan approved by the Cabinet in August 1979 was resubmitted in revised form six months later, with the forecast annual growth rate over the seven years reduced from 5.7 to 5.5 per cent, this both reflected and fed into an increasingly sombre appraisal of the effects of the oil-price rise.

The second EPA contribution to opinion formation is the annual Economic White Paper. Although no longer having quite the authority that it had in the 1950s and early 1960s, its annual publication is the occasion for considerable reflective debate on the economy and its overall direction, both in the general as well as in the specialist economic press – the more so because in addition to the charting of annual trends, the document takes up some long-term theme for more searching analysis. Much importance is attached, also, to the title of the document which is supposed to encapsulate that theme. 'The road to advanced country status' in 1963 was followed in 1965 by 'The problem of stable growth', in 1968 by 'The Japanese economy in the process of internationalization', in 1969 by 'The challenge to (sic) affluence' (it was never clear whether it was 'Tackling the problems of affluence' or 'On to affluence: the challenge' which was intended). 'The building of a new type of welfare society' came in 1972 and 'Towards welfare without inflation' followed a couple of months before the oil embargo. 'Beyond the growth economy!' and 'Looking for a stable [growth] trajectory' were the reactions to the next two turbulent years. Since then the titles have been: 'Preparing the ground for a new development', 'Steady adaptation to stable growth', 'The Japanese economy and structural transformation', 'Admirable adaptability for a fresh start' (as optimism came flooding back in 1979), then 'The testing problems of Japan, the advanced country' (a reflection of the pressures Japan felt herself to be under from the other members of the 'advanced country' club at economic summit meetings, etc.) and, in 1981, reflecting the new confidence in Japan's technological capacity, 'For the promotion of creative activity in the Japanese economy'. The 1982 title reflected the dominant strengthen-the-supply side: cut-back-government mood with 'The road to greater economic efficiency', and in 1983 came: 'The foundations of sustainable growth'.

There is no mention in these titles, it is worth remarking, of the NICS and the adaptation of Japan's economy to their growing industrial power. There was a good deal of talk in the late 1970s about 'pressure from the developing countries as they catch up' (encapsulated in the neat word *oiage*, meaning something like 'down-neck-breathing'), but it was never selected for a major theme, as Japan's relations to the other industrial countries was (e.g. in 1980).

From the early 1970s, however, these guiding statements have been somewhat upstaged by 'forward looks' published at two–three year intervals by MITI, or rather by the Industrial Structure

Council which is very largely a creature of MITI, although its members and the members of its industry sub-committees include a number of businessmen and some academics. These statements, or 'visions' as they are called, have not been concerned so much with overall growth rates, etc., but have specifically addressed themselves to the question: what *shape* should our economy take over the next ten years or so, given the pattern of our present, and probable future, problems, constraints and opportunities? These have been the documents which have most clearly spelt out the 'adjustment' themes, beginning in the early 1970s with emphasis on welfare and quality-of-life issues (see also the titles of the White Papers of 1971 and 1972 quoted above) as a reaction to growing concern with environmental pollution, and the prospect that the 'information industries' could offer a new cleaner path to higher added-value production. This general direction was reinforced with respect to the 'light rather than heavy and chemical industries' dimension by the new importance of energy costs after 1973, and with respect to the 'high value-added and technology-intensive, rather than low value-added, labour-and-materials-intensive' dimension by the growing awareness of the economic strength of the NICs towards the end of the decade.

All this has (a) established a consensus about where the growth areas are, which has functioned to guide the investment of private firms, and (b) helped to create a receptive climate for measures to promote the 'frontier' industries and run down those in which Japan is losing comparative advantage.

Promoting new developments

Measures to promote the frontier industries during the 1970s have included the following:

1 Support for R & D. Government expenditure on R & D increased some 3.7 times between 1970 and 1979, while GNP grew 2.9 times (both figures nominal), just about matching a similar increase in the expenditure of private firms. The R & D effort has been concentrated in fields like electronics and bio-technology, aerospace (so far in a modest way) and alternative energy development, not in the traditional areas of steel, cars, etc. Computers and the wider application of electronics technology (e.g. in machine tools) has been a dominant focus of attention, that being

the major battleground in which the endeavour to 'catch up' with the USA was concentrated. (It having, at successive earlier stages, been ship-building, steel, automobiles, chemicals, etc.) Setting priorities, picking the next likely winners, has not been difficult throughout the post-war period when the objectives of policy were primarily 'catching up' objectives. That period is not entirely over, though now that Japan has achieved a solid competitive position in electronics, the only major field left to conquer is aerospace. As yet there is no evidence of a consensus forming around the ambition to mount a major challenge to the USA in this field, though the steady accumulation of expertise continues and the government contributes its support to the development of a high-performance jet engine.

Research policy has necessarily to change somewhat now that Japan has in most fields 'caught up' and can no longer imitate and try to improve on existing models of 'more advanced' nations. At the frontiers, 'picking winners' becomes harder. The recent emphasis has been not on the development of existing technologies, but on identifying strategic research projects – the development of certain materials and processes – with fairly foreseeable industrial applications likely to become important in the next couple of decades. In the summer of 1981 MITI announced a 10-year programme of what is called 'The Development of Next-Generation Base Technologies'. Close to half a billion dollars was to be spent, over 10 years, on 10 programmes – fine ceramics, separation diaphragms, crystalline macro-molecules, conductive macro-molecules, lightweight high-strength alloys, bio-reactors, accelerated cell culture, genetic recombinatory engineering, super-lattice elements, stacked ICs, environment-resistant elements (Dore, 1983).

The role of the government has not been simply to finance research, but also, on occasion, to direct and co-ordinate the research effort of private industry. In the computer and machine tool fields MITI took the lead in bringing the major firms together for joint research projects into basic technologies which the separate firms have then individually taken over to bring to commercial viability in competition.

The role of the government in the research effort should not be exaggerated, however. Only 2 per cent of the cost of R & D within private firms is financed by the government, compared with 25–30 per cent in Britain and France, and 16 and 35 per cent in such bastions of free enterprise as West Germany and the USA

Table 5.1 Share of government expenditure in estimated total R & D expenditure (%)

	Including defence	Excluding defence
Japan (1979)	28	27
France (1979)	58	47
UK (1976)	52	35
US (1980)	49	34

Source: Kagaku Gijutsucho, 1981, pp. 338–48. If one adds the tax forgone by the tax incentive scheme for R & D (see below), this would increase the Japanese government's share by 2–3 percentage points.

respectively. Differences in defence spending are a partial explanation, but far from being the sole one, as is clear from the table 5.1, which relates to total (industry, university, etc.) R & D spending.

It is worth remarking, too, that while most of the government's research expenditure is indeed directed towards creating a more internationally competitive industrial structure by giving a lead to private industry or by financing projects whose development costs are very large and risky, some of it is also prompted by the divergence between public and private costs and benefits in certain areas – e.g., energy conservation, urban transport systems, etc., – where improvement in Japan's international trading position is hardly at issue.

2   A second set of measures involves the fiscal and monetary incentives to private enterprises provided by tax measures and the lending policies of the major state banks. Accelerated depreciation allowances linked to exports were discontinued in 1972, but given, instead, for pollution control and energy-saving investments and research-laboratory equipment. A new tax provision in 1976 allows reduction of taxable income by 20 per cent of new R & D expenditures (i.e. expenditures exceeding the highest year's expenditure since 1976). The distribution of preferential credit by the state banks has also changed with changing priorities. Fed with funds from the postal savings account and the accumulated reserves of various state pension funds, these banks – the Japan Development Bank (JDB), the Export Import Bank, the Small Business Loan Fund and the People's Finance Corporation (for the very smallest businesses) – dispose of sizeable amounts of credit, the first two about 4 per cent each of the total credit

supplied by the Japanese banking system at the end of 1979.

These banks lend at up to 0.8 per cent below the prime rate (2–3 per cent below commercial rates), the rates for different categories of loans being adjusted from time to time in accordance with changing perceived priorities. The JDB has been putting a higher proportion of its funds in recent years into regional development, the development of urban transport systems, etc., but also into high-technology development areas. In the export field, a major emphasis has been on promoting the export of complete plants, and on the support of overseas investment projects. The changes in the distribution of outstanding loans between 1970 and 1979 are shown in tables 5.2 and 5.3.

3   The third means of promoting the development of 'frontier' industries is through direct intervention to reduce internal competition and co-ordinate rationalizing measures to enhance the international competitiveness of a Japanese infant industry. Magaziner and Hout describe developments in the industrial machinery industry in the late 1960s:

> . . . a cartel was formed to allocate product categories among companies, group enterprises, and to establish joint ventures. In some businesses, like chemical machinery, individual

Table 5.2   Japan Development Bank: distribution of outstanding loans

	1970	1980
Electricity generation	19.5	13.1
Petroleum	3.1	3.6
Shipping	33.8	10.5
Improvement of technology	7.3	7.8
Special machines	1.9	—
Private enterprise railways in urban areas	5.3	9.3
Modernization of the distribution system	2.4	2.4
Metropolitan redevelopment	1.5	8.2
Regional development	11.4	12.7
Pollution control	0.5	14.1
Other	13.7	18.1
	100.0	100.0
Total (internal loans) (Ybn)	1,766.0	5,384.6
Total lending	1,814.0	5,390.1

Source: KY, 1982, pp. 246–7.

Table 5.3   Export–Import Bank: distribution of loans for exports and overseas projects

	1970	1980
Ships	57.5	11.1
Aircraft	1.6	—
Railway trucks and other vehicles	1.9	1.8
Electrical machinery	4.0	9.7
Communications machinery	1.2	1.3
Textile machinery	4.8	2.5
Steel products	1.2	0.8
Other engineering goods	18.7	43.3
Overseas contracting and investment	7.0	29.8
	100.0	100.0
Total (exports and overseas) (Ybn)	1,246.0	2,395.3
Total lending	1,597.0	5,101.7

Source: KY, 1982, pp. 246–7.

producers were encouraged to co-operate in the development of new products; in other businesses, like machine tools, certain enterprises were encouraged to drop certain products. In other cases such as printing machinery, joint ventures and mergers were sponsored. (Magaziner and Hout 1980, p.75)

These initiatives, though prosecuted in informal talks between the relevant department of MITI and industry associations or individual firms, are not without due legal process. There are numerous pieces of legislation which allow formal exemption from the provisions of the Anti-Monopoly Law for cartel arrangements deemed to be in the public interest. Some of the 19 separate provisions counted in one survey (Uekusa, p.207) have some special purpose in view – agreements between exporters which become necessary to allocate quotas when voluntary quota restrictions have been accepted, for example (70 cases in 1980), or agreements among fishermen to restrict catches for conservation reasons. More than half of the 491 cases in 1980 (the peak was reached in 1965 with 1,079 cases) concerned the formation of co-operatives among small businessmen (of which more in the next chapter). (Kōsei, 1981, p.190) Some of the rest relate to the rescue of a particular problem industry – such as the Fertilizer Price Stabilization Law which dates back to 1955. But the bulk of the provisions are elaborations for particular industries of the two exemption clauses already included in the original Anti-Monopoly Law of 1953 – namely the 'recession cartel' for temporary agreed production cutbacks in times of recession, and the 'rationalization cartel' for agreements between producers which can be deemed to serve, as the law says, 'the advancement of techniques, the improvement of quality, the reduction of costs or improvements in efficiency'. The particular piece of enabling legislation for the computer industry which has served to promote a number of useful schemes during the 1970s, including the founding of a government corporation to undertake the leasing of (Japanese-made) mainframe computers, is the Law for Emergency Measures to Promote Particular Branches of the Electronic and Machinery Industries of 1971, itself a revamping of earlier pieces of legislation going back to the 1950s. These special bills provide for a certain amount of expenditure as well as for exemption from anti-trust suits.

Even outside such enabling legislation, however, there is a good deal of cartel activity under the informal 'administrative guidance' of the relevant MITI bureau. In the 1960s, for instance, there were industry-wide investment plans negotiated for steel, vinyl chloride, synthetic fibres, pulp, paper, cement, petroleum, petro-chemicals, cars, machine tools and certain branches of electronics. They were seen by MITI sometimes, primarily as a means of preventing over-expansion, sometimes of promoting specialization within an oligopoly framework in order to get bigger plants and achieve economies of scale which would enhance international competitiveness. The practice of these informal investment cartels caused a certain amount of friction between MITI and the Fair Trade Commission which was resolved by a formal 'peace treaty' in 1966 – 'an agreed set of guidelines for the application of the Anti-Monopoly Law with respect to the measures to improve the structure of the economy' (Uekusa, pp.210–11).

Declining industries

The civil service head of MITI said the following in a speech to the OECD Industrial Committee in 1970:

Industrialization in developing countries will stimulate competitive relations in the markets of advanced nations in products with a low degree of processing. As a result, the confrontation between free trade and protectionism will grow more intense.

The solution of the problem is to be found according to economic logic, in progressively giving away industries to other countries much as a big brother gives away his outgrown clothes to his younger brother. In this way, a country's own industries become more sophisticated.

A solution to the North–South problem depends not only on internal development for developing nations but also on giving them fair opportunities in the area of trade. To do this, the advanced nations must plan for sophistication of their industrial structures and open their market for unsophisticated merchandise as well as offer aid in the form of funds and technology (quoted Magaziner and Hout, 1980, p.6).

There, at least, was a brave statement of principle. That Japan should have had such a positive attitude towards handing on the cast-off clothes of unsophisticated industries to younger-brother late developers may be partly explained by the fact that Japan was not such an older older brother itself. Some indeed in the audience for that speech might have wondered whether it was saying that *Japan* ought to be given more access in the markets of countries more advanced than itself or that Japan should give market access to others.

There is no doubt about the consensus around these ideas in principle. In practice, as the next chapter will show, there has not been any unseemly haste to hand on the old clothes of the textile industry to Japan's NIC competitors. The industry has fought back against NIC competition (with some success), and the government has given it some encouragement to do so, though encouragement which *has* been balanced by measures to reduce capacity through exit compensation, and encouragement which has stopped short of the protectionist measures available under the Multi-Fibre Arrangement which other countries have used.

In fact, however, the main problem industries in which the government has sought to intervene have not been industries where the *main* cause of decline was competition from the NICs. The 1978 Law for Special Measures to deal with Particular Depressed Industries was initially aimed at several specific industries: in the first instance, artificial fibres, aluminium smelting, ship-building and open-hearth and electric-arc-furnace steel-making, but subsequently extended to ammonia, urea, spinning, ferro-silicon, corrugated cardboard, and wet process acid-making.

NIC competition in world markets was at least an element in the plight of three of these – spinning, steel and ship-building. But these are problem industries for other reasons also. Some of them had been marked out as undesirable for Japan on environmental grounds since the early 1970s. Clearly they were also – and this was the dominant perception of the problem in the late 1970s – victims of world recession following a period of world-wide over-expansion of capacity, while for some key industries – aluminium, fertilizers, electric-arc-furnace steel, for example – the absolutely decisive factor in destroying their competitiveness was the change in relative costs of energy or naphtha. Only towards the end of the decade was it generally appreciated that the basic-materials industries were industries with low-income elasticities anyway. The Industrial Bank of Japan has produced the sobering table 5.4.

Adding the declines in consumption together with the inability to compete with imports produces a sombre story for the basic materials industries. A classification of industries into 'basic materials' and 'transformation and assembly' categories by the Industrial Bank of Japan is striking. With an average output growth for manufacturing of 50 per cent, 1975–82, 'basic materials' grew by 16 per cent while 'transformation and assembly' grew by 113 per cent (FT, 16 December 1982).

Whatever the source of trouble for the problem industries, however, the measures used to tackle their problems have been the same, and they have been rather more deliberate, more thorough-going and more closely planned with the whole industry

Table 5.4 Domestic consumption of major basic materials (tons per Y100m of *GNP* at constant prices)

	1970	1975	1980	1981
Textiles	1.21	0.87	0.90	0.82
Paper	10.55	9.11	9.39	8.85
Ethylene	2.96	2.78	2.88	2.50
Steel	41.01	33.28	32.60	28.87
Ferroalloys	1.40	1.43	0.98	0.84
Aluminium ingots	0.74	0.78	0.86	0.81

Source: FT, 16 December 1982.

than in most other industrial countries. The 1978 Law could be activated when 'as a result of some marked change in economic conditions whether at home or abroad, there is a severe over-capacity of production facilities . . . , and when, moreover, because of the likelihood of a long-term continuance of that situation, there is a danger that a considerable proportion of the enterprises concerned will, over a prolonged period, suffer severe destabilization' – and on the petition of the industry concerned.

The schemes devised to cut back capacity in some of the more severely affected industries have been most easily and inexpensively carried out in industries with a small number of producers. In such industries, one or two pieces of major surgery have generally been enough. A special sub-committee is set up within the Industrial Structure Commission as a forum for dialogue between MITI and the Industry Association, but with the participation of unions and representatives of customer or supplier industries. Then, usually starting with a recession cartel as a holding operation, a scheme is worked out, either to scrap or to mothball a certain proportion of existing capacity, the cutbacks being allocated among firms in a manner acceptable as fair. (Mothballing means stripping the equipment down and concreting in the mountings 'so that it requires a good deal of expenditure of time and effort to rehabilitate' as the man-made fibre agreement said.) In this way, ship-building capacity has been cut by nearly 40 per cent leaving the industry in much better shape, with a more recent average capital vintage, than its competitors. Synthetic fibres were cut back in 1978 by 16 per cent – largely by mothballing. Then, in 1981, the mothballed equipment had to go and another 3 per cent of capacity with it. For aluminium smelting, a second cutback to 45 per cent of 1977 capacity was finally decided in 1981, and here it was suggested that a quota tariff system (the Japanese producers having the right to import quotas at reduced tariff rates) would have the minimum adverse impact on the domestic selling price and be a way of raising revenues for the remaining high-cost producers.

The aluminium industry is worth looking at in a little more detail, perhaps, since it reveals certain limits placed on Japan's adherence to the principle of comparative advantage, arising from the importance attached to 'economic security' as a policy objective.

A first-round cutback in smelting capacity engineered under

the 1978 Law scrapped some half million of a total of 1.6 million capacity. By July 1980 the industry was back to working at 97 per cent of capacity, but already demand was falling off and stocks rose. The American recession brought down spot prices which widened the price differential and strained the loyalty even of loyal domestic purchasers. Imports were running at 58 per cent of total demand by the second quarter of 1981. The aluminium companies had made losses of $140 million in 1980 and were expected to lose $150 million in 1981: their accumulated debts were over $4 billion.

It was perfectly obvious to the Aluminium Sub-Committee of the Industrial Structure Council that with electricity prices making up 40 per cent of costs at Y14–15 a kWh compared with Canada's Y2–3, there was no hope of the industry being internationally competitive in the foreseeable future. Nevertheless the conclusion was that the industry should be persuaded to scrap only another 400,000 tons, and that by various devices it should be made possible for the industry to maintain a viable 700,000 tons' capacity – about a third of the projected 1985 demand. Six reasons were given why the free play of market forces should not be allowed to wipe out the domestic industry.

The first was security of supply. Although it is expected that a further 0.7 million tons out of 1985 total domestic demand of 2.15 million tons will be provided by 'development imports' – captive imports from Japanese-financed enterprises in Australia, Indonesia, Brazil – even they might be interrupted by long-term strikes. Secondly, some domestic production gives bargaining power in negotiating long-term contract prices. Thirdly, imports cannot provide some very high-quality types of aluminium needed for high-pressure condensers and some automobile parts, nor provide the sort of service required by some small producers of alloys and billets which require small batches of special products. Fourthly, there is a need to maintain an R & D capacity in the industry as a precondition for regaining competitiveness if the cost situation changes in future. Fifthly, there needs to be a solid home industry from which to mount overseas development projects, and finally, the smelting industry is by its nature scattered and often the staple source of employment in otherwise non-industrial local communities (Sanshin, 1981). Needless to say, these arguments were reinforced by a good deal of high-pressure lobbying, of a not wholly disinterested kind, on behalf of the six aluminium companies.

At the end of 1985, with world prices lower than ever, there were still five companies in the refining business with accumulated losses since 1981 double their paid-up capital. (Y234bn. only half covered by sale of assets, the rest by loans.) A new reconstruction plan called for capacity cuts from .7 to .35 million tons, though production was running at only .22 million tons. The capacity cuts were to continue to be financed by an import tax rebate to the refiners of 8 per cent. (Business Japan, November 1985)

Aluminium-smelting posed few administrative problems, once the political decisions over the degree of protection and state assistance to be afforded had been settled. Other more complex and heterogeneous industries, whose decline had more widespread employment effects, required more complex measures. Ship-building, subject of the first of the comprehensive rationalization schemes, is a good example.

It was in one sense an easy industry to handle since it had always been a closely regulated one. All investments in shipyard facilities had required a licence since 1950 and so, even, after 1953, had the acceptance of all orders for ships of over 2,500 tons. The controls on entry and expansion were used effectively to build up a competitive industry (and on one notorious occasion in the 1950s, corruptly to feed the venality of politicians). They were justified – and made enforceable – by the other arm of the policy, a system of low-interest loans for ship purchase from the Japan Development Bank for domestic ship-owners and from the Export-Import Bank for foreign purchasers. The volume of preferential loans for domestic ships was equal to more than 50 per cent of value-added in the mid-1950s and again in the mid-1960s, but tailed off to almost zero ten years later; the export credits were equally of considerable proportions (Yonezawa, 1981).

The industry was not, therefore, unused to the idea of regulation, but its diversity made regulation complicated. The central arena for the political bargaining over the extent of the cuts and the extent of compensating state assistance was a Shipping and Ship-building Rationalization Council set up under the aegis of the Ministry of Transport (though as always, of course, the real bargaining went on in the dressing rooms rather than in the arena of the Council itself). The size of the problem was considerable. New orders had amounted to 34m. tons in 1973 (ships built, 17m. tons; work in hand, 52m tons). By 1978 orders were down to 3.2m., production to 6.3m. and work in hand to 6.5m. That growing competition from the nics, as well as the world recession, was responsible was apparent in the decline in Japan's share of world production: from 50 per cent in 1974 to 35 per cent in 1978. The diversity of the industry complicated the search for a solution. The large companies and efficiency-oriented civil servants wanted to see the big companies cut capacity, and many of the small companies to close down. The small companies wanted the large ones to take all the cuts. Companies which had newly invested in up-to-date berths from which they expected to gain competitive advantage wanted special exemptions. And all companies wanted government assistance in the form of early retirement and replacement of government ships, schemes to supply ships as foreign aid, advance orders for LNG tankers, as well as a restoration of the earlier interest rate subsidies for ship purchase which the industry had enjoyed in the days when it was at the frontier of progress. There was also considerable horse-trading over the extent of direct aid to one particular ship-building firm (Sasebo Heavy Industries) which was on the verge of bankruptcy in early 1978 (Magazine and Hout, 1980, pp.69–70).

Temporary measures beginning in 1976 and using the provisions of the 1950 laws had 'urged' on the 67 largest firms cutbacks in production over the next two years. They should plan, it was prescribed, to use only 72 per cent of the 1973 peak manhours in 1977 and only 67 per cent the following year. A more thoroughgoing rationalization plan was eventually devised under the Depressed Industries Law of 1978. It had the following elements (*Kampō*, 14 November 1978; *Hōrei*, 1978, pp.79,227):

1   An agreed programme of cuts in capacity, graduated to the size of firm, ranging from 40 per cent for the 7 biggest firms and 30 per cent and 27 per cent for the 33 firms in the intermediate size classes to 15 per cent for the 21 smallest firms. The actual legal order only specified the *total* volume of capacity to be cut (3.4m. out of 9.8m. tons) collectively by all firms capable of building ships of more than 5,000 tons, and also the complex formula by which annual capacity was to be calculated from the size of the largest ship which a dock could hold, a prohibition on disposing of the property for sale except (see below) for sale and destruction, and a prohibition on any investment which would involve an increase in capacity before June 1983. The actual quotas for individual firms were left to a gentlemen's agreement within the Ship-building Industry Association.
2   The establishment of a new quango, the Association for

Special Stabilization Measures for the Ship-building Industry, to provide scrapping compensation by buying out complete ship-yards or building berths from small and medium firms – the land at market prices and all the equipment on it at book value. The equipment was to be destroyed or sold for non-ship-building purposes, and the land redeveloped for subsequent sale to other enterprises. The government provided half of the initial capital of Y2bn. ($10m.), the rest being provided by the industry and banks, while funds for purchase operations of up to another Y96bn. ($48m.) were to be borrowed from the Japan Develop-ment Bank and the private banks. Further income to repay the loans (on the assumption that the equipment purchase, unlike the land purchase, was irrecoverable) was provided by a cess on all subsequent ship sales, initially set at 0.1 per cent (a version of the 'survivors are gainers: survivors should pay' principle of which more in the next chapter).

3   Two special laws and additional funds to provide (a) assist-ance to small and medium enterprises affected as sub-contractors by the closure of shipyards (special tax concessions, loans and interest guarantees to help them develop a new line of business) and (b) assistance to workers who lose their jobs (enhancement of unemployment insurance benefits and special attention from the organizations set up in the mid-1970s recession to provide re-training and employment subsidies for workers who are victims of bankruptcy or redundancy cuts).

4   Production cutbacks were continued and formalized this time in a recession cartel, with the planned reduction in hours worked being graduated, again, to size of firm: 34 per cent of peak year for the seven largest, 45 per cent for the seventeen medium and 49 per cent for the sixteen smaller firms.

5   It was also agreed to help the industry by a generous program-me of interest rate subsidies to ship-owners for a 'scrap-and-build' operation.

The scheme appears to have worked according to plan. Some sixty building berths were scrapped and the total reduction of capacity (allowing for a small permitted increase for the smaller firms building ships of less than 5,000 tons) was slightly greater than the target – 3.6m. tons. The Association's buying-out scheme applied only to about half a million tons of this total and all for smaller firms. The labour-force which had been 229,000 at the end of 1947, 68 per cent of them production workers (the 1973 peak had been 253,000), was down to 162,000 (60 per cent of them production workers), at the end of 1979. The 88 berths which remained were, of course, the most modern and best equipped of the original 138. The industry was in a good deal better shape as a result and, with an additional million tons of domestic orders from the scrap-and-build plan in 1979, the leading firms were making profits again by 1980.

The ship-building rationalization scheme is the most complex of the operations carried out under the 1978 law. It shows certain features in common with other schemes, notably those of the textile industry which will be considered in the next chapter; the mixture of public and private industry initiative, of voluntarism, compulsion and financial inducement; the important role played by the relevant industry association; the variety of institutional devices resorted to; the relatively low cost to public funds, and the clash between the 'rationalizing' principle of favouring the larger firms and the 'justice' principle of favouring the small firms which are worst hit – a clash resolved in a compromise which is certainly not neglectful of the small firm interest.

Summary

It will be apparent by now why some observers of the Japanese scene speak, with varying degrees of scorn and envy, of Japan Incorporated, why the committee hearings in the us Congress should abound with complaints about Japanese 'industrial targeting' (i.e. of us industries for destruction) and why the Japanese business federation, the Keidanren, should seek publicity for speeches at Harvard by its senior members under titles like 'No need to apologize: explaining Japanese "industrial policies"' (Ikeda, 1981). The close co-operative relations between government and business have a quality apt to be missing in countries where individualistic versions of 'free enterprise' actually constitute an article of faith as well as of rhetoric. The division of labour in the achievement of 'efficient' structural change (i.e. change which maintains or enhances the nation's competitiveness) is not easy to chart. The development of new branches of production owes most to private initiative, though both the exhortatory and predictive effects of government objective-setting and consensus-creation and a variety of fiscal and monetary incentives are important stimuli to such intiatives. Some of the other preconditions for those initiatives, both cultural and institutional – the educational system and attitudes to intellectuality, the level of savings and the banking system, the life-time employment system and the propensity to cartelization – have all been mentioned.

In the running down of branches of production which are losing comparative advantage, the role of the government in resolving conflicts of interest and devising incentives for exit from the industry has been more central, though again the initiative of private industry acting through its trade associations has been important. Inevitably political compromises have had to be made, and the small businesses by no means always come off worse than big businesses when the bargains are struck. Their ability to mobilize politicians through their voting strength can outweigh the obligations created by large firms' donations of campaign funds. But total expenditure on declining industries has not been large: the larger share of state funds for industry has been reserved for the growing ducklings rather than for the lame old ducks.

The consensus shared between government officials and corporate managers is shared also by the leaders of labour unions. This predisposes them against any wholesale defence of the status quo and inclines them towards compromise compensation-seeking solutions when their members are affected by change and their interests are threatened. Other features of the labour economy also facilitate structural change; the fact that Japan is still not wholly an employee economy and that the approximately 30 per cent self-employment sector can expand or contract to cushion changes in employment levels in the large enterprises; the enterprise bargaining system in which both bargainers accept the survival of their firm – if necessary at the expense of painful surgery or wholesale reconstruction of its business – as an overriding objective; and the life-time employment guarantee together with the seniority wage system which (i) gives assurance to workers that neither their jobs nor their wage and skill status will be threatened by wholesale technical change within the plant, and (ii) establishes an accepted sense of job property. This last leads to levels of compensation for job loss through voluntary early retirement schemes which are genuinely attractive – compensation at levels found exceptionally in Britain only in a few nationalized industries where it is seen, not as an act of justice but as an unfortunate concession to trade union blackmail. (For it is still held, as it is not held in Japan, that hire-and-fire at a week's notice is the normal condition of a *properly* functioning job market and the concept of a job property right represents one of those creeping rigidities which radically-reforming Tory governments must try to cure if the economy is ever to be made efficient.) The high levels of compensation both express and reinforce the assumptions of managers that, as between their duties to their employees and their duties to shareholders, the former should take precedence – at least in the early stages of crisis. Many Japanese firms allowed profits to fall or disappear, cut dividends and ran down assets for a year or two before they cut employment. Another effect of the very high cost of the mass redundancy option (including the faint air of moral failure which surrounds it) is to prompt the most vigorous management efforts to diversify, to find new fields and new products and to invest in the retraining of their workers for new ventures rather than dismissing them.

III   A case study

7
Textiles: How much adjustment?

The best starting point for a study of adjustment in the Japanese textile and clothing industries is a puzzle. Why is it that, when imports of textiles into Europe and the USA, particularly those from Third World producers, have captured a good deal of those markets, and in some countries, such as Britain or France, would have almost entirely wiped out the domestic industry, were it not for the import quota protection legalized by the MFA (the Multi-Fibre Arrangement), import penetration into the Japanese market, both for textiles and for clothing, remains at relatively modest levels despite the fact that:

(a) Japan has no import quotas under MFA or otherwise, except to protect domestic production of extremely high-priced raw silk and silk thread.
(b) Japan's tariffs on textiles, averaging something like 7–8 per cent, are lower than those of other industrial countries – a good deal lower than the US 20–25 per cent range, for example;
(c) Japan is sitting within half a day's 'plane ride of Korea, Hong Kong and Taiwan, the most efficient of Third World producers; whose exporters
(d) have less difficulty than their European counterparts in understanding and coping with some of the cultural characteristics of Japanese markets which constitute 'non tariff barriers' for Europeans – at least those characteristics which derive from their shared 'post-Confucian' culture; and
(e) Japan has a per capita income and wage rate a good deal higher than e.g. Britain or Italy?
The following chapters will attempt to answer that question and thereby given an account of adjustment in the Japanese textile industry over the last ten years.

Some basic facts

First, some basic facts about the industry, starting with trends in production, consumption, export and import.

Table 7.1 Production, demand, exports and imports of textiles and clothing: all forms (imports exclude raw cotton, wool, ethylene-glycol, etc.)

	Production		Consumption			As a percentage of domestic production			
	Tons (1000s)	Index	Total volume (index)	Per capita (kg) (garments only)	Share of man-made fibres %	Consumption	Imports	Exports	Of which, garments
1960	1,270	100	100	6.981	40.9	58.5	0.3	38.3	9.1
1965	1,566	123	142	9.575	50.8	67.4	0.4	31.6	9.2
1970	2,040	161	195	12.146	56.7	71.0	3.1	29.9	7.6
1975	1,776	140	176	10.276	50.4	73.7	7.4	36.0	7.0
1979	2,072	163	254	14.406	57.9	91.1	16.4	24.5	4.5
1980	2,050	161	230	12.654	58.0	83.2	13.6	29.3	5.6

Source: Seni Tōkei-hyō (Textile Statistics).

Table 7.2 Production, demand, exports and imports of textiles and clothing: all forms: cotton and cotton goods only

	Production		Consumption		As a percentage of domestic production			
	Tons (1000s)	Index	Total volume (index)	Per capita (kg)	Consumption	Imports	Exports	Of which, garments
1960	544	100	100	2.589	51.8	0.0	44.3	6.8
1965	567	104	121	3.215	60.1	0.0	36.3	9.3
1970	526	96	155	3.928	83.1	6.3	21.3	7.2
1975	460	85	165	4.058	101.1	14.6	16.0	4.6
1979	508	93	228	5.423	91.1	38.1	9.8	2.8
1980	504	93	204	4.801	114.3	29.7	15.5	3.8

Source: Seni Tōkei-hyō (Textile Statistics).

Table 7.3 Production, demand, exports and imports of textiles and clothing: all forms: man-made fibres

	Production		Consumption		As a percentage of domestic production			Of which, garments
	Tons (1000s)	Index	Total volume (index)	Per capita (kg)	Consumption	Imports	Exports	
1960	512	100	100	2.745	59.4	0.1	37.1	8.6
1965	795	155	175	4.528	67.0	0.3	31.3	9.9
1970	1,290	252	265	6.259	62.6	1.1	35.9	8.7
1975	1,149	224	217	4.575	57.4	3.5	48.0	8.8
1979	1,420	277	360	7.693	77.0	8.2	31.3	5.4
1980	1,406	275	326	6.665	70.4	7.5	32.5	6.5

Source: Seni Tōkei-hyō (Textile Statistics).

Table 7.4 Share of textiles and clothing (%)

	In total manufacturing production	In total manufacturing employment	In total employment	In exports	In imports	In bankruptcies
1960	13.8	18.9	4.1	30.2		14.7
1965	11.7	17.5	4.2	18.7	0.7	10.1
1970	8.9	15.9	4.2	12.5	1.6	6.0
1975	7.4	15.2	3.8	6.7	2.3	7.9
1980	6.3	14.0	3.3	4.9	2.5	

Source: KY, 1984, pp. 181, 164.

Table 7.5   Yarn production by type of fibre (1000 tons)

	1970	1980
Man-made filament	593	761
Man-made staple	710	649
Mixed cotton/man-made	12	31
Cotton	495	473
Hemp	4	1
Wool/man-made mixed	40	30
Wool	142	89
Silk	23	18
Other	139	26
	2,158	2,078

Source: Kasen Kyōkai, *Kasen Handobukku* (Man-made Fibres Handbook 1982) pp. 62–3.

The structure of production

The outstanding characteristics of the Japanese textile industry which differentiate it from the industries of other advanced countries (with the exception, perhaps, of Italy) are the dominance of the small-scale enterprise in all except the spinning and fibre-making sectors, and the contract arrangements which often bind these small-scale producers to larger firms.

Even upstream where the big firms predominate, concentration is not so very far advanced. In cotton spinning, the so-called Big Nine shared about 75 per cent of the market for cotton and cotton-mixture spun yarn, with the largest taking some 16 per cent. There is a greater concentration in man-made fibres where the three biggest firms account for a half the total ton-days of installed capacity and the Big Ten (three of which figure also in the spinners' Big Nine) have about 90 per cent of the market. But still the biggest Japanese firm is smaller than the UK's Courtauld, or the USA's fifth largest, Celanese.

But weaving is dominated by the small family concern. Altogether there are over 50,000 weaving enterprises in Japan, found, geographically, in over 50 *sanchi* – concentrated, and usually organized, local areas each with their own narrow range of specialties. For cotton and allied textiles alone – now of less importance in the total picture than silk and synthetic filaments – there are over 16,000 enterprises with an average of between 19 and 20 looms each. The modal firm as a couple of family members and 2–3 employees, a weaving shed which is adjacent to or an extension of the proprietor's home (usually in a rural area), two or three of the proprietor's family actively and flexibly engaged in the business, a considerable willingness to work long hours, and very flexible income expectations.

Some vignettes
An idea of the enterprise structure of the textile industry can perhaps best be given through sketches of a number of individual firms.

1 *Teijin*   Teijin is a fibre-maker with interests in a wide variety of chemical products (its diversification policy will be considered later). It produces mainly nylon filament, polyester filament, polyester staple and acetate filament. Formerly it produced a higher proportion of staples and until 1978 had its own spinning mill in Nagoya. The mill became uncompetitive for wage-cost reasons. This had nothing to do with the characteristics of Nagoya as a labour market. Teijin's 'home industry' is plastics/ chemicals and it is the wage levels of that industry's leading firms which shape Teijin's workers' – and their trade union leaders' – wage expectations when they negotiate their *uniform* wage levels for all Teijin's employees, irrespective of where their plant is located or what is its line of business. (Uniform wage levels, that is, for comparable age and education levels, though there might be small local cost-of-living allowances for particular plants.) Teijin's main competitors were spinners belonging to the spinning industry whose wage levels, geared to the lower profit levels experienced by that industry in recent years, were lower than in chemicals. Hence Teijin had too much of a cost disadvantage *vis-à-vis* its competitors for it to be worth continuing.

A relatively small proportion of Teijin's textile production is sold as yarn, the bulk is processed into cloth through a contract-weaving, dyeing and finishing process, the whole of which is overseen by Teijin. The Fibre Association Handbook's dictionary of brand names ascribes 139 to Teijin, or to its subsidiary Teijin Acetate, ranging from Rosel, an acetate filament cloth, either woven or knit with a high shine and good draping properties, to Poemee for lingerie, the suede Maxi, Franky for warp knitting 'with a drapy hand-knitted look', and the stitch-bonded Unicel for industrial and agricultural use. Only twelve of the brands are listed as yarns, though some thirty are listed as also available as yarns.

The brands are about equally divided between those available as cloth and those produced in knitted garment form, in either case being produced in close co-operation with nominally independent weavers and finishers and knitters. Great emphasis is placed on co-ordinated research into fibre-making and dyeing and finishing. When new processes are introduced, Teijin will give careful guidance to 'its' weavers (if they are using a specially processed yarn that requires a certain adjustment of warp tensions, for example) and to 'its' dyers and finishers. One of their main brand lines is a fine crêpe georgette which requires a difficult 'peeling' process using caustic soda to give a silky finish. They have a small subsidiary in the garment industry specializing in men's suitings, but do not plan to move further in that direction.

2 *Yoshioka* is a weaver in Nishiwaki, one of the 62 sanchi, or textile 'producing areas' (each organized into one or several producers' co-operatives). It is an area where cottage industry weaving dates back to the eighteenth century. In recent years it has specialized in yarn-dyed colour-weaves for shirting and especially for ginghams for Europe and the USA. About 80 per cent of the area's production is exported, nearly half of the exports ending up in the USA, the bulk of them after being made up (mostly by independent apparel makers, but sometimes by contractors working with Japanese trading companies) in Hong Kong or Korea. Yoshioka's father, a farmer, started a little weaving as a secondary activity in 1927. Cotton stopped coming and the looms were scrapped for guns during the war, but he re-started again, with 36-inch looms in 1948, in time for the big post-war textile boom. They changed most of these looms at various times for wider widths in the 1950s and early 1960s and finally, in 1969, took a large bank loan and re-equipped completely with a new set of forty 56-inch looms, non-automatic but with colour boxes to use up to four different weft colours and dobbies that permit relatively simple woven patterns.

They have six employees, two men and four women. The men are in their late thirties – younger than most wage employee textile workers of either sex in the area – and between them do all the loom maintenance, reaching, drawing in and beam-gaiting as well as helping out with the weaving. Three of the women work from 8 a.m. to 5 p.m. At any one time, two of them are looking after the looms and one either pirn-winding or inspecting the cloth. The other woman comes to help Mr. Yoshioka or his wife who work the looms rather less intensively (they might keep 35 of them going most of the time) from between 6 and 7 a.m. in the morning and until 8 or 9 p.m. at night. He gets about 60,000 yards a month off his forty looms (90–100 picks to the inch.)

Once the family bought yarn and sold cloth, doing all the intermediate processes themselves, but gradually specialization set in. Yarn dyeing was the first specialist occupation – all the more necessarily specialized as production became adjusted to fashion shifts and the area co-operative began to set annual colour ranges. Yoshioka still made his own warp beams and did the sizing, but in the 1960s new large-scale and cost-saving sizing equipment came in and he decided around 1970 that he would do better to get his beams from a specialist beamer who had the equipment. Already, by that stage, he was a contract weaver, getting his yarn from, and contracting to hand his products to, one of the area's *sanmoto* ('converter' but actually a good deal more than a British converter.) But he still contracted for the whole preparation and weaving process and made his own bargain with the beamer. Since 1975, however, he has moved to a 'net-net' basis with the sanmoto. The latter takes care of the beaming and orders delivery of the beams with the warp dyed and sized for the cloth he wants. Yoshioka is responsible solely for the weaving. He still does his own reaching and drawing in, but even that is a specialized sub-contracting operation in Nishi-waki. His business simplified, his business targets are equally simple. He is a satisficer rather than a maximiser, who calculates that if he can keep wage costs to 40 per cent of receipts, and divide the rest about equally between other costs and profits plus depreciation, he should be satisfied. But at mid-1981 prices – only double 1954 prices, he claimed, in spite of a quadrupling of general price levels – this was a difficult target to reach.

3 *Hyōgo-shōten* is a sanmoto in the same colour-weaving district of Nishiwaki. The firm was started before the war by a local merchant-entrepreneur – now in his active mid-80s – who developed a profitable line in exporting sarongs to South-east Asia. It was incorporated into the residual state-controlled weaving system during the war, but its present pattern of business began to form in the years immediately after the war ended. Only the Big Nine spinners had import licences for raw cotton. Hyōgo established itself as contract converter for one of them, organizing

the transformation of the yarn which the spinning firm supplied, into cloth which the spinning firm marketed. Such a 'loyal' contracting relationship was the only way merchant-converters could survive in the situation of yarn shortage, and they were able to impose the same loyalty requirements on their weavers, claiming prior or exclusive right to the weavers' production capacity (which is known as their 'supeesu' – the English word 'space').

The system of 'relational contracting' thus created out of shortage has persisted. (In the pre-war system the production stages were linked not by such enduring ties but by more competitive markets and shifting, often one-off, contracts.) The advantages of predictability, reliable expectations of a fair share of orders even in times when business is slack, the saving on information-search costs and transaction costs, are seen to compensate for the lower prices which the subordinate contractor may sometimes be forced to accept – as they are in Britain by Marks and Spencer's sub-contractors who operate under a very similar system. Negotiations, in these cases, are a matter of constrained haggling and moral pressures, conducted, at the sanmoto level at least, in fairly full knowledge of relevant factors. A Hyōgo manager said, for instance, that they know the price at which the spinning company has contracted to sell the finished cloth to a trading company. They also know the price which the yarn concerned is fetching on the open market (including 3- and 6-month futures). They might well be pressured into settling for a contract processing price which, in effect, (when subtracted from the cloth-selling price) gives the spinning company Y340 a pound for its yarn when the market rate is 330. But they accept that for the other advantages, and they can, of course, to some extent pass the squeeze on down the line to the dyers and weavers who take their work.

When the system started after the war, each sanmoto was tied to one and only one spinner. Loyalty had to be exclusive. When a second wave of spinners got cotton import allocations, however, thus adding to the total supply, the Big Nine were obliged to allow 'their' sanmoto to break their vows of monogamy and take a secondary relation with one of the 'New Spinners'. And so with the third wave of import licensees, the 'New New Spinners'. Hyōgo now contracts only for the New Spinner and the New New Spinner which it acquired as partners at that time in the late 1940s. Its relation with the original Big Nine spinner was at some stage dropped.

However, Hyōgo has diversified its business portfolio. It now does only about a half of its business on contract from one of these two spinning companies. The other half is done on its own account, buying yarn and selling cloth in the market. The split gives them both swings and roundabouts: the security of the contract system on the one hand, the opportunity for bigger gains from shrewd handling of market fluctuations on the other. Only two of the other 30 sanmoto in the Nishiwaki sanmoto co-operative union do as much 'own account' trading.

Some of their weavers, too, run 'own account' weaving operations as well as working as dependent sub-contractors for Hyōgo, with an (unwritten) obligation to take so many yards a month. Others keep a proportion of their 'space' for shifting competitive-market contracts over and above their basic long-term contracts. Hyōgo sometimes bids for this 'space' too, when it needs more than it can call on 'as of right' from the 50 dependent weavers to whom, in the Japanese phrase, it can 'give a shout'. There are, perhaps, another 50 weavers with whom it deals in this arm's-length market fashion. Altogether, for its one-and-half million-yard monthly production (about 5 per cent of the whole Nishiwaki-sanchi output) it has 10 employees who are engaged in production planning – negotiating contracts and supervising the journey of the yarn from dyer to beamer, to weaver, to finisher. Total employees, including three design developers, number 33. Lot sizes are typically 40–50,000 yards, but they will come down to a thousand on occasion.

One other, rather unusual, thing about Hyōgo, is that it has its own factory – one of only two weaving factories of any size which have survived from the days when most production was concentrated in large factory units, and have managed to remain competitive with the family establishments like Yoshioka's. The factory is, in fact, operated by a subsidiary jointly owned by Hyōgo and by one of its patron spinning companies. It manages to operate at a small profit by dint of having some efficient rapier looms, by very efficient labour utilization, and by substituting, among its 70 employees, local part-time housewives who do not have to be paid the union rates now required by the unmarried dormitory-housed girls who were the traditional core of the labour-force.

For finishing its cloth Hyōgo uses all of the sanchi's three finishing factories. So does practically everybody else. Once there was competition for business, but at some stage the weavers' co-operative established its own brand-new finishing mill to compete with the two existing private-enterprise establishments. Being owned by the weavers and able to command their loyalty it was in a strong position. Cosy cartelization, or what might alternatively be called sensible give-and-take arrangements, soon settled in. Prices are agreed, competition (apart from the latent threat of price competition from finishers at a greater distance) is in quality and service, the stakes only marginal shifts in market share. Hyōgo, for example, uses all three and – a condition for being able to claim priority attention – divides its business between the three in approximately equal proportions every month. 'Everybody is very well-behaved in the finishing business' said a Hyōgo manager.

4 The *Nisshin Spinning Company*, founded in 1907, is the third biggest of the Big Nine spinning companies with total sales in 1979 of some Y163bn ($740m.) and the only one to have returned a net profit in each of the post-oil crisis years. It is a very traditional firm; in ethic (a great emphasis on thrift, responsibility and free competition in the image it presents externally and in its internal exhortatory literature); in its business practices (an unusually low (4:6) debt–equity ratio, its strict control over staff junketing at the firm's expense under the guise of entertaining customers); in its rejectionist attitude to corporatist arrangements by MITI (on its approach to recession cartels see later); and in its determination to retain its traditional interests in weaving.

Six of its eight spinning mills are integrated spinning and weaving operations. They have about 700,000 spindles. They bought 70 open-end spinning machines in the expectation that the technology would develop, but it has remained suitable only for coarser counts and they have sold off all their equipment. Their 6,340 looms are nearly all Unifil automatics (plus 40 Swiss Sulzers). They have cut costs by greater efficiency, relying on natural wastage to reduce their labour-force. According to the union's survey, 45 per cent of their 6,200 workers are girls who left school at 15, another 10 per cent girls who graduated from high school. The remaining 41 per cent of men include 3.5 per cent who are university graduates and 18 per cent high school graduates. Of the remaining 1,281 men (who completed only compulsory schooling) only 28 per cent have less than 11 years service with the firm and a third have more than 30 years. Of the 2,464 girls in the same educational group, 90 per cent have been with the firm for less than 5 years. Wages for these girls range in 1980–81 from Y71,000 a month ($325) at age 15 to Y90,250 ($410) after 5 years; for high school graduate men Y83,300 ($380) at age 18, and Y114,000 ($520) 5 years later. (University graduates after 12 years and high school graduates after 25 were getting about Y225,000 ($1025). There was an 8–9 per cent increase in all these figures in April 1981, and total cash incomes were made about 40 per cent greater by the year-end and mid-summer bonuses. Adding these in, the 1981 starting wage would be the equivalent of $485 monthly, the 35-year-old university-graduate wage $1,430 (at Y220 = $1).

In their own weaving mills they concentrate on plain standard poplins and broad-cloths – mostly shirtings and plain cotton or polyester-cotton dress fabrics. Only a portion of their output is finished off in their own bleaching and dyeing works, which they keep partly for experimental reasons to be able to give guidance to the small finishing firms which handle the rest of their production. They have a 40 per cent share of the Japanese shirt market which they attribute to their Silbright soft-wash-and-wear process. They also, largely through the *sanmoto*, contract out a fair amount of more expensive yarn-dyed and fancy weaves (ginghams, etc.).

They do not shop around for their polyester staple. They buy it all from Teijin with which they have a long-standing arrangement, but they have a third share in one of the smaller of the Big Ten fibre-makers which specializes in cellulosic fibres, and they also have their own texturizing plant to give nylon a woolly texture.

They attributed their ability to stay in the weaving business to, in the first place, their relentless pursuit of efficiency: their weaving girls look after 100 to 150 looms each, and loom efficiencies (even including in down time the necessary time for beam changes) average 92 to 93 per cent. Secondly, they achieve scale economies by high volume. Given the contraction of the domestic market, this makes their exports (20 per cent of their textile production is exported) even more important. They adopted the strategy of sticking with their export markets through the high-yen-value years of 1978–9 on the grounds that markets once lost were not easily regained. They were justified when the dollar came back a year later.

5 *Fujiwara*   is a weaver in Kishiwada, a sanchi within local-call

telephone distance of the Osaka markets, which, largely for that reason, has no sanmoto. A half of its weavers are entrepreneurial weavers, buying yarn and selling cloth on the Osaka market, some of whom also sub-contract to the other half. Whether one is a subcontractor or a sub-contractee seems to be largely a matter of personality. Those who fancy themselves at bargaining on the phone tend to become the organizers. The more introverted settle for a quieter life, albeit at somewhat lower income levels.

The firm was started in 1955. Fujiwara's adoptive father had been a greengrocer who envied the weavers' 'more flamboyant' trade. Fujiwara was a machinist in an automobile factory until he was adopted into the family to marry the daughter, take the family's surname, and inherit the business. He is still running the same seventy 56-inch automatic looms which the old man bought between 1955 and 1960, banked in four rows and driven by overhead drive from an electric motor on each row. The looms do only 140–150 picks a minute, but they have been equipped with an electronic warp stop motion (stopping the loom when a warp thread breaks; the electronic device eliminates the laborious business of putting drop pins on each thread when the loom is set up) and with another electronic device which stops the shuttle before the thread runs out, thus eliminating the danger of that slight quality defect of a missed weft thread and the labour of turning the loom back a throw or two.

Fujiwara buys all his yarn but sub-contracts all his beaming and sizing, though he has one-third of the equity of one of the beaming firms. He weaves just two sorts, both all cotton; a 44-inch broad cloth for quilt covers, and a 49-inch cambric for outer wear. He has been weaving these for over ten years during which time he has tried three other sorts; a poplin, also for bedding covers which stayed at too low a price for too long to be worthwhile, and two synthetics for export: one, a synthetic cashmere of fine acrylic fibre, was very profitable until the Iranian revolution wiped out the market which a Japanese trading company had created.

He gets his orders – mostly quarterly contracts for so much cloth a month – mainly from four convertors/makers-up in Osaka and Nagoya. He takes a good deal of pleasure in exercising his judgement as to the right time to strike a contract. He had, for example, his April–June order book nearly filled by mid-February. But in mid-May he still had not made any July–September contracts. The cold summer of the previous year had lowered demand and prices and scared the current price lower than he expected it later to rise to. He was fairly secure, however, in the 'expression of intent' he had got from his buyers. There was enough un-impacted information and sufficiently large numbers around in the market for them to reach what they would both acknowledge as an acceptable-in-the-circumstances price when the time came. He buys his yarn mostly from one trading company, but has other sources too, including a Korean importer. Transactions are in 10-bale lots of which he needs about six a month.

Some of his contracts he makes through one of three brokers he also deals with. Brokers really know the market. They act as middlemen negotiating a contract price between the parties and taking a small transaction fee. When Fujiwara has got a broker-broked contract for a certain cloth/period, he can then confidently settle another contract with a different buyer for the same price directly and thus save the fee.

Yarn is paid for with 30-day bills, but cloth with 90-day bills – a difference which reflects in textbook fashion degrees of monopoly power and numbers in the market. The weavers' co-operative will discount these bills at a favourable rate. Cloth-price fluctuations are considerable: cambric at Y138 a metre in July 1980 was Y175 by the following March and down again a few months later. The broad cloth moved between Y113 and Y130 in the same period. Contracts are firm once made. The only point in the Japanese textile-clothing chain at which a stronger party reserves the right to cancel a provisional order (for which the weaker party may have had to make considerable investment in preparation) is in relations between a department store and a small apparel-maker.

Fujiwara gets up, crosses the yard from his house-office to the weaving shed and sets his looms going at 5 a.m. each morning. His wife joins him at 6 a.m. and they keep as many of the looms working as possible until the hired labour comes at 8 a.m. There is one 65-year-old man who is a loom mechanic hired at Y650 an hour – at 1981 exchange rates approximately $140 for a 48-hour week. Then there are 11 women, all of whom have been working with them for more than five years: local housewives, friends of the family, slightly status-subordinate, but friends of the family nevertheless, whose standard of living (if not net worth) is no more or less petty bourgeois than the Fujiwaras'. One of them is a general overseer, and at any time three weavers look after 23–24 looms each – a load which would be unthinkable in Lancashire for non-automatic looms that require the weaver to change shuttles: it is made possible by the care with which Fujiwara buys reliable yarn and by careful temperature and humidity control – at a very humid mid-eighties. Women's wages are Y460–Y500 an hour (weavers' fluctuate slightly in that range since they are paid by the pick) – $100–$110 for a 48-hour week. These payments should be increased by 14 per cent for the 1½ months' bonus he pays in two annual instalments. He decides wage increases by looking at newspaper advertisements for supermarket help, etc., by asking what friends pay, and by the outcome of the annual Spring-Offensive all-industry synchronous wage negotiation. In 1981 the monthly average increase for 40-year-old middle-school-leaver males was, the newspapers reported, Y14,000. His women's wages are half that level so he paid a proportionate Y7,000 increase.

After 8 a.m. Fujiwara moves on to the telephone to do his business negotiations, works on the books, helps the loom mechanic in changing warp beams on the looms that have run out – two or three a day on average – takes a nap, calls on friends, and at 5 p.m. when the employees go home, is back at the looms with his wife keeping them going until 8 p.m. in the evening.

The structure of his costs (operating and overheads) for 1980 was as follows:

	%
Yarn	58.4
Labour	12.8
Beaming and sizing contracting	15.8
Utilities	1.8
Cloth inspection	0.8
Directors' fees	3.4
Other costs	7.0

Subtracting yarn, beaming costs and electricity from sales for gross value added, that was divided as follows:

	%
Labour	46.1
Directors' fees	12.2
Depreciation	1.8
Interest	8.0
Operating profits	6.3

Reserves	1.7
Services and other costs	23.9

His immediate business ambition is to get into a debt-free position: his debt–equity ratio being at present exactly 1:1 and interest payments were about three-quarters of his director's fee. He is not particularly worried about the future; they have contained the threat from Korean imports so far and he does not see why they should not do the same for the Chinese. It is unlikely he will find replacements for his weavers when they get too old to work and then he will think about re-equipping with air jets – but not until he has got his debt ratio down: the air jets will be proved by then. Otherwise he does not expect any big changes: 'It's places like this, working the way we do, that keep the Japanese economy going. I am supposed to be the management. Actually I am a labourer jack-of-all-trades. There are thousands of little family businesses like this that work all the hours that God gives for a pittance. That's what keeps the automobile industry going. Foreigners can talk about economic animals and rabbit hutches. Well, let them. That's fine. That's the way it has to be with us within the country if we are to defend our family's livelihood, and we've got nothing to apologize about.'

6 *Furuike*   is one of the three brokers with whom Fujiwara deals. Twenty-five years ago he left a large trading company (in his early thirties) and decided to capitalize on the expertise he had acquired and the force and charm of his telephone personality to set himself up as an independent broker. He sits in a cramped, stuffy office at the back of a dingy early post-war building at a large table bearing six telephones. Opposite him sits his partner and another older man whose subordinate status is clear from his silence and from the fact that it is he who gets up to make the tea. Furuike buys and sells nothing. His job is to put willing sellers in touch with willing buyers and negotiate a price between them. Transactions cover future deliveries sometimes up to nine months ahead, the futures usually being for monthly deliveries over the next or the next-but-one three-monthly period into which the textile year is divided. He deals with about 50 yarn suppliers and three times as many weavers. The actual contract is made between the parties directly concerned (he receiving a commission) but he may be asked to mediate claims – attempts to return defective goods (which tend, such is the venality of man, says he, to increase at

times of falling prices: if one can return a few bales of high-priced cotton and replace them at the new lower price, one is doing well: the trust which reigns in Japanese markets is not absolute).

As a guide to prices he has his neat loose-leaf notebook and three textile newspapers published daily or every other day. Most of these published figures are offer prices gleaned by telephone from brokers like himself, but for three kinds of standard yarn – 20s, 40s and 60s – there actually is a physical market – a beautifully appointed well-lit room (with spectators' gallery as well as the latest electronic equipment) at the top of a new tall building where 32 member dealers balance bids and offer to find the price that clears the market 18 times a day (twice for each type of yarn, for immediate delivery and for three- and six-month futures). The total volume of sales in this market exceeds the volume of production by a fair margin (by 30 per cent in 1980), but at monthly settlement day, when dealers deliver or collect their *net* sales or purchases, to or from the market warehouse, only a tiny fraction – often less than 2 per cent of the gross volume put through the market actually changes hands.

An essential part in the efficient functioning of this market is played by the inspection system. All transactions in the market are in 'standard' yarn. Every major Japanese manufacturer's production (43 brands of 32 spinners) is sampled monthly by an organization run by a committee of traders, brokers and weavers, and graded in terms of so many yen discount below the standard (which is currently Tōyō Bōseki's Goldfish brand). Only these yarns are eligible for deliveries at settlement day, at the discount designated.

In addition to the cotton-yarn market, there is also a less important market for staple fibres, but this is all that is left of the once flourishing Three Goods' Market – for raw cotton and cloth as well as for yarn – in its heyday as bustling and as 'real' a market as the Manchester 'Change. Even the yarn market, of course, is a shadow of its former self; once a market through which a good deal of yarn actually flowed from spinner to weaver, now a tiny spot market fringe which sets guide prices for the 98 per cent of yarn transfers which move along the channels of established relations, or channels created by men such as Mr Furuike. The big spinners, who are also the organizers of production of brand cloth by satellite contract weavers and who market the bulk of their yarn in this way, are keen to see this market abolished; the publication of its fluctuating prices lends an instability to their relation with their dependent weavers. In late 1981 they were feeling strong enough to press their case in the major Spinning Industry Association, but were still resisted by the biggest spinner of all (Kondo) which sells most of its yarn production on the open market, as well as the Weavers' Association and the market itself.

Mr Furuike is merely an observer of the Three Goods Market, not a participant. But like that market, he does not deal in imported yarn. The whole network for imports is different. The yarn department of Marubeni or Itochu, the big trading companies who act as agents for most of the Japanese spinners, does not handle imported yarn; that is handled by a separate department of the same trading companies who sell through a different network. Likewise the brokers who sell Pakistan or Korean yarn, or who have sales agencies for Korean spinners. The problem of Korean yarn is, as Mr Furuike will explain, its uneven quality and the difficulty of making claims against defective yarn stick. The risk premium is about 3½ per cent. When the Japanese price is around Y130,000 a bale, Korean yarn has to be Y5,000 cheaper to sell. Since Korean yarn is quoted in dollars (and the yen tends to move with the dollar), yen-dollar exchange fluctuations which have reached 20 per cent in a single year are crucial determinants of the viability of imports.

Mr Furuike has a strong historical sense. 'We are going the same way as you, but you still have it much better. Look at the houses you live in. How long will it take us to build up a stock like that? You tell those people in England that we need to export to live. And we haven't got *all* that much time. What we did to Lancashire, Korea and China will do to us. Already Chinese qualities are very good. They are bound to win. Sheer quality of labour will give them an edge. It's the same in China and Korea as it was in Japan before the war. A textile job is a prize job: the brightest girls go in for it. In Japan now, though, we've only got a few old ladies left in the business: any younger ones who go into it are the ones who aren't bright enough to do any better. Our generation will be the last in a whole range of the industry. The younger generation want a job where they can take all their holiday entitlement: they're not interested in working. Nobody's going to want to inherit my business.' An exporter came in and spoke of his student son just off for a postgraduate course in Manila, after which he was going on to study in London. 'See what I mean?'

7 *Fukui*   is on the North Japan coast, as area where the weaving industry is at least twelve centuries old and where the weaving of cloth from spun silk has been a cottage industry by-employment for farmers (and for a while for indigent warrior families) since the seventeenth century. The silk-weaving tradition translated easily into skill in weaving nylon and polyester and acrylic filaments, and most of the fibre-makers have brought a factory to the north coast to serve the weavers of Fukui and its neighbouring prefecture, Ishikawa. Fukui, with its 800,000 population, had 4,342 textile and 355 garment-making establishments in 1980, producing about 40 per cent of the prefecture's manufacturing output. (Ishikawa, with 1.1m. population, had nearly 7,000 establishments.) About 60 per cent of these establishments were weavers.

Hishiyama and his wife live in a large concrete building in a village half way between Fukui city and a famous Zen temple, now a thriving tourist spot on the foothills at the rim of the coastal plain. They built it in the late 1960s as a dormitory for young girls recruited from the rural extremities of Japan – areas where still 20–25 per cent of the 15-year-old age group did not then follow their nine years' compulsory schooling with three years at regular high-school and were prepared to be recruited by employers such as Hishiyama who could offer them a comfortable dormitory, paternal care and the chance to attend a part-time evening high school which the weavers' co-operative in the district had helped to finance. (Graduation took four years after which most of the girls went back home or on to a better job.) As the high-school attendance rate increased and the supply of 15-year-olds dried up, some textile areas ratcheted their recruiting effort up a notch, sought 18-year-old high-school-leaving weavers, turned the local high-school into a junior college and offered, now, the prospect of a nursery-school teacher's certificate after four years' work and part-time study.

But that did not happen in the Hishiyamas' district, and in any case the Hishiyamas were out of that particular market, for by the early 1970s they had gone bankrupt. They were the victims of the pioneer spirit: one of the first to take advantage of a government re-equipment scheme and replace most of their automatics with a set of the latest and newest looms – the much faster water-jet looms made by Enshū, a firm with many years' experience in the loom-making business. No one foresaw then that, partly because the new technology marked such a radical break with the old, by

the end of the decade Enshū, the traditional loom-maker, would
be completely outclassed as a manufacturer of water-jet looms by
Nissan and Toyota, the automobile manufacturers. But so it
proved. The Enshū looms were lemons; they did not earn enough
over the cost of repaying the large debts their purchase incurred
to keep the business going.

But the Hishiyamas were still left with their skills, Mr
Hishiyama in particular with his highly developed knowledge of
loom mechanics, and a considerable reputation for tinkering
dexterity, finely honed by his experience in trying to keep the
Enshū looms going. It was around these skills that a local sanmoto merchant converter built a two-tier organization which took
over the assets of the bankrupt Hishiyama enterprise (the former
concrete dormitory now becoming the Hishiyamas' home, for the
bankruptcy left them unable to keep their mortgaged house).
Hishiyama became the Managing Director of the Fujishima
Weaving Company. At the same time (partly because this was a
precondition for cheap government finance) the Polaris Weavers'
Co-operative was created – a joint venture of Fujishima and 11
other weaving firms. The co-operative made sense because they
were all converting to water-jet looms, and could gain scale
economies by providing certain facilities on a co-operative basis.
Between them they have 265 water-jets. Fujishima Weaving
Company has 77, a second firm has 96 and the others have
between 10 and 30 each. The common facilities are, first, for
drying and then inspecting the water-jet woven cloth, secondly a
new and very complex Swiss machine for reaching and drawing
in – the final stage in the preparation of warp beams (the beams
themselves still being bought in from specialist beamers).

Hishiyama is Managing Director of both the Fujishima Weaving Company and the Co-operative; his wife is in charge of the
drawing in. The company has built a new light and airy weaving
shed. In addition to the 77 water-jet looms weaving a straightforward polyester taffeta twill, there are another 53 automatic looms
with dobbies which are weaving more complex weaves more
slowly. The weaving staff was 13 strong: one mechanic and two
women for each of the two-day shifts, three men on the night
shift, plus one additional helper to cover the (staggered) rest
days. The factory operates seven days a week, the workers 18
days out of 21. Women earn about Y130,000 a month, men on
average Y180,000 – night weavers Y160,000 to Y170,000 and
mechanics up to Y230,000 at the age of 40, though the starting

wage for a high-school leaver would be less than Y120,000. Bonuses as well as seniority differentials are of large corporation levels – mid-summer and year-end bonuses combined equalling five months' salary. Adding the bonus in, average cash wages were the equivalent of $827 for a month of 48-hour weeks for women (£104 a week), $1,145 for men.

The office was spacious, with stylish modern furniture and a microcomputer whose visual display shows which looms are working, which have stopped, and what the percentage of stoppage time has been on the shift so far. A print-out (back numbers are filed – another 'modern' touch – in a folder labelled, in English 'Dayly Data') summarizes the information for each shift and for weekly or monthly periods (but with no analysis of stoppages into warp breaks, weft breaks, etc. as in some European computer systems), When he gets round to programming it, it will be possible to use the computer to check which looms need beam changes within the next x days. The previous month's records showed loom efficiencies of 97 per cent for the water-jets, 94 per cent for the other looms, 95 per cent overall, the 5 per cent stoppage time including the time necessary for changing warp beams. (This is less than it would otherwise be for the fast-weaving water-jets by virtue of the specially big, one-metre-diameter beams which they can take.)

Their problem now is not weaving efficiency but prices. The contract weaving price for a standard length of polyester taffeta was Y2,200 in the spring of 1980, down to Y800 fifteen months later. The price of the more difficult fine georgette crêpe which is harder to handle on water-jet looms has held up better: Y2,200 compared with a Y3,200 peak.

The problem is domestic over-capacity, plus competition in export markets. Just under 51 per cent of Fukui's 1981 production was exported: a half of that to the USA, either directly or via Hong Kong garment-makers. Fukui alone by October 1981 had 11,000 shuttle-less looms out of a total of 72,000 looms weaving filaments (mostly water-jets, about 9 per cent rapiers) compared with 4,600 in 1974. Under government schemes to be described later, water-jet looms could only be installed if 2.4 times as many automatic looms of comparable width were simultaneously scrapped, and 1:2.4 is about the right output ratio: 600 picks a minute on a water-jet compared with 220–240 for an automatic. But water-jet owners, having spent $16,000 on a loom ($24,000 with dobbies) are more keen to work them for three shifts than they were to get the maximum out of their fully depreciated automatics. Hence a considerable rise in production – 42 per cent higher in Fukui in 1981 than in 1975, and Ishikawa showed a similar increase. The other thing that has changed is the external competition. The USA had only 1,500 water-jet looms in 1974, and 7,500 by 1981. Korea and Taiwan between them had 12,600, having had none at all in 1974. Korean competition is reaching the domestic market too, plain woven cloth from Korea is being brought to Fukui for finishing and re-export to the USA where it counts towards the Japanese quota which still has space, rather than the filled Korean quota (Kuroki, 1981; Fukui-Ken, 1981; Fukui Textile 1982).

The Hishiyamas hope to avoid bankruptcy a second time. They hope that perhaps the quality premium which their best fine georgette crêpe can command will see them through, though their two sons at the Tokyo University of Foreign Languages, one doing Chinese, the other German, are perhaps a better bet. 'We're urging them to get a job with the government. The security is important. You don't get that in the textile industry.'

8 In the same village is *Kanefuji Sizing*. It director and principal owner, Mr Aoki, was once a 'salary man' with one of the big fibre-makers. There were times after he left the firm in 1964 when he regretted his temerity in choosing the small-firm option, but not since the oil crisis, as he has seen one after another of his contemporaries – not dismissed, for the big corporations do not do that even when they are grossly overmanned, but 'farmed out' to make-shift jobs in the firm's 'colonies', their pay part-subsidized by the parent company.

The firm was created when the new large-scale sizing machines arrived in the 1960s. Capital was provided by a group of weavers, all of whom were contract weaving for the fibre-maker Kanebō, Kanebō itself providing technical advice and a firm promise of future business which helped persuade the banks to make loans. For some years he worked only for the participating firms, only on Kanebō business – with continuing Kanebō advice on sizing techniques. At the low point of one recession, however, Kanebō pushed the weavers too hard in price negotiations and the connection was broken. Some of his shareholder-clients switched to other makers which had their own exclusive contract beaming arrangements, so he became a freelance contractor, relying on his own resources of skill and experience to keep up with advances in technology. Those resources seem considerable to judge from the products of his attached machine shop. He has made his own creeling cages, and all the tracking on which he moves beams around the factory; he has some special devices of his own invention – for loading creels, for cutting threads, for patrolling the creel cages on any-height-adjustable moving platforms, all of which gives him a good deal of satisfaction as well as saving money. His two large sizing machines, one of which sizes straight from special high-quality cones, the other a more conventional one, are of recent vintage and have automatic stop devices to prevent any slubs from getting through. They are operated for three shifts by a total of 15 employees: wages are at approximately the same level as at Fujishima Weaving. His production schedules are planned in detail two weeks in advance: in outline three months in advance.

The structure summarized
The main features which have emerged from these descriptions may be summarized as follows.

The more powerful concentrations of capital are to be found upstream in the spinning and fibre-making companies.

The process of transforming yarn into finished cloth is highly fragmented with large numbers of specialist beamers and sizers, twisters, doublers and texturizers, yarn-dyers, weavers and dyers and finishers, working in what are predominantly small-scale enterprises built around the nucleus of a single family.

Co-ordination is effected less by markets than by inter-enterprise ties of organization and enduring partnership. The December 1976 special industrial census produced the following figures. Of the 104,000 firms in textiles with fewer than 300 employees, 67 per cent delivered more than four-fifths of their production to a single purchaser. (A third of those purchasers were wholesalers and nearly a half were other small manufacturing firms with fewer than 50 employees.) For the 65,000 firms with three or fewer workers, the proportion of 'tied' firms was 79 per cent (MITI, Tōkeibu, December 1976). When the survey was repeated five years later (by which time the number of firms enumerated had fallen to 98,000), the figure had marginally dropped to 65 and 76 per cent respectively (MITI, December 1981).

The key co-ordinating role in the processing of yarn into finished cloth may be played:

by a large spinning company or fibre-making company directly commissioning manufacturers (rarely);

(more commonly) by a large spinning company or fibre-making company operating through a sanmoto convertor in one of the textile producing areas;

by a sanmoto convertor buying yarn and selling independently to a cloth wholesaler;

by a large Osaka, Nagoya or Tokyo-based trading company operating independently or through a sanmoto.

The chains of enduring relations involved can be several steps long: spinner → trading company → sanmoto → weaver → sub-contract weaver. Such chains are often called the X Keiretsu, X being the dominant firm at the top of the hierarchy. The chain *is* a hierarchical one in the sense that the contracting parties do not have equal power to influence the terms of the contract. (The difference in the payment practices where co-ordination is still via the market – 30-day bills for yarn, but 90-day bills for cloth – indicates the different initial positions from which they enter these relationships.) The sources of differential strength are fairly clear. Difference in *numbers* in the market is one element: there are few spinners and trading companies, many weavers. Other elements are differences in capital resources, difference in knowledge of final markets, and control over technical innovation (particularly in synthetic fibres where the fibre-makers are the source of the product-differentiating innovations which offer the best opportunities for enhanced profits).

As in other countries, there is very little vertical integration across the textile-clothing line; only one of the larger clothing companies was actually set up by a textile company, but the pattern of enduring trading relations is still found across the textile-clothing divide. A survey of the apparel industry found that a high proportion of garment firms were taking 70 per cent of their cloth from three or fewer sources (Tomizawa, 1980, p.99).

The structure of the garment industry is similar to that of the textile industry in its widespread use of sub-contracting. The industry is becoming increasingly dominated by large-scale 'apparel firms'; the top 25 have increased their collective turnover by 10–15 per cent a year over the last few years, but still have only about one-third of the market with the biggest; Renown, having about 6 per cent (Tomizawa, 1980, pp.53, 85; Nihon Orimono, 1982, p.33). Although none has yet got the Levi-Strauss kind of stature with a one-and-a-half billion-dollar turnover, the three biggest are at least half that size. These garment firms are responsible for design and planning, either directly commissioning the makers-up (there were some 42,000 garment factories: their numbers and their total employment having increased by 26 per cent and 28 per cent respectively between 1970 and 1977, at a time when the number of textile enterprises fell by 5 per cent and textile employment by 28 per cent (Tomizawa, 1980, pp.36, 43)), or leaving the actual manufacturing to be organized by the wholesalers whose pattern of organization has evolved from the traditional trade networks of the days when Japanese-style clothing dominated the scene.

The structure of the industry resembles that of Britain rather than the United States in that it is usually the clothing firm which decides the dyeing and finishing specifications; only about 10 per cent of the cloth is offered ready-finished, dyed to what the *textile* producer decides is to be the fashionable colour. (The actual organization of the finishing – to order – is usually by the same convertor as organizes the weaving, however, though sometimes by the cloth wholesaler.) Indeed, the clothing firms also interest themselves greatly in the structure of the cloth as well as in its finish and may specify variations in the weave, apparently attaching some importance to having their very own cloth, even if it differs from others' cloth only in having 58 threads to the inch instead of 56.

The other feature of these garment firms worth mentioning is that they deal with their main outlets, the department stores and supermarket chains (which sell about half of Japan's clothing) on a sale-or-return basis – which means that they get heavily involved in the retail process (Tomizawa, 1980, p.128). The leading firms in men's suitings and women's clothes are also very active in licensing European and American designs, though how far the benefit of these licences lies in access to design skill, how far in the glamour of an exotic brand name is a moot point. These firms are also the major organizers of imports of cheap garments (underwear, some shirts and men's suits, children's wear) from the developing countries.

Producers' co-operatives

One final element of the structure of these industries somewhat modifies the picture of a set of vertical hierarchies. It is the important role played by the *horizontal* organization of producers' co-operatives. These proliferate in a complex network. For example, the prefecture of Shizuoka with 3½ million population and (1979) about 7 per cent of its manufacturing employment and 3 per cent of its manufacturing output in textiles (the output including 90 per cent of Japan's production and a sizeable proportion of world exports of velveteens and corduroys) has no fewer than 33 co-operatives formally organized enough to be constituent members of the Shizuoka Textile Association. They are organized partly on trade, partly on a regional basis. For example, there are three weavers' co-operatives for three different districts, plus a weavers' federation of all three; three for dyers and finishers; three for corduroy cutters and so on. The specialities separately organized include the sanmoto convertors, yarn twisters, beamers, sizers, garment-makers, garment wholesalers, yarn dealers, knitters.

The scope and effectiveness of these organizations vary widely. To take only weavers' co-operatives as an example, at one end of the spectrum are the local weavers' co-operatives of large parts of Ishikawa prefecture on the north coast where (a) weavers are scattered in smallish concentrations of a few score, (b) all of them are contract weavers rather than independent sellers in the market, and (c) the sanmoto convertors are relatively few in number and quite large operators in consequence. Here the co-operatives are little more than friendly societies of weavers incorporated into the Keiretsu of the same sanmoto. As such they can sometimes bargain collectively with the sanmoto over contract prices, and it is as difficult to assess the clout of their collective bargaining strength as it is that of an enterprise union in a small or medium firm. Suffice it to say that they can rarely push the dominant sanmoto very hard, though they may at least marginally restrain the latter's ability to play fast and loose with their members.

At the other end of the scale is the Senshū co-operative of the thousand weavers in the suburban area centred on Kishiwada, to the south of Osaka, who specialize in cotton sheetings and shirtings and gauzes. These are for the most part independents weaving for the market, not doing contract weaving, so that the co-operative performs no collective bargaining function, but the size of its membership, the relative homogeneity of the members and their sense of being under threat give the co-operative plenty of scope for useful activity to keep its 18 full-time officials and 9 supporting employees busy. Among the functions which this and similar cooperatives perform are the following:

Organizing training programmes in new techniques, lectures on markets, fashion prospects, gathering information on the performance of new looms and other machinery.

Publishing a monthly newsletter carrying similar information.

Organizing exhibitions in major centres (usually in conjunction with garment-makers, showing the cloth and finished products).

Organizing study tours, including, in the case of Senshū, a tour of China to assess the import threat and to try to persuade the Chinese export agency to limit the increase in exports.

Discounting bills.

Mediating loan applications to the special small and medium industry banks.

Providing contract pro-forma in an attempt to 'modernize' trading relations to strengthen the hand of the weavers.

Collecting and distributing price information.

Fixing minimum contract weaving prices for standard cloths (which contract weavers are not supposed to under-cut).

Running a Young Weavers' Association (their equivalent of Young Farmers' 4H Clubs, designed to 'keep the youngsters down with the looms').

Running collective fire, life, sickness and accident insurance schemes.

Operating collective purchase schemes for yarn, size, packing materials; collection and return of used cheese spindles.

Offering a personnel management consultation service, and a technical advice consultation service (in conjunction with the prefectural Textile Technology Research Institute and the Cloth Inspection Service).

Performing delegated functions under government measures for the restructuring of the textile industry – loans and capacity reduction grants, facilitating mergers, etc.

Lobbying the government for protection and aid schemes, primarily through the national Cotton and Staple Fibre Weaving Industry Association to which the co-operatives are affiliated.

Decreeing short-time working at times of slack demand – as when the Senshū cooperative declared a five-day week in the summer of 1981 as the figures for cloth stocks reached dangerously high levels.

Sending out elaborate questionnaires to collect detailed statistics for the information of its members and of government.

Preparing long-term development plans for the industry.

In Nishiwaki, a country area closer to the groupish traditions of rural Japanese culture, the co-operative also exercises permanent control over hours of work – no Sundays or after 10 p.m., and a summons to the office if a patrolling official catches you at it. Exemptions are allowed for Sundays if you have to miss a working day to, say, attend a funeral. (One reason for the regulations is to mitigate neighbours' criticisms against weavers collectively for their noise pollution.)

These co-operatives usually have a dual personality. Outside the Senshū offices, for instance, two signboards proclaim the one that it is the Senshū Weaving Industry Co-operative Union, the other that it is the Senshū Structural Improvement Industrial Union. In its first capacity it is a voluntary organization, with 684 members owning 749 factories, which operates an annual budget of Y113m. ($514,000). In its second capacity it is the organization which exercises a variety of functions as an agent of the government, ranging from the registration of looms, which is compulsory, to administering various grants and loan schemes to its own members. It has somewhat more members – 931 owning 1,001 factories and has an annual budget of Y164m. ($742,000). In effect, since all its 30 elected board members and its 130 representatives are members of the voluntary union, it behaves as a single organization with a single budget, some of whose functions (of which more later) are delegated to it and some of whose funds are granted to it, by government.

8
Textiles: The sources of viability

We are now in a position to enumerate some of the factors which account for the low level of import penetration. A large part of the explanation (but not all) lies in the industry's competitiveness – as is indicated by the continued retention of substantial export markets. Japanese producers can compete in foreign as well as in domestic markets. The sources of that competitiveness are several.

1 Innovativeness

Japan is perhaps the most future-oriented of all industrial societies. This came out clearly in an international comparative study of civil servants and the content of their work and concerns (Kubota, 1981). It comes out in the frequency of 'next ten years' forecasts (or 'visions' as the Japanese say, borrowing the English word) published by various ministries, industries, municipalities – and textile weavers' co-operatives. It comes out in the frequency with which newspapers carry articles about technology and the rapidity of change and the way the next few years are going to be vastly different. It comes out in the steady increase in expenditure on R & D by Japanese enterprises – not least in the textile and clothing industries. Here one has to take account of two kinds of innovation – what the Japanese call hard and soft: innovation in material processing and product technology on the one hand, and, on the other, the process of creative design, forecasting and engineering of taste and snob values which goes into fashion innovation.

To take the former first, most of that research is concentrated in the big fibre firms, and to a lesser extent in the spinning firms and clothing firms, but there is also a not insignificant structure of central government and prefectural research laboratories which work together with 'study groups' set up by the co-operatives. Some of this activity generates more enthusiasm than concrete research ideas, but nevertheless it and the mental set that goes with it give the Japanese industry certain keen advantages.

First, in the development of new fibres, new ways of texturing yarn and finishing cloth, the Japanese are scoring notable successes. Their georgette crêpes, for instance, command a large market and are the product of ideas first conceived in the USA, but only developed to production viability by Japanese research.

Secondly, the keiretsu structure of tied sub-contracting carries with it a good deal of 'guidance' – uncosted technical advice from the research-strong fibre firms down to the weavers and finishers. Likewise, the tied collaborative relationship between textile firm and clothing firm extends that guidance across to the garment-makers. Hence the diffusion of new fibres, finishing techniques, etc., can be rapid and (the appropriate treatment for the appropriate material) efficient, while the back-flow of information – from the final market to the research effort – is also facilitated.

Thirdly, where people are always looking for something new even quite outside these keiretsu structures the diffusion of best practice can be rapid: the small family weavers with the electronic device to stop a shuttle loom before the pirn runs out in order to safeguard product quality are an example.

As for fashion innovation it is hard to generalize, except to say that the Japanese are highly clothes and fashion conscious and that the business of fashion innovation seems to be discussed with a rare seriousness in Japan. So far the snob appeal exerted by Paris and New York fashion names far outweighs that exerted by Japanese names, both in Japan and in the world at large (and the fact that nearly all Japanese cloth brand names are European loan words is indicative of that). On the reasonable assumption that this is not so much a matter of intrinsic quality as of the diffuse prestige of these places as centres of civilization, the steady rise in Japan's reputation for creativeness and artistic imagination offers the prospect that this situation might reverse itself and what is now a competitive disadvantage of the Japanese industry might be turned to an advantage.

2   High investment rates

Much innovation requires investment; a high investment rate is a precondition for maintaining a stock of recent-vintage equipment. A high savings ratio, a relative abundance of capital and low interest rates, plus a considerable optimism about the future have led to high rates of investment in Japanese industry in general, and in its leading sectors in particular. Textiles is obviously not one of these. Estimated to have 7.2 per cent of the manufacturing sector's fixed capital investment in 1965 and 6.9 per cent in 1970, it had only 5.0 per cent in 1979 (*Kōgyō Tōkei*. The MITI survey of large firms shows lower proportions in textiles, but the same trend. KY, 1984, p.113). This comparative decline masks an absolute increase, however – a 40 per cent increase, in fact, in the estimated value of the capital stock in real terms during 1970–79 (28 per cent of that before 1973) (KY, 1981, p.74). With capacity cutbacks in both fibre-making and spinning toward the end of the decade, most of the new investment was replacement investment – as also were the fairly large-scale purchases of shuttle-less looms – firms were in fact required by government legislation to replace, not add to, capacity. Hence the effect of this investment on the vintage average was all the greater – with considerable pay-off in product quality and cost reduction.

3   Product quality

The third element in competitiveness is difficult to analyse and certainly to quantify. It consists in a concern for quality, the pursuit of perfection, the careful conscientious attention to detail which economists find it hard to take account of except by including it in the general category of X-efficiency. The spread of the electronic device mentioned above for avoiding a possible missed weft thread when changing shuttles on shuttle looms is one example of this close attention to detail. The speed, deftness and care with which weavers tie broken ends are less easily measured or described, but nonetheless important and manifest in the high loom efficiencies recorded in weaving shops. These high efficiencies are partly a matter of this conscientiousness and deftness – of the fact that weavers see a stopped loom as a nagging accusation and proprietors do not sleep well at night when they are behind with their deliveries – and partly of the fact that the same conscientiousness in spinners and sizers (*plus* investment in spinning and sizing machines with automatic control devices) has produced yarn of high quality which is not liable to frequent breaks.

A phenomenon related to this high level of quality conscious-ness is the frequency of references to 'making claims' – sending back defective materials or claiming compensation for losses caused by defective material. One of the reasons for the electronic devices for avoiding problems of shuttle change-over is because, with plain-colour dyeing being more commonly done by roller-printing than in vats, doubled threads and turned-back ends stand out undyed and the finisher is likely to 'make a claim'. I have no statistical evidence that this happens more frequently in Japan than elsewhere, but that is certainly the impression one gets, and it coincides, also, with everything one hears about the extremely rigorous quality controls over components purchased from sub-contractors by large engineering and domestic appliance firms. It is particularly with reference to imports that one hears a great deal about 'claims'; the fact that claims cannot be easily made to stick against distant importers is a frequently cited reason for not taking imported yarn or cloth.

This concern for quality is sustained by an important institutional factor – the extensive inspection system. This has a long history. Its inspiration lies not so much in the public interest which society has in ensuring that *caveat emptor* is not the only check on shoddiness or dishonesty, but in a national concern with the nation's reputation – and business success – as an exporter. Most of the cloth produced by Japan's weavers goes for inspection to an inspection station run by the quasi-governmental Cloth Inspection Association. Inspection systems of this kind go back to the early nineteenth century. In their modern form, they date from the early years of the century, and inspection for export purposes – where *the nation's* reputation is at stake – became legally compulsory in 1919. There it is graded A, B and C, according to the number of faults discovered. A good deal of cloth goes through as many as three inspections in addition to the weaving firm's own – once after weaving, once again after finishing, and possibly once again by the export inspection service when it gets to the docks. Yarn outputs are subject to a monthly check, it will be recalled, as part of the organization of the Three Goods Market.

These quality factors have a good deal to do with the low penetration of imports – in two ways. First, Japanese qualities are such that domestic producers have a real competitive advantage. Korean yarn is said to have improved very considerably over the last seven or eight years in both quality and in producers' ability to keep to delivery schedules, but still it is only the coarser counts, 20s and 40s, that are imported: from Pakistan only 20s. A Kishiwada weaver with nearly 200 looms and brave plans for steadily re-equipping with air-jet looms claimed that he would always be able to withstand Chinese competition because he could, and the Chinese could not, produce cloth of the faultless quality that could be dyed a plain colour. The Chinese might sweep the board with prints, but cloth for plain-colour dyeing would always command a high price. Trading company experts declared that he was deluding himself: Chinese qualities were well up to Japanese standards because their old equipment was compensated for by highly labour-intensive care and attention. China's selling price was set at the maximum, which would still clear all they had the installed capacity to produce, over and above domestic requirements, and was well above production costs – so that they could take as much of the market as they wished in standard cotton lines as soon as they could install the necessary capacity. Korean cloth, on the other hand, was said to be much less reliable. One might order 1000 yards in 100-yard lengths, only to find that some were 30-yard and some 150 (they would have let the loom get into a bad smash and have had to cut the beam off and start again). Moreover, the number of faults was unpredictable. For finishers or makers-up whose production system was set up to deal with 100-yard lengths without serious faults, this could be a very grave disadvantage.

Secondly, in addition to such real substantive quality defects as imported yarns and cloths may have, the exclusion of imports from the inspection system has hitherto meant that even if qualities were first-rate, importers could still not offer the same guarantees as domestic producers and consequently would have to take a sizeable risk discount. However, there are signs that this may be changing. The Senshū weavers have set up their own yarn inspection system at the centre recently built with government funds under the Structure Improvement Scheme. In the first place they set little store by the official inspection system for the Three Goods' Market. Test data is never revealed – only the decisions of the committee after considering the test data. And it is mighty curious, they point out, that quality differentials should so exactly mirror the feudal hierarchical structure of the industry; the yarn of all the original Nine Great Spinners is counted as equally of top quality; and with some few exceptions the New Spinners come below that and the New New Spinners below that. The Senshū Centre, instead, publishes comparative measurements for thread length, dry weight, tensile strength, frequency of reps and thin patches and the consistency and variability of all these characteristics – 13 measurements in all. And they include in their samples 20s imported from Pakistan and 40s from South Korea – the which, as it happens, three or four Senshū weavers have recently entered into a partnership to import directly.

4 Cost reduction

Many things have contributed to the ability of Japanese producers to remain competitive in price as well as quality. Price comparisons overall are difficult to make, but if one takes standard cotton cloth as an example, the average 1980 price, deflated by movements in the general wholesale price level, represented a reduction of 23 per cent over the 1970 price, and it remained at that relative level over the next three years (KY, 1984, p.166). Faster and more efficient spindles and looms, more reliable materials, as well as improved – and intensified – work practices have all contributed to the increase in efficiency which has made this possible.

Productivity changes are, of course, very difficult to measure when there are large fluctuations in capacity utilization but the following figures for hours of labour input per unit product, though based on larger firms, suggest a rate of progress equal to or better than the national average.

By another measure of labour productivity, used by the Japan Productivity Centre, the improvement worked out at 5.5 per cent

Table 8.1   Productivity indices (1975 = 100)

	All industry average	Cotton spinning	Wool spinning	Cotton, etc. weaving
1970	125.0	117.5	134.2	130.4
1974	101.5	98.5	115.8	107.4
1975	100.0	100.0	100.0	100.0
1976	87.6	85.7	87.9	89.5
1977	87.1	86.0	83.1	82.6
1978	80.0	77.1	80.6	75.1
1979	73.3	62.1	75.4	72.9
1980	73.1	64.1	73.6	68.3
1981	74.6	65.5	70.4	69.1
1982	75.2	60.5	71.0	67.5

Source: KY, 1981–2, p. 202, KY, 1984, p. 186. Weightings are based on the product mix as at 1970, 1975 and 1980 for those and subsequent years.

per annum in the textile industry as a whole between 1973 and 1978 (8.3 per cent in spinning, 6.3 per cent in weaving, 3.6 per cent in finishing) and 1.9 per cent in the garment industry (Zensen Domei, 1981, quoting figures of Productivity Research Institute, Japan Productivity Centre). To take a more local, more detailed figure, between 1975 and 1980, the weaving labour-force in the Enshū Sanchi of Shizuoka Prefecture fell by 29 per cent, and the number of looms by 17 per cent, but at the same time, total production (in square metres) fell by only 6 per cent: production per person increased by 24 per cent. Manning levels of 25 non-automatic looms per weaver would seem incredible from the vantage point of, say, New Delhi where two weavers for three looms is a common ratio, even in comparison with Lancashire where nimble-fingered old ladies would be likely to feel pressed if they were expected to manage more than seven or eight. And that – in the case of automatic looms, 75 to 100 can be left to a single girl – suggests that quality is built into the machinery and the precision of its settings, and the yarn itself, of a quite high order.

Another ingredient in the low-cost recipe is flexibility of labour use – a marked contrast with the UK where beamers, twisters and drawers are in one union, the loom-repairing overlookers in another, and the weavers in yet a third, and (in most factories at least) there is no way a 'knotter' who has several hours of a shift left and no knotting to do would ever leave his cribbage game to cross demarcation lines and help with a broken loom.

Job categorizations are pragmatic and shifting, being based on the general assumption that employees are there to further the work of production in whatever seems, at the time, the most efficient way of doing so. In weaving firms, loom mechanics take a hand in tying up a broken end when they pass a stopped loom, and are willing to take a weaver's job entirely in an emergency; women are happy to rotate between pirn-winding, weaving or inspecting, and even do a good deal of the setting of their own looms. There is no problem of unions based on occupational divisions strengthening class consciousness and insisting on the sacred importance of job demarcation. Zensen, the Japanese textile workers' union federation (its full name is the Japanese Federation of Textile, Garment, Chemical, Distributive and Allied Industry Workers' Unions) is primarily, like most Japanese unions, a federation of enterprise unions organized in the major firms, but it does also have regional unions for smaller firms, and unionization stretches further down the scale spectrum in textiles than in most other industries. But Zenzen is primarily concerned with wage bargaining rather than with job control; its annual survey of textile wages categorizes workers only by sex, by age, by educational status (into three groups – graduates, high-school leavers, middle-school leavers) and by seniority in the firm; not by occupation.

Labour costs per hour are also low compared with Japanese average wages. Discussion of wages falls into three parts. First, there are the unionized employees in the large firms. As a comparison between the figures given earlier for the unionized Nisshin Bōseki and those for other small firms will indicate, employees in these firms get considerably higher wages. They are, however, lower wages than in more prosperous industries: for example, according to the figures of the government wage survey, for regular workers in enterprises of 30 or more employees the average textile wage for males was only 83 per cent of that in the man-made fibre industry in 1969 and the differential remained the same in 1979, though it had narrowed to 90 per cent before, and gone down to 74 per cent after, the oil crisis.

The second category is the lowest paid of all. These are the employees in small firms. The men have often retired from a career job at normal pay and are glad to have the chance to prolong their working lives even at pay rates a half or two-thirds of what they were earning before retirement. Middle-aged women are a second category tending to surplus in the Japanese labour economy and their wage rates are generally low. They may be willing to take wages even lower than average for the advantage of a congenial neighbourhood atmosphere, the ability to pop back home occasionally to look after a sick member of the family, etc.

The third category is the proprietors and their families – what the textile co-operative officials call 'our Viet Cong'. They have the incentive to work long hours – not, usually, at a furious pace; the ability to take a nap when they feel like it is one of the attractions of their way of life – and often do so for total incomes that are not very much higher than their employees receive, which means that in terms of returns for their labour and entrepreneurship they may, especially in times of recession, actually be getting less per hour than their employees. Their incomes tend also to fluctuate seriously with business conditions. Left to themselves they would have a backward-sloping supply curve – 'I'd get up and start the looms at half-past-five instead of at half-past six', said one man, when asked what he would do if Chinese competition brought the price of cloth lower – but the co-operatives' limitations on production save them from that.

A large proportion of the proprietors are middle-aged and hooked into the industry by virtue of the fact that they have no other skill and no way of realizing the capital invested in their equipment other than by using it. In that sense, the economic and social problem of decline in the textile industry is analogous to that of the inefficient family farmers in Japan or in Southern Europe.

One plausible scenario in such a situation is for a steady decline in the number of weaving families as that older generation dies off. A number of the co-operatives have carried out what are known as 'successor surveys', asking proprietors whether they expected a son to succeed them when they retired or died. In the plain-cottons-weaving area of Senshū, for example, only 29 per cent of proprietors said that a successor for the business was assured; 20 per cent said they would have no successor and the other 51 per cent were not sure. Whether the succession was secure or not depended a great deal on the size of the firm. Among the 49 proprietors of establishments with a total labour force of 20 or more, the percentage expecting to hand on the business was 68 per cent; among the 336 with three or fewer workers, only 10 per cent.

It is possible that, just as farmland tends to get aggregated into larger capitalist units as the older generation of family farmers dies off, so the generation change may produce a tendency for small family firms to become merged into larger units. In fact, over the last decades, the trend has been all the other way – towards the dissolution of large weaving establishments into congeries of specialist family firms linked in a complex division of labour – very much the same process as has been seen in the Prato woollen weaving industry in Italy. The proportion of cotton looms operated by the generally large-scale cotton spinning companies was 25 per cent in 1952, down to 16 per cent by 1969 and to 13 per cent by the end of 1979.

This trend needs to be disaggregated into two separate aspects. The first is specialization of function – the integrated weaving mill being replaced by a plethora of beamers, warp sizers, yarn dyers, drawers in – and the second related trend is the replacement of large aggregations of looms by small family-size aggregations of looms. Technological change has something to do with the first process. As preparation becomes more capital intensive, with large sizing machines, or the new drawing-in machines, the designing of an integrated mill such that *all* its capacity can be fully utilized becomes increasingly difficult; the possible economies of scale can only be realized on a cross-enterprise basis.

But the competitiveness of the small family firm as opposed to the large corporate firm in weaving proper has, presumably, other sources. It is not hard to guess at what they are: proprietor families are prepared to exploit themselves to a greater degree than the law or convention or trade unions now permits employers to exploit paid employees. In particular they can sit out recessions by tightening their belts and eschewing some luxuries in a way that firms with large fixed wage bills cannot.

The same competitive advantage partly explains the specialization of function just attributed to technological change – as is evidenced in the way some spinning companies have, over the last five years, hived off their texturizing, doubling and twisting processes to independent family firms. One might ask: why now? Surely the self-employed have always been ready to exploit themselves more than employers could exploit them? What is new, one might guess, is three things:

(i)   Affluence with union power has made the differential greater than when everyone was close to subsistence survival,

(ii)   There is now a much wider diffusion of technical and business expertise which is the *other* precondition for the small firm besides a willingness for self-exploitation, and

(iii) The tax-avoidance and tax evasion advantages of the family enterprise become more telling as the tax take rises in affluent societies.

The extent to which the proportion of proprietors and families in the total workforce has increased in recent years seems to vary in different sectors of the industry. There is a difference between the two weaving areas in Shizuoka (Shizuoka-ken, 1981, pp.12, 24). Both have seen a considerable decline in total employment between 1975 and 1980 – by 29 per cent in Enshū and by 17 per cent in the Tenryū area. But whereas Enshū lost considerably more paid employees than family workers, so that the latter made up 36 per cent in 1980 compared with 26 per cent in 1975, the proportion of family workers in Tenryū actually declined – from 68 per cent to 65 per cent. The fact that Enshū weaves the simplest kind of plain cotton, whereas Tenryū produces velveteens and corduroys with higher value added, a large proportion of them for export, may be a partial explanation for the difference. In five silk-weaving areas, the proportion of family workers rose from 28 per cent to 31 per cent between 1975 and 1976 (Shōya, 1978, p.20).

Most of the new entrants come from weaving families: often someone who has been in an employee job and, reaching middle-age and the prospect of retirement, puts his savings into buying the looms of someone who is getting too old to manage them and starts up – at first with the safer alternative of contract weaving. Thereby he extends his working life 15 or 20 years beyond the 55–60 age at which he would be retired from his employee job.

It is hard to get an overall measure of these trends, but there is a strong probability that the proportion of proprietors and their families has increased in recent years, and that this has been a powerful factor in keeping labour costs down. That it is not the only factor, however, is evidenced by the fact that Nisshin Bōseki still manages to operate large weaving establishments entirely with hired labour paid at union rates. The looms in such establishments may account for only 13 per cent of the operating looms in the country, but they produce over 20 per cent of the cloth – the usual practice of such firms being to do the long runs of basic shirtings and sheetings on their own looms and to rely on the sanchi small weavers, through the sub-contracting system, for the smaller more specialized lots. Nisshin itself is re-equipping and has recently replaced 600 of its 6,300 looms. Its choice was not the newest, fastest and most expensive shuttle-less looms, but the (cheaper) best available automatic shuttle looms (imported Picanols: Japanese loom-makers have concentrated their R & D on air-jets and water-jets and cannot compete in plain automatic looms). This represents their optimal solution to the balancing of three main parameters – capital cost, loom-speed and – a good deal more important to them than to the small weavers – the reliability which permits three-shift working and manning levels of 100 looms per weaver. The other element in the renewal strategy is steady investment in the newest spinning equipment to produce the yarn quality which is the second crucial element in reliability and hence in very high output per man-hour.

5   Exclusively domestic factors

So much for the factors which have sustained competitiveness in *all* markets and kept Japan in the textile export business, albeit with somewhat declining export volumes. There are certain other factors which operate to the advantage of domestic producers in the home market: one is the structure of the Japanese market for clothing, a second the structure of production already described. The third is the protective action occasionally taken by the Japanese government.

People engaged in the textile and clothing industries frequently assert that Japanese consumers are more fastidious and more fashion conscious than most populations – certainly more than the American or British publics. This is the ultimate justification for the concern for quality in the intermediate goods market and the carefulness in sending back defective goods which was mentioned earlier. How far the ultimate consumer does examine carefully the structure of the cloth, the evenness of the dye, the immaculacy of the stitching, is not entirely clear, but I was assured that the up-market stratum of people who do care about these things – the purchasers of the European brand-name clothes etc. – is a good deal thicker, and the stratum who 'would wear anything provided it was serviceable, and the cheaper the better' a good deal thinner than in, say, Britain. Consumers of that upper stratum are also the fashion-conformers, ready to discard a wardrobe for a new one of the right colour or shape – and the people who are keen to try the latest innovations: the mock suede, the wool-like nylon, etc. It is certainly true that the Japanese consume a higher volume of textiles a year than most other peoples (in spite of a shorter average stature!): by 1975 they were spending 12 per cent of personal income on textiles, and that figure was still 10.8 per cent in 1977 when even the Germans were spending only 9.6 per cent, and the less affluent British and the more affluent Americans only 7.9 and 6.8 per cent respectively (Tomizawa, 1978, p.33; Tōyō Bōseki, 1980, p.17) – eight shirts a year compared with the Englishman's five. And it is reasonable to suppose that this indicates a fastidious willingness to discard clothes at an earlier stage of wear rather than, say, a greater propensity to tear the clothes off each other's backs.

At any rate, the belief that (pricey European/American clothes apart) imported clothes and cloth (and yarn) are inferior to Japanese products is strongly held and makes a big difference to the market structure. This is even true for underwear, which one would have thought might be exempt from the earnest pursuit of quality. Gunze, one of the largest clothing firms, markets two types of briefs which an electron microscope might possibly tell apart. One has a green label indicating that it was made in Japan and is priced at Y550. The other with a brown label comes from Korea and sells for Y380 or three for Y1000. At that price differential both lines will sell equally well.

This mechanism – the final consumer's snob discount against imports – does not apply directly to Chinese cloth or Korean or Pakistani yarn since there is no obligation to specify on labels the origins of intermediate products (or, as a matter of fact, of final products either). But the concern with quality in the final market almost certainly feeds back into intermediate markets and induces a quality consciousness such that perceptions magnify substantive differences to the detriment of imports.

The second powerful factor which gives some natural protection against imported yarn and cloth intermediates is the structure of the industry already described at length above. According to some estimates only 20 per cent of the cotton and cotton-mixtures cloth woven in Japan is woven by weavers who are *not* tied into some dependency relationship which inhibits their freedom to buy yarn in the open market. Perhaps another 20 per cent are linked by hierarchical ties to a trading company which is not in its turn dependent on Japanese yarn suppliers and could conceivably switch to imported yarn. The proportions for synthetic filaments are almost certainly a good deal lower. The way in which this reduces the possibilities for foreign suppliers to penetrate the markets should be obvious.

With respect to synthetic fibres, some people in Japan argue that there is a technical inevitability about such arrangements; it is not a mere matter of cultural preferences. This was advanced as a reason why, during the several years when American natural-gas-based polyesters were a good deal cheaper than Japanese naphtha-based equivalents, there was little penetration of American imports into Japan. Subtle differences in the degree of polymerization between makers can cause a difference in the response to dyes; it is therefore a risk to switch away from a Japanese supplier who provides a careful handbook specifying optimum pressures and temperatures for the finishing processes to something that might be difficult to handle. The differences in the oiling of polyester staple very much affect the way it should be treated in the spinning process. It is difficult for an outsider to estimate the importance which should be attributed to such factors.

6   Domestic factors: government protection

The third and final factor which gives some advantage to Japanese products on the domestic market is a range of government protectionist measures.

These are, let it be said clearly, of quite minor importance when compared to the extent to which tariffs and MFA quotas are used by the other industrial countries to protect their textile industries, but they are nevertheless significant enough to be worth recording in detail.

To begin with tariffs, Japan's import duties are lower than those of the USA by a considerable margin. There is, also, a fairly wide range of 50 per cent reductions in tariffs for developing countries under the General Special Preference (GSP) scheme. The only deterioration in conditions in this regard came with the removal of Korea and Taiwan from the GSP country list in the spring of 1981, putting the tariffs for raw silk up from 3.75 to 7.5 per cent, for silk cloth from 5 per cent to 10 per cent and for cotton yarn from 1.4 to 2.8 per cent.

Secondly, Japan has no origin-label legislation.

Thirdly, Japanese textile exports are still subject to quotas or standing safeguard arrangements of one kind or another in 13 countries, but Japan has no quotas of her own – except in the single field of raw silk where the interest being protected is not that of the textile industry but rather of the remaining few thousand farm families which still depend for a part of their income on raising silkworms, and whose interests are, in fact, being protected *at the expense of* the textile industry.

That story can be briefly told. A Raw Silk Industry Control Agency had been in existence for some time to intervene in the cocoon and reeled silk market for price stabilization purposes when its operations were increasingly undercut by imports from Korea with prospects of further imports from China. As a temporary one-year measure, the Agency was given in 1974 a monopoly over imports of cocoons and raw silk. Two things happened as the temporary arrangement gradually became permanent. The silkworm-rearers, spread in significant numbers over a large number of constituencies, were able to demand an annual redefinition of the 'just price' for their labours (and for those of the reeling industry) which by 1981 had made the domestic price of raw silk double the international price. Secondly, the Agency's stocks and stock financing costs inexorably mounted as it found itself caught between the Ministry of Agri-culture's requirement that it purchase all domestic offers, the Ministry of Foreign Affairs' requirement that it should keep up its quota of purchases from friendly neighbours, and on the other side a decline in domestic demand as (in spite of some cross-subsidization by average pricing) the rising cost of raw silk and the further development of competing synthetics reduced de-mand for silk products and put silk weavers out of business. To prevent imports of silk cloth from undermining the scheme, bilateral quota arrangements were negotiated with Korea and Hong Kong. By 1981 it was reputedly worthwhile to take silk cloth from Hong Kong to Spain for light dyeing and import it as (un-quotaed) Spanish produce for washing and unpicking and sale as 'black market' silk filament cheaper than the Agency could provide. If Japan had wanted to teach itself a lesson in the convolutions and unintended consequences of quota controls it could not have chosen a better place to start.

There are two other forms of direct action which have a protectionist effect. The first affects the garment industry and is the strict control exercised over outward processing. These con-trols have their origin in the commissioning of embroidery and garment-making in Japan by American clothiers who provided materials or semi-finished goods. Whether to keep control over possible exploitation, or because the arrangements lent them-selves so easily to under-invoicing and secret transfers of curren-cy at a time of strict exchange controls, these arrangements were subject to licensing scrutiny. When Japanese manufacturers moved into the position from which they could naturally become the organizers of such activity in Asian countries, 'outward processing' as it is called in Europe, or 'reverse international sub-contracting' as it was called in Japan, came under the same licensing controls as the 'original inward' international subcon-tracting. Nowadays, unlike in the 1950s, no American in his right mind would go looking for Japanese housewives to embroider pink roses on fancy bedsocks and in 1979 the law (the Foreign Exchange and Foreign Trade Control Law) was amended and inward sub-contracting was freed from control. Outward sub-contracting, however, for dyeing and finishing, embroidery, knitting, tie-dyeing, garment-making, hooked rug-making and leather work, remains subject to licence – 'in view of the effects on domestic industry' as a MITI document explaining the position puts it. Permission has been sought and given in one or two cases for processing in China, but generally the procedure is sufficiently cumbersome to be an effective deterrent. It is possible, of course, to circumvent the provision by selling the materials with the promise to buy back after processing, though the law does try to control such loopholes. The fact seems to be, however, that there is not a very great deal of interest in these arrangements for reasons which were suggested to be:

(i)   The quality of materials available in Hong Kong, Korea and Taiwan are now for the most part quite adequate for the sorts of garments which Japanese consumers are ready to take from low-wage-cost countries.

(ii)   Even if the materials do have to be imported from Japan, the garment-makers in those countries are perfectly capable of bearing the risk of organizing production and assembling materials.

(iii)   Japanese trading companies – and the overseas agents of clothing companies if they do not use a trading company – are fully accustomed to providing the full specifications, guidance and quality checks necessary to ensure that the products by overseas producers are up to specification.

It is not easy to conclude that the limitations on outward processing seriously restrict imports into Japan. A recent sample survey of the contemporary practices of 50 firms in the clothing import business (Seni Kōgyō, 1981) made the following points:

In only two out of fifty cases (special texture lingerie) were the necessary materials exported from Japan, and there was little indication that others were keen to make such arrangements.

The business of importing garments is a risky one: there are foreign exchange risks (many Japanese firms were insisting on CIF contracts so that they could book foreign exchange for the whole transaction and shift the risk of rising freight rates to the exporter), there was the risk of the supplier's bankruptcy, of war, etc., which may need the potential cover of an alternative source of supply, and there was the risk of quality defects (one sleeve shorter than the other, stripes not matching, etc.) which could be coped with only by factory gate inspection – reckoned on average by one firm to turn a 10 per cent defective rate into a 0.7 per cent defective rate.

Quality problems are greater in Korea and Taiwan than in Hong Kong. In those two countries a 10–20 per cent cost advantage was necessary to justify the risks involved, and the recent rise in wages in those countries was eroding that margin. China, where wage rates were still one-fifth to one-seventh of Japanese levels, still offers very big cost advantages, though poses considerable quality problems.

These were three responses to the Korea and Taiwan trend: one was to turn back to home producers, as one firm reported 'sub-contracting rates in Japan, after all, are not all that high'. The other was to cut out the trading company middleman. Typical margins were for the trading company to buy at 40–45 per cent of the final price and sell to the department store or supermarket chain at 60–65 per cent. Direct purchase by the department store could make current Korea and Taiwan cost margins profitable. The third response was to carry on on the assumption that Japanese wage costs were anyway going to stay ahead.

Few firms seemed to consider the non-Confucian countries of Asia – Malaysia, Philippines, Sri Lanka – to have much potentiality to provide them with decent clothes, except, of course, of the 'ethnic' kind popular in New York or Paris.

Overseas purchases made sense particularly for large-volume items – items which might have seasonality, but only marginal fashionability, and where prices could be calculated on the assumption that 20–30 per cent would be sold off at half price in end-of-season sales – winter underwear, slacks, sweaters, etc.

The final form of government protective action affects the upstream fibre-making and spinning industries only and consists of the well-known recession cartels and the less well-known 'administrative guidance' import controls which frequently accompany them. The best way to give an account of these practices is probably to describe what happened in the cotton and mixed cotton-synthetic spun yarn industry in 1981.

Prices of yarn had been steadily declining since mid-1980 (and, in spite of the nature of intermediate markets in Japan, it still remains the case that the accelerator effect on stocks produces wider swings in the price of yarn than of cloth and of cloth than of finished garments). In the spring of 1981 the price at which 40s were being traded on the Osaka market was such as was generally acknowledged, given the price of raw cotton, to leave the average spinning company 5–10 per cent below break-even point. (There were still profits to be made on, say, double-twist

70s where Japan's superiority was not assailed by imports.) Stock
figures were still steadily rising.

Discussions between the Spinning Industry Association, MITI
and the Fair Trade Commission led, on 24 April, to a formal
request from the Industry – referred to as 'The Nittō Spinning
Company and seventy-eight other firms' for reasons which will
appear later – to the Fair Trade Commission to organize a recession cartel. This permission was granted for two months from 1
May. Each of the seventy-nine firms was to (a) formally seal up
the gearboxes on 20 per cent of its spindles and (b) reduce its
production to 15 per cent less than the daily average for the first
three months of the year. Ten inspectors were recruited from
member firms to make spot checks that the seals were not broken,
three times a month. The co-operating firms were calculated to
have a 67.5 per cent share of total Japanese production.

The next step, on 12 May, was for the head of the Basic Consumer Industries Bureau of MITI to address a letter to some
seventy trading firms. The courtesy copy of the letter which was
sent to the secretary of the Japanese Textile Importers' Association is reprinted in *Textile Import News*. The letter announces that
the recession cartel has been permitted under the appropriate
section of the law to deal with the supply demand imbalance in
the price of yarn and goes on:

> In order to achieve the objectives of this collective action, this
> Ministry considers that an assurance of orderly importing
> arrangements is essential. It consequently expects all firms
> concerned with imports to trade with the greatest conscien-
> tiousness, and, as far as imports in the near future are con-
> cerned, calls on them to exercise the utmost restraint.
>
> We do, therefore, though with great regret knowing how
> many things there are to keep you busy, ask you to fill in the
> attached form reporting your importing activities for the four
> months April to July, the April form to be returned by 20th
> May and the forms for later months by the 10th of the following
> month.

The textile press commented that this was a harder sell than
usual – to be precise than on the two previous occasions of 1975
and 1977. To begin with, the letter had gone out in the name not
of the Textile Products Division Chief, but of his superior, the
Bureau Director. Secondly, after the April report was received,
twenty of the major importers were summoned to MITI at the rate

of four firms a day for 'hearings' ('*hyaaringu'*) – personal meetings at which the importance of restraint was urged on them and they were asked to explain their intentions. And thirdly, for the first time, import restraint was requested for cotton cloth as well as for yarn, although the cartel applied only to yarn (oss, 12 May, 21 May 1981).

There were two other prongs to MITI's attack on the problem. First, it tried to tighten up its import-contract reporting service. All importers are required to make monthly returns of forward contracts for the import of textiles and clothing. Some were doing so conscientiously, others – as the customs records of subsequent transactions showed – were not. Each received a letter either congratulating it on its conscientiousness, or remonstrating about its lack thereof, with a chapter-and-verse table showing item by item what the firm had imported in a particular month and what proportion of those imports had been reported when the contract was made.

Finally, MITI sent officials to Korea and to China to explain the measures taken, to ask that they should not be taken amiss, and to request co-operation in securing an 'orderly' solution of the market problem. In Korea an arrangement had already been established in September 1980 whereby the Korean Spinners' Association, under the guidance of the Korean Government, fixed a minimum export price – a device which suited both established Korean exporters and the Japanese authorities (oss, 20 May 1981). The Korean authorities made it very clear that they were not very happy about what was going on, but there was no indication that they had any intention of lowering that minimum export price (oss, 19 May, 28 May 1981).

The application for the cartel had had formally to be made in the name of 79 firms, not of the Japan Spinning Association (JSA), because not all its 85 member firms was in favour of the move. Nisshin Bōseki, the firm described earlier, was the only one of the major firms to argue very strongly against it in the committees of the JSA. It did so on the good classical grounds that it was precisely in the testing times of a recession that the sheep should be sorted out from the goats – a case argued from the strongest possible conviction that Nisshin would never be one of the goats, it being common knowledge that it was in a healthier state than any other spinning firm. On previous occasions Nisshin had allowed itself to be over-ruled. This time it held out and remained outside the cartel. 'However', a senior manager told me, 'we did not think it would be right to take advantage of our position, so we have in fact cut back production by 15 per cent.'

The price per pound of 40s had been Y335 on 1 May. By mid-June it was down to Y305 and stocks were not declining. The case for renewal for a further two months was obviously strong, and MITI insisted this time that the production cutback should be 20 per cent and not 15 per cent.

By the end of August the price of yarn was beginning to climb back, if only on 20 August to Y345. There was still strong sentiment in the Spinning Association for continuing the cartel for another two months, but now the weavers were getting squeezed; the price of cotton cloth was still falling while the price of yarn was rising. On 28 August a delegation from two cotton-weaving sanchi with the largest proportions of independent (i.e. cotton-buying, not contract-weaving) weavers went to MITI to protest strongly against the prospect of an extension. The National Weavers' Association also got into the negotiations (OSS, 1 September, 2 September 1981). It was put about that the July stock figures, which would not be available until 9 September, would have to be decisive. This allowed a healthy ten days' pushing and pulling. The Spinners' Association Executive declared after a meeting on 3 September that, since only 20 per cent of their cotton was sold on open market and 80 per cent went through 'tied' channels, the weavers 'belonged to the same family', and their interests could not be ignored (OSS, 3 September 1981). They obviously had decided to lose the battle gracefully; the cartel was not renewed, but the guidance to exercise restraint over imports continued to operate for several months.

How effective are the measures to restrain imports is anyone's guess since there are no 'policy-off' periods from which to derive price elasticities of imports. There was some fall-off on imports of both cotton yarn and cotton cloth in the second half of 1981, but this would arguably have happened anyway as a result of the fall in Japanese prices. A surge in the last two months of 1981 in Pakistan imports of the coarser 20s count (for which the price recovery was greatest) left the total imports for the year slightly greater than for 1980.

It does seem, at any rate, that the cartel arrangements have lost their effectiveness. MITI calculated that the seventy firms which received a restraint request and were asked to send monthly reports accounted for 89.5 per cent of yarn and 87.5 per cent of cloth imports (OSS, 12 May 1981). This may be the case, but what seems generally agreed is that the 'community pressure' on importers have weakened since earlier cartels. For the first time the letter was sent not only to leading importers who were members of the Japanese Textile Importers' Association, but also to 'outsiders' who were said to have made up at least one-third of the yarn importers who received the MITI letter and one-half of the cloth importers. What seems to have happened is this.

Importing is, to begin with, a slightly disreputable activity and has become more so as the industry has got into worse trouble. (The Importers' Association used to have regular meetings with the National Weavers' Federation but these have become more and more ritual and the importers are not invited to the formal meetings of textile groups which MITI organizes – 'After all: they're the enemy," said one MITI official, joking with a sizeable grain of truth.) However, the Association dates from the days when there were very few low-cost imports from Asia, and textile importing was largely a matter of bringing luxury goods from Europe and North America. This is the image it still seeks to cultivate. Its office has sporting-trophy-like plaques bearing Union Jacks, and photographs of Savile Row tailors and Beefeaters and Japanese gents in horsey tweeds. It is hard, however, to maintain that bearer-of-all-that-is-best-in-civilization image when a large proportion of your membership is engaged in the grubby business of importing Korean underwear. It would not be surprising if the latter group of importers (and the smaller firms *are* specialized in that business) felt somewhat like second-class citizens in the organization, particularly since all the pressures on the organization – exerted by MITI, for instance, or in the regular meetings with the Weavers' Federation – concerned *their* activity and were transformed into pressures from the Association on *them*. (One has to remember when thinking of these pressures, that industry associations in Japan are a little more like communities and a little less like mere interest associations than in most countries. *Textile Import News*, for instance, not only contains a lot of hard business information but also chatty accounts of the Association's outings and even a *haiku* corner with offerings like: 'The age of passports. Even my little grandson, Gets the foreign signature habit.' As an importer one is in some sense a brother to all other textile importers and a cousin of everybody else in the textile business.) At any rate the number of outsiders has grown. The Association estimates that its 210 members now handle about 50 per cent of total import trade and that there are probably between three and four thousand outsiders. For cotton yarn there are probably about 100 importers of which about 20 or 30 are members. This represents a big change since 1975 when a recession cartel/import restraint scheme was operated rather more effectively. A MITI estimate was that between about 90 per cent of the relevant imports were handled by big firm insiders, compared with the present 50 per cent. That is why outsiders were brought into the reporting scheme in 1981 for the first time.

But there is little that can be effectively done to bring pressure on the outsiders – or on the *insiders* who set up dummy outsider companies to handle the suspect trade. Even an outsider firm whose main business was importing Korean yarn was trading under two names. It received 'restraint please' letters to both addresses, obediently reported its import record and intentions in its own main persona, but ignored the letters sent to its other address.

So, in the end, the effectiveness of these import restraint tactics was highly suspect. One MITI official suggested that the main purpose of the whole exercise was to 'sustain the face' of the Spinners' and Weavers' Associations – to allow them to represent to their members that they had secured a tactical victory and had prevented matters from getting worse. Thus the benefits of comparative advantage could be achieved by the inevitability of gradualism, the virtues of solidarity and compromise could be upheld, and the transitional decline of the industry could be managed with the minimum amount of political fuss.

That, however, was not the way the spinning industry saw the matter. It wanted maintenance of the status quo, not graceful decline and it continued to press MITI to activate the MFA to keep yarn imports to a lower level. 1982 saw imports nearly doubling in the first half of the year, and in December, emboldened by Australia's imposition of an anti-dumping duty against Korean yarn, the spinners made a formal request to the Ministry of Finance for a similar duty (NBG, April 1983, p.34). The final result was an emergency meeting of the two countries' spinning associations and an agreement – which the Koreans, however, insisted was not an agreement but an *ex gratia* promise on their part – to limit exports to Japan for three years to a figure 10 per cent below the 1982 level (20 per cent below the peak 1979 level). The Japanese side withdrew its proposal for an anti-dumping tariff (NBG, May 1983, p.78). The Pakistan threat remained and, as quality improved, extended to finer counts. The Japanese government was persuaded to take proceedings under GATT to require Pakistan to withdraw an export subsidy system, and negotiations were still dragging on in the spring of 1984.

Meanwhile the Kishiwada co-operative testing station began to test samples of Chinese yarn. Imports of Chinese yarn, of insignificant quantity in 1982, began to grow steadily in 1983. The spinners are clearly worried that this new hole in the dyke will require a bigger finger than they can command.

9
Textiles: Adjustment policies

The last chapter has outlined the reasons why, as compared with, say, the UK textile industry, the threat from low-wage foreign competition has not been so acute. There is no doubt, however, that the textile industry has been under pressure, is commonly seen as a declining industry and a proper object of adjustment policies. Over the last decade the import threat has been compounded by a number of other serious challenges. For example:

The sharp increase in external competition which resulted from the sharp revaluation of the yen against the dollar in the early 1970s and the prospect that the continuing all-round strength of Japanese high-technology exports will steadily raise the value of the yen.

The problem of declining aggregate income elasticities of demand for textiles in the domestic market and the changing structure of that market: the relative growth of the garment trade (less home dressmaking) and increased fashion differentiation, and the growing importance of household furnishings and other industrial uses.

The particular loss of competitiveness of fibre industries dependent on expensive imported naphtha facing competition from fibres derived from natural gas and other cheaper or subsidized raw materials.

The problem of rising labour costs as productivity improvements in leading industrial sectors raise average incomes (in a situation of competitive pressure even in up-market textile products from advanced country producers with less rapidly rising costs). This problem is manifest partly as labour shortage, exacerbated by the social definition of the industry as a declining industry.

The prospect of the nation not reaping the potential advantages of living in an age of high technology, as a result of being hooked into (hooked into by political mechanisms) a labour-intensive, low-value-added industry.

These response-demanding challenges are not all of one piece: some are challenges for *firms*, some are challenges for *industry associations*, some are challenges for *unions*, and some are challenges for the national economy and for the *government agencies* which seek to manage it. These are the four categories of actors whose *adjustment strategies* in response to these challenges have to be considered.

Firms

The adjustment problem for the large-scale spinning and fibre-making firms was, indeed, a real and present problem particularly in the years 1974–5, and indeed for some of them until 1978–9. A surge in imports and considerable difficulties in export markets in 1973 as a result of the revaluation of the yen was the first cause for alarm. Overall textile imports rose from 5.8 per cent of total internal demand (11.1 per cent for cotton goods, 2.2 per cent for synthetic fibre goods) in 1971 to 16.2 per cent of demand (28.3 per cent for cotton, 8.9 per cent for synthetics) in 1973. Since internal demand rose 30 per cent in those two years and the increase in imports was a quarter of a million tons less than the increase in consumption this was not immediately serious, but it suggested that the writing was on the wall.

The oil crisis brought an altogether more serious message. Total demand since the peak year 1973 is shown in table 9.1.

Export markets, of course, have been similarly depressed. The problem was exacerbated for the man-made fibre sector, as in every country, by the steep rise in raw material and energy

Table 9.1   Trends in domestic demand 1973–80

	Cotton goods	Man-made fibre goods	Goods based on other fibres	Total
1973	100 (33.2)	100 (54.3)	100 (12.4)	100 (100.0)
1974	78	70	75	73
1975	72	62	76	67
1976	77	81	76	79
1977	70	76	66	73
1978	81	92	60	85
1979	99	103	62	97
1980	89 (33.7)	94 (58.0)	56 (8.2)	88 (100.0)

Source: MITI, *Seni Tōkei.* Figures in brackets show weight in total.

prices, and by the fact that it had a much greater momentum of plant construction because (a) it was the most rapidly expanding sector of demand, and (b) its faster pace of technological advance provided additional arguments for replacement of existing capacity.

Firms responded by: cutting production and seeking to shed labour; diversifying out of textiles; seeking to minimize production cuts by increasing their textile market share; exit.

The last was the option, obviously, chiefly of the small family-based enterprises. Surveys (see table 9.2) show a loss of 6,000 firms in the two smallest categories. The increase in garment firms has, however, more than compensated as far as numbers of firms is concerned, with, again, the growth being concentrated in small firms.

The patterns of response of the small and medium firms – for the majority gritting the teeth and weathering it out, but for a not inconsiderable number a continuing search for more profitable textile opportunities and a willingness to invest in new equipment – can only be left to the illustration of the case studies included earlier; the data are not available to give analyses by scale category.

The published accounts of major spinning and man-made fibre firms for the period 1973–9, however, do permit of a certain degree of generalization.

Table 9.2   Textile and clothing industries: firms by size: 1971, 1976 and 1981

No of workers (family and wage workers)	Textiles			Apparel		
	1971	1976	1981	1971	1976	1981
1–3	60,614	65,189	63,648	10,843	14,385	22,313
4–9	34,296	26,270	24,262	9,564	11,249	14,913
1–9	94,910	91,459	87,910	20,407	25,634	37,228
10–19	7,854	6,140	5,370	4,293	4,451	4,876
20–29	1,879	2,313	2,212	878	1,588	2,304
30–99	3,268	2,911	2,376			2,301
100–999	965	811	731	1,959	2,659	599
1000+	65	39	33			11
	108,941	103,743	98,632	27,537	34,332	47,319

Source: MITI Tokeibu *Dai-4-kai (Dai-5-6-kai) Kōgyō Jittai Kihon Chōsa Hōkokusho: Seni Kōgyō* (base date 31 December 1971, 1976 and 1981 respectively).

If we take the Big Nine Spinning Firms, for example, ranging from Kanebō with a 26 per cent share of their combined textile sales (and 29 per cent of combined exports in 1973) to Omi Kenshi with a 5 per cent share, it is clear that they follow a common pattern. All made a reasonable operating profit margin on sales in 1973, ranging from Daiwa's 11.8 per cent to Kanebō's, 5.6. All made a loss in 1974. Two of the nine struggled back to an operating profit the next year. Another followed in 1976; four made losses for four consecutive years and the ninth, Kanebō, finally made a bare profit in 1979. In man-made fibres the worst years were 1975 and 1977 – years when only one of the Big Seven (a different one in each of the two years) managed a profit. Over the whole seven years 1973–9 the most profitable firm achieved only a 3.5 per cent margin on sales: one achieved an overall loss, and three others of the seven had margins of less than 2 per cent.

How far was it a viable strategy for these firms to seek to compensate for the overall decline in demand by increasing their market share (by greater efficiency or improved products) at the expense of their competitors? How competitive were their markets: how far was that competitiveness limited by the patterns of 'sewn up' tied relations which have been described earlier? One can only judge by results which suggest a fairly rigid market structure. Among the Big Nine Spinners, the average percentage movement in market share (share of combined textile sales, domestic and overseas) was three percentage points over seven years. The biggest movement was Kanebō's loss of 9.1 per cent (from 26.1 to 17.0 per cent overall, but 29.0 to 28.1 per cent of exports), followed by Tōyōbō, the firm with the second biggest initial share which went from 26.4 to 22.4 per cent. The gains were distributed fairly evenly among the others. (Even Kanebō's large loss may be partly spurious since it appears that some subsidiaries whose results were consolidated in group results in the earlier years became unconsolidated later.)

Among the man-made fibre Big Seven, by contrast, the biggest, Tōrē, got bigger, going from 21.2 to 27.2 per cent, which suggests, possibly, a greater importance of technological advantage in artificial fibres, except that the other gainers were the third largest, and the two smallest (Kurarē going from 10.2 to 11.1 per cent and Tōhō Rayon from 5.0 to 5.4 per cent).

The main point is that none of these movements – over seven years – was spectacular or suggests a very fluid market structure.

Cost reduction: labour-shedding

It was common ground throughout the large-firm end of the industry that a crucial form of adjustment was to reduce the labour force. Total employment in spinning firms with 20 or more employees fell from a peak of 183,000 in April 1974, to 108,000 in December 1977. Weaving establishments with ten or more employees reduced their labour force from 328,000 to 257,000 over the same period – 41 per cent and 22 per cent reductions respectively – according to one estimate (Yoshioka, 1978, p.39.).

The reduction in weaving was probably predominantly of non-unionized workers in small firms (plus some family workers) and is less surprising than the 41 per cent reduction in spinning, given that the spinning firms are mostly of sufficient size to be in the unionized 'lifetime commitment' sector. How was it done?

Partly by bankruptcy, especially of small-firms. According to Chamber of Commerce figures textile bankruptcies, which were running at less than 500 a year in 1973, rose gradually to a peak of 1,388 in 1979 – though that represented a rise only from 6 per cent to 9 per cent of total bankruptcies (KY, 1981, p.180). The number of jobs lost thereby and the proportion which would otherwise have been subject to no-redundancy guarantees cannot easily be estimated.

Something more is known, however, about the methods used to reduce the labour-force in the larger unionized firms, thanks to a survey commissioned by MITI (Nōritsu Remmei, 1979). Reductions in this sector were large. The survey chose a random sample of large firms employing between 7,255 and 23,481 workers in October 1973 and found that by April 1978 the smallest reduction in the labour-force was 13.2 per cent and the largest 66.2 per cent.

The first measure to reduce labour costs was reduction in overtime, used by nearly all the firms, but since the overtime worked at the October 1973 peak had been only between two and ten hours a month in most of the sample of 38 large textile firms (maximum 16 hours) there was much less scope here than in, say, automobile assembly or machinery manufacture where 30–35 hours a month had been common.

A second temporary measure was the lay-off which was normally at 90–95 per cent of regular salary. The Government subsidy scheme (see chapter 5) which paid up to two-thirds of the cost of such measures for firms with fewer than 300 employees made this a distinctly more attractive measure than it would otherwise seem to be. Fourteen textile firms which had used this device (out of the same 38) up to April 1975 had laid off for up to 27.3 days per employee – either closing whole plants for a period or, more usually, rotating employees 'for morale reasons'.

The next measure enquired about in the survey was the reduction of annual April recruitment plans, and here the surprising thing, perhaps, is that 16 of the 38 firms said that they did not do so in 1974 and 11 were still saying the same thing about the two succeeding years. There are two elements in this. One is that some firms still had enough faith in the long-term future to continue full-scale recruitment of lifetime male employees (in the belief that not to do so was a bit like eating your seed corn); the other is that many firms' main recruitment drive was for 15-year-old girls (with a very short employment life cycle) and the overall shortage of such labour – which continued unabated during the recession, being the product of long-run secular trends such as increasing high-school enrolments, and the declining prestige of the textile industry, etc. – meant that for many years they had been operating with a vague 'as many as you can find' recruitment target which there was no reason to change.

Teenage female labour was slowly being replaced in a majority of firms by older married women, often working shorter than normal shifts and, whether they were or not, collectively referred to as 'paato' (part-timers). These, and the 'temporary employees' – older unskilled males, often part-time farmers – had no union membership or lifetime employment guarantees and could be easily dismissed. (The Textile Workers' Union had, in fact, resolved at its 1973 Conference to begin the organization of part-time workers. The supporting documents for a resolution reaffirming this stand at the 1980 Conference studiously avoids any indication of how much – or if, indeed, anything – had been done on these lines. One imagines it would go very much against the grain. Regular tenured workers in the union are well aware that their privileges depend in part on the existence of others less privileged.) Twenty-four of the 38 firms replied in the survey that they had run down their numbers of part-time and temporary employees in 1974, but two said that they increased their recruitment of housewife part-timers to replace teenage school-leavers. One other firm developed a new form of contract labour, letting on-site contractors employ the part-timers, but using them in the same shop and on the same jobs as their own direct girl employees.

The next device, of distinctively Japanese invention, is the 'external posting' – usually of senior male workers – who are for a period 'loaned' to another firm while remaining tenured members of their original firm. Since many of these loans were to related or subcontractor firms which might often be paying lower wages than the parent firm, the parent firm financed the difference (some workers continued physically to draw their wage packet from their original firm). If holiday provisions were less at the new work place than the worker's entitlement in his home firm, the difference was settled in cash or the forgone holidays saved up to the end before his return. One firm which resorted to the measure as an emergency device at first regularized it in a detailed collective agreement with its union in 1977; 504 workers were loaned in that year, some to related firms, but most to entirely unrelated nearby firms, 200 to a motor-car assembly works, these firms being glad to get experienced workers of a probity guaranteed by the loaning firm. The period was set at three years with possible extension for a further two if all parties were agreeable, but at any rate with a right to go back 'home' after three years.

Plant closures were dealt with by 'voluntary early retirement' schemes and by 'internal posting' – the offer of a place at another plant. The early retirement offers provide something better than normal separation allowance entitlement, and, even though union bargaining power is not strong in the industry, such is the premium placed on the lifetime guarantee that the inducement has to be fairly great to persuade workers to surrender it, even if the alternative is a very inconvenient transfer to an unattractive job in a distant plant in the full knowledge that the company considers you a bit of a nuisance in not quietly taking your retirement and getting lost. The offer of early retirement clearly becomes less attractive with age and declining prospects of re-employment. That it proved more attractive to younger workers is clear from the fact that all the firms which had substantially reduced their labour force had simultaneously seen an increase in the average age of their employees: from 29 to 35 for a firm with a 52 per cent cutback (over 2½ years), from 34 to 37 for one which lost 13 per cent – and so on.

In principle, at any rate, everyone had a right to refuse early retirement and to claim an internal or external posting if his plant was closed, the 'internal posting' to another plant of the same firm being an arrangement, as in every country, more common for managerial and technical than for manual personnel, but still very much resorted to for the latter also. Transfer, says the report, posed some problems.

> First, there were no great problems about work conditions since the wage structure was nearly always standard across the enterprise, but most of the jobs workers were posted to were in the preparation or inspection or canteen services: few could be moved to a job comparable with their original one. Some had difficulty adapting to a new hierarchy of authority.
> As for housing, those who were in company housing could usually be put into comparable housing at the other end, though older workers who owned their own houses posed some problems. The company usually either rented his house from the owner, or helped him to rent it or sell it, but house-ownership, especially among those who had lived all their lives in the district [one might add particularly those who were commuting from farms which still had a little land], was often a potent reason for choosing the early retirement option. In one case the textile firm closing the plant arranged for such workers to be re-employed by the canning company which bought the factory.
> Schooling was also a considerable problem, not so much for the compulsory nine years during which every child has a right of entry to the nearest school, as for high-school children who may not be admitted in the new area to a school comparable in quality to the one they had succeeded in entering originally. The resolution was frequently for the father to go alone to the new job and be accommodated in a bachelor dormitory, or the child might be left behind with friends, or accommodated in a dormitory provided by the company.
> Married women usually took the retirement option. Working wives of employees who could not find comparable jobs in their new place of residence were in some cases found new jobs by the company.

The final means of reducing labour costs was 'the creation of new companies' which, not quite as entrepreneurial as it sounds, may better be described as transforming an employment relation (with predictably mounting costs, thanks to the seniority wage system) into a sub-contracting relation (with initially perhaps equal or greater, but stable or even squeezable costs); in other words the hiving off of certain functions to independent creature firms. (Whether there were also tax advantages the report does not make clear.) Examples were firms which took over the sales function for a particular region or product, maintenance, warehouses, security, canteen and other welfare services, staff training, etc. These enterprises have the considerable attraction, particularly for the managerial and white collar workers who predominated in them, that, although they had to take lower wages and faced more uncertain prospects, they could fix for the new firm a retirement age much higher than the 55–57 of the large firms. Since it is common practice for workers in their last few years to be looking round for a small firm to move to with this in mind, the arrangement suited many purposes.

A rather different form of hiving off was practised by certain spinning firms which created, and shunted workers into, new companies to take over certain processing functions – especially, for instance, spinning companies setting up independent texturizing, twisting and doubling firms. Here we see the results of competitive pressure. These are functions (unlike spinning proper, or, *a fortiori*, man-made fibres) which are well within the scope of the family enterprise division of labour. It is no longer possible to compete in that field with labour paid at factory rates. How far the new firms created were single-owner family type or organized on a co-operative basis is not made clear. What is clear is that labour costs per hour were lowered, again acceptably for middle-aged workers who gained the prospect of prolonging their working life in a field of their own speciality.

Cost reduction: overseas location

There was some growing interest on the part of Japanese firms in investing overseas during the late 1960s and early 1970s. But the effect of the mid-1970s recession was to choke off, rather than to accelerate those tendencies. The official figures recorded 686 licences for direct overseas investment in textiles and clothing up to March 1977, but the vast majority predated 1974. There was a sharp decline thereafter and only three new licences in the last year, April 1976 to March 1977. Meanwhile there had been 86 disengagements from overseas joint partnerships between 1973 and 1976. The total accumulated overseas investment of textile firms in 1977 (about $4.5bn.) was roughly estimated to be about 5 per cent of accumulated investment at home (Yoshioka, 1978, pp.

61–4), and Yoshioka, 1979, pp.24–5.) According to another set of figures relating to 436 of the firms actually operating overseas in 1977 (310 of them in Asia), the biggest single speciality was garment-making (81 firms) followed by fibre staple spinning, followed by knitting. The largest category were joint ventures in which the Japanese partners were a large Japanese manufacturer and a Japanese trading company, but over a quarter were joint ventures of Japanese small firms operating independently (Yoshioka, 1979, pp.34–5).

It seems, in any case, that the search for cheaper sources of labour supply was only one, and that not the most important, of the motives for direct investment in textile and clothing production in Asia. Several government-sponsored surveys in the mid-1970s, when there was some expressed concern about the 'export of jobs', suggested that the substitution of exports to Asian countries by local production – at a time when those countries were pursuing import-substituting industrialization policies and when Japanese reparations and aid programmes were offering favourable terms – was a more important motive. Not a great deal of total production was for export to Japan, though rather more for export to third countries, and the ability to share in the host countries' GSP advantages and quotas under the MFA (or rather its predecessor the Long Term Agreement) was an additional attraction. For Japanese textile firms in Asia surveyed in 1976, 23 per cent of their product was exported to Japan, 26 per cent to third countries and 51 per cent to the local market (Yoshioka 1978, p.67); 37 per cent of their materials came from Japan. South Korea, with the highest density of investment, however, had a much higher ratio – 69 per cent exported to Japan. (The source does not make clear whether the overall Asian figure is a simple or a weighted average of country figures or, indeed, whether the country figures are simple averages of the firms in those countries or weighted by the volume of production.) The investment in the Middle East and Central and Latin America, not to mention North America, was even more heavily directed towards service of the home or neighbouring third-country markets.

The decline in interest in textile investment overseas in the mid-1970s is attributed not so much to a general loss of investment confidence, though that may have been part of it, as to the fact that the advantages of such investment in the post-Confucian countries had much diminished with their industrial progress; textiles could not any longer cream off good labour at low rates and local capitalists now had the technical know-how, the capital, the confidence and the nationalistic motivation to squeeze their Japanese collaborators out of joint ventures. The alternative opportunities in the other countries – Malaysia, Indonesia, Sri Lanka, Philippines – were less attractive in terms of political stability, labour force quality and the reliability of business relationships. There was some thought that only as China 'settles down' is there a chance of rediscovering the favourable investment conditions of Korea and Taiwan in the late 1960s, and by the end of the decade joint ventures were already getting under way in the Shanghai and Canton areas.

As for international sub-contracting, or 'outward processing', the reasons for its limited extent – and for its limited appeal anyway – were discussed above in the section on government protectionist measures.

Diversification

Very few of the small enterprises among the 100,000 in textiles have other interests outside the industry; very few of the leading firms do not. To take the prominent case of Kanebō (prominent because it operates in highly advertised consumer-goods areas), it has gradually diversified its interests since the 1960s and now has five main divisions: cosmetics (in which it has the second largest market share), pharmaceuticals, foodstuffs, housing (including building materials, glass fibres, etc.) as well as the whole range of textiles and a small line in Christian Dior brand-name clothing and accessories. It sees a rationale in its diversification – getting close to the whole range of consumer wants with high income elasticity – 'bringing beauty into human life' as the firm's slogan has it. Another spinning firm, Nisshin, has been more pragmatic and opportunistic; having woven asbestos to make firemen's suits before the war, it woke up one day to find all the firemen equipped with durable suits and a familiarity with asbestos which they needed to put to good use, so they went into brake linings and clutch facings. They also are now in paper, rubber and synthetic foams, machine tools, plastics and printing machinery. Some of the fibre-makers have capitalized on their strength in basic chemicals to move into resins, plastics, molecular biology and new opportunities thrown up by the development of materials science.

If one looks at consolidated accounts of the Big Seven and the

Big Nine, there is fairly clear evidence of an effort to increase the diversity of their interests between 1973 and 1979. For the Big Nine spinners, non-textile sales averaged 12 per cent of total sales in the former year and 16 per cent in the latter. For the fibre-makers the shift was from 21 to 37 per cent. These figures are not definitive since some of the groups' companies are not consolidated, the boundary between the consolidated and the unconsolidated shifts over time and the accounting system does not always allow for a clear division between textile and non-textile areas, but they are indicative of where efforts have been directed. Nisshin, generally reckoned the most successful of the spinners, set a target of 30 per cent of sales outside textiles in the early 1970s, but had only achieved 25 per cent (starting from 16 per cent in 1973) by 1982–3 – but partly because textile sales had expanded better than expected.

Keeping ahead

Japan is a society given over to belief in the supreme virtues of science and technology to a greater extent, perhaps, than any society since post-revolutionary Russia. In Britain we have recently become accustomed to hearing the pundits who seek to exhort the nation to greater competitiveness talking about the importance of 'the management of change'. The phrase is difficult to translate into Japanese. The Japanese assumption is that all good management is about change. The emphasis on continuous product and process development in all rhetorical talk about industrial strategy is striking.

One of the major forms of government finance flowing to, say, the weavers' co-operatives, is for R & D. The co-operative in the corduroy–velveteen area, for instance, with some 1,400 members, got subsidies of some $65,000 (Y13.8m) for a total of fourteen different development projects over three years (organized jointly with the corduroy cutters' co-operative, and the sanmoto, the dyers and others' co-operatives). (Tenryusha, 1979). They ranged from developing new cloths with multiple materials, trials of the capability of the Nissan air-jet machine (lent by the company), experiments with weft-colour variation on air-jets, energy-saving measures in the finishing process, the development of warp-pile corduroy and exploration of new garment conversions for local cloths, to market research, questionnaire studies, and exhibitions of products. There may be a whiff of ritualism about some of these activities, and a Public Accounts Committee might see the cost-effectiveness of the subsidies as lying in a political rather than an economic dimension, but they do reflect an urge to progress and improvement which is widespread even in the family-enterprise sector.

Likewise, at the other end of the industry, the brochures of the leading companies give great prominence to photographs of the firms' research laboratories. In the man-made fibre industry, certainly, great store is set by the development of new types of fibre – especially by exploiting the possibilities of varying the cross-section of the constituent sub-threads within filaments, though it does seem to be a field in which the notion of 'breakthrough' is highly subjective, and one where it is as much commercial persuasiveness as scientific ingenuity which decides the competition. However, textiles is not an R & D-intensive industry, and it would be surprising if it were. Textiles are reckoned to have 2.2 per cent of the scientific manpower in industry (2.3 per cent of that in manufacturing) compared with its 7 per cent share of manufacturing output (Kagaku-Gijutsuchō, 1981, p.156).

The trade union response

The Japan Federation of Textile Workers' Unions (Zensen) is the only union of any political or business-strategic consequence in the Japanese textile industry. It is a somewhat unusual industrial federation in that it exercises a good deal more control and guidance over its constituent unions than most, and its constituent unions include a certain number of area unions organizing small-firm workers as well as the independent enterprise unions of the larger firms which dominate the Federation in the standard Japanese pattern. That some of these smaller unions were of not negligible importance is suggested by the fact that in the 1980 wage negotiations, while the big unions were doing their usual decorous ballet, setting a series of staggered strike dates and then settling the midnight before, the textile firms which did actually have to go on strike for at least a day to push obdurate employers closer to what they hoped for (68 firms with an average of 140 workers each) were all in the small-firm sector.

The textile industry has the longest tradition of continuous organization in Japan and its unions (from the very beginning in the 1920s organized on an enterprise rather than on any craft basis) have generally been counted on the right wing (Gompers-inspired business-unionist wing as it was called before the war) of the labour movement. This meant that they were incorporated more easily into the war-time patriotic workers' organizations than those of the revolutionary left, and had some organizational continuity out of which to construct a post-war union organization. Like the British textile unions in recent decades, Zensen has had a high proportion of women members and generally been counted as 'weak' or a 'reasonable' union depending on the point of view – a tendency which the decline of the industry and a prevailing sense of the need to stave off inevitable decline has – if not to the same extent as in Britain – made more pronounced.

Zensen today has some 50 per cent of all textile workers and 23 per cent of garment workers as members – about 85 per cent of all union members in those two industries. It is the leading union in Dōmei, the right-wing one of the two politically oriented national federations, which is closely linked to the Democratic Socialist Party. Three of the 33 members of that Party elected to the Diet in June 1980 were former full-time officials of the union, and several more owed significant segments of their support to it. Most of the other 15 per cent of unionized workers in the industry are linked to one of the left-wing federations.

Unions' adjustment: getting the best deal out of the run-down in the labour force

The union's main adjustment concern over the last decade has been the reactive concern to 'struggle against rationalization'. In fact, in line with the union's history of reasonable compromise, the concern has primarily been to improve the conditions under which rationalization takes place without permitting any deviation from the *principle* that a firm owes all its regular employees a working lifetime's work, and has to make handsome amends if it cannot provide it (though working lifetime, of course, means until the mid or late fifties for men, but only until marriage or first childbirth for women). The translated record of the appendix makes clear how successfully a union could make that principle stick if a firm was unwise enough to put itself in the wrong by not following proper formalities and so producing a bitter conflict situation rather different from the compromise-seeking negotiation more common in Japanese industrial relations.

Much of the union's effort was devoted to trying to safeguard the position of workers in bankrupt firms, and at an early stage it drew up a very detailed document for the guidance of its members and officials, setting out the legal position, and the pitfalls and possibilities of the various alternatives to bankruptcy – reconstruction under a receiver, etc. It advises on the legal priority of debts to workers, and how the union should calculate entitlements, and get a written agreement from the management recognizing these prior claims, allocating realizable assets to meeting them, and putting those assets under the union's effective physical control by sit-ins, etc. (Zensen, 1980a, pp.69–75). A record of the union's negotiations during 1979–80 includes, for instance, a bankruptcy in a provincial town in which the settlement for a garment firm's eight workers allowed for the current month's wages, plus one month in lieu of notice, plus 1.35 months in lieu of the year-end bonus, plus a 50 per cent increment to the accumulated retirement bonus formally due under the firm's contractual scheme (Zensen, 1980b, p.68). In another case in Shizuoka the union had got the contractual retirement bonus plus an additional 20 per cent ex-gratia payment in cash and was negotiating to persuade the firm to pay an additional 80 per cent to make a total of double entitlement, but the receiver disallowed it in the interest of other creditors. The union took the receiver to court and an additional 20 per cent (making, that is, an ex-gratia payment of 40 per cent over entitlement in total) was granted in an out-of-court settlement with the judge acting as mediator (Zensen, 1980b, p.71).

In the case of plant closures and other occasions for reducing staff the main objective of the union has generally been to secure generous terms for voluntary retirement. Standard Japanese labour practice is to provide a lump sum bonus at a retirement age (which in textiles has slowly been raised from the original 55, and according to agreements reached in 1980 will be 60 in all the big firms within a few years). The bonus is calculated according to years of service, and after 25 years' service, may amount to 3–5 years' wages. Smaller sums are available for those who leave before retirement age, *less* than the full sum pro-rated to years of service for voluntary leaving, and *more* than the pro-rated sum for departures 'at the firm's convenience'. (This is the sum referred to as the 'entitlement' in the bankruptcy cases mentioned above. No third category of termination through unavoidable circumstances is recognised.) The standard negotiating objective for the union was that voluntary retirement should be at *double* the

entitlement, the 'firm's convenience' figure. Sometimes, as in the
case described in the appendix, where the company put itself in
the wrong, they did better than that (3.6 times entitlement in that
case). Sometimes, when firms were clearly struggling to keep
nose above water, the union settled for less. An example was a
garment firm which was undergoing an emergency reconstruction. One-hundred-and-forty union members with eight non-
members accepted a scheme which the union agreed (with cuts in
directors' and managers' salaries as one condition) under which
full entitlement was paid plus a special redundancy bonus which
worked out at 37.6 months' salary for a 51–55-year-old with 20
years' service – rather less than double entitlements (Zensen,
1980b, p.71). Larger firms with remoter managements sometimes
found it easier to be tougher as in the second case reported in the
appendix which paid only 23 per cent. Other additional elements
in the settlement may be equal per-capita payments under the
guise of 'job search money' or 'apology' money. How much this
meant in total is difficult to calculate from the accounts given
because sums are averaged across sex and age groups, but it
appears that older workers in the most favoured firms received
4–5 years' wages as compensation (6–7 years if one does not count
bonuses as part of a normal year's wages). In the first appendix
case, compensation amounted to about $15,000 per person, aver-
aged over the 129 leavers which included a good proportion of
young girls.

The union also got involved on occasion in negotiating the
arrangements for hiving off certain functions to subsidiaries.
When Unichika set up four new companies in 1980, the agreed
terms were that they were to be manned by volunteers only and
the opportunity restricted to those over 45 years of age; that the
retirement age should be 60 in the new firms, with the option of
re-employment up to 65, and that the retirement entitlement plus
a supplement should be paid on entering the firms, as if for
normal voluntary retirement.

Unions' adjustment: diversification

The adjustment behaviour of a union is partly a matter of reactive
protection of members' interest. But it must also be remembered
that the union itself – or, more concretely, its full-time officials –
have a constellation of interests of their own. The union members
collectively may have no particular interest in how many textile

workers there are in total – provided that any reduction in numbers is on favourable terms to the people actually involved. To the union officials, however, total numbers may be a crucial concern as a determinate not only of the organization's power and effectiveness, but also of their own income.

Zensen has 170 persons permanently employed by the Federation, including 20–30 regional organizers. In addition, there are some 4,700 full-time union officials in the constituent enterprise unions (about one per 400 members). The latter, almost without exception, are 'on leave' from a tenured position in the company to which they can return. It is the officials of the Federation who have the personal 'livelihood' stake in the Federation itself. (Though some of them too may have the possibility of returning to their original firms.)

They have been pursuing the objective of organizational survival with some imagination. Accepting the decline of the textile labour force as inevitable, they decided as a matter of strategy to diversify into a growth industry to compensate and found that the steadily expanding, and very largely unionized chain-store business answered their needs. The transition was not unnatural since some of the clothing wholesalers and garment-makers had got involved in the chain-store and supermarket business, so they already had an entrée into the field. As a result their membership figures, having once fallen to 445,000 in 1978, had climbed back to 460,000 in 1980. Having lost nearly 100,000 members in textiles, the union gained 60,000 in distribution and has a declared aim of getting back to the half-million mark, partly by developing this line, partly by concentrating on improving organization in the garment small-firm sector where the organization rate is estimated at 30 per cent – compared with 55 per cent in textiles proper.

Government adjustment policy

We turn now from those whose adjustment behaviour has been concerned with the survival of individual firms or the welfare of individual workers to those with broader interests. First there are those whose ostensible concern has been with the health of the 'industry' (or sections of it) – the business associations and, in some capacities, politicians from textile constituencies and officials of the textile divisions of MITI. Secondly, there are those whose business is to be concerned about the 'economy as a whole' – the same officials and even politicians in some moods and circumstances, together with other officials of the Economic Planning Agency, the Ministry of Finance and those in MITI – such as the secretariat of the Industry Structure Council, whose business it is to take an integrated, and long-term view of the economy.

The account which follows will concentrate on the evolution of government measures, as a concrete expression of the compromise bargains struck among all those involved of both categories, with such explanation of the nature of the negotiations as is necessary to understand the purpose of the measures and their effects.

Deliberate adjustment policy towards textiles starts early in Japan, and was solely prompted by external events – by alarm in the American textile industry as imports from Japan rose from 33m. square yards of cotton cloth in 1953 to 140m. in 1955, of women's blouses from 5,000 dozen to 4m. dozen. By December 1955 it was quite clear that voluntary export restrictions were the only solution and temporary measures were followed by a five-year restraint agreement in 1957, which led into the 1962 initial Long Term Agreement, later revamped as the MFA.

The resultant check to the growth of the textile industry had serious internal effects which called for counter measures. The first such measure was the law of June 1956, the main purpose of which was to freeze total capacity. All equipment in spinning, weaving and finishing was required to be registered. The co-operative organizations in the various *sanchi* were given legal status, and became the agency for maintaining the register. Henceforth the installation of new equipment required permission which was granted only on condition that an equivalent volume of capacity was scrapped (in the presence of inspectors).

Spindle registration ceased in 1970 at a time when it was thought that the dangers of over-capacity had passed, but has continued for looms and for other equipment to the present day. Its application in practice loosened during the 1960s and some looms found their way to the scrap-heap several times over, so that the system had to be revamped, with an amnesty for unregistered looms, in 1974. The result was an immediate 10 per cent increase in registrations.

The Chairman of the Overview Sub-Committee of the joint Government–Industry Textile Council was to call these 1956 measures, in a personal introduction to his Sub-committee's influential report on the state of the industry some 20 years later, 'the missed opportunity'. 'Both the Government and the industry wanted the status quo policy of the registration system, and both thought that was enough, but it had the effect of delaying the modernizations of the industry.' (Inaba Hidezo in MITI Seikatsu, 1977, p.iii).

By the mid-1960s, however, industrial policy towards industries like textiles had begun to move forward as the decade of high growth began to induce a general forward-looking mood of optimism and focus attention on the structural problems of Japan's dual structure. A series of measures between 1963 and 1967, notably the establishment of the Agency for the Revitalization of the Small and Medium Industries, focused on what was called, at first, the 'promotion of modernization' and later 'structural improvement' in industries with a high concentration of small (often family-owned) firms of low productivity and low potentiality for development. Textiles was clearly one of these, and was the subject of the Law for Special Emergency Measures for the Structural Improvement of the Textile Industry of 1967. It involved compensation for the scrapping of old machinery, grants for the purchase of new equipment and to facilitate the grouping and combining of small firms, and the establishment of a special agency, the Textile Industry Rationalization Agency to carry out these tasks.

The legal and financial structure thus created for an initial period of seven years has since been several times revised and revamped, most recently in 1979 for a period of four years. From time to time the emphasis has changed. The tightened American import restrictions of 1971 brought a special 'political pay-off' compensation element into the system for a temporary two-year period (see Destler et al, 1979). In the early 1970s the concerns with pollution and urban congestion and the current talk about the need to up-grade the industrial structure towards the 'knowledge-intensive' industries, combined with a further tightening of export markets, brought an emphasis on 'computerisation' and 'quality' and 'high fashion'. The import surge of 1973 brought a concern with viability in the face of 'catching up' competition from Asia, which was again reinterpreted by the Textile Council as a reinforcement of the need to modernize in a knowledge-intensive direction in order to stay ahead – this time with an emphasis on vertical integration as a means. But the actual instruments of policy and their general effects remain today those that were introduced, in textiles and more generally in the small-firm sector, in the mid-1960s.

The major measures have been:

1   Finance for collective developments, organized by co-operative organizations in the textile sanchi.
2   Modernization grants, partly for the same purpose, partly for re-equipment of individual firms.
3   Exit compensation.

Collective sanchi development

First there is a range of survey, study, planning and training schemes financed under a special law for the promotion of the development of sanchi (The Law for Emergency Special Measures to Develop Small and Medium Enterprises in Concentrated Sanchi, 1978). A typical story of an initiative undertaken under this law might be as follows. The exercise begins with the establishment of a committee of twelve to twenty knowledgeable people of the locality headed by textile specialists of a local university, and including technical experts from the local cloth inspection offices and, usually, a government research station, as well as leading members of the co-operative – proprietors, usually, of fairly prosperous local firms. The committee then commissions a survey, a detailed statistical exercise and questionnaire about business practices and intentions, which may be carried out by one of its professor member's students. The survey report, with a concluding chapter of recommendations, is then produced by the committee under such titles as 'A Vision (Bijion) of the Way Ahead for . . .', 'The Path to Revitalization of . . .' or 'Plans for the Promotion of . . .' the sanchi in question, on the basis of which application is made for funds on a modest scale ($50,000 to $100,000) for a series of small ventures, trying a new kind of loom, marketing surveys, experimentation with new yarns, exhibiting at trade fairs, etc.

It must be admitted that none of these reports and plans seems to the outside observer to carry much promise of the sort of transformations implied by their brave titles. Let us take, for example, the 1979 report for the Senshū area which has one of the worst problems, being specialized in plain grey cloth of types with which Chinese imports directly compete. After an extremely informative statistical survey of the enterprises in the district, the final chapter is devoted to 'a vision of the future' (Senshū Orimo-no, 1979).

The sanchi is, it begins, 'destined to lose its power of survival in competition with developing country exports unless we develop our orientation towards high value-added products as befits an advanced industrial country.' This is then translated, apparently quite arbitrarily, into the objective of finding new products for 30 per cent of the output. It then begins to look at various concrete policies.

What should that new 30 per cent be? Yarn-dyed colour weaving is considered and ruled out because other sanchi start too far ahead in an uncertain market and water resources are not good enough. Maybe with modern finishing techniques more could be made of the very narrow widths traditionally woven for kimono material (the narrow-loom sector was in particular trouble because of disposable paper napkins etc.).

Weavers should get closer to their markets. The survey showed that two-thirds of them did not know the final use of the cloth they sold. They should diversify. Seventy per cent of them were only weaving a single sort. They should learn to combine standard year-through lines with short-cycle fashion-catching lines in a flexible mix.

And so the recommendations continue with a mixture of the concrete and somewhat trivial with the vague and rather grandiose. There is the thought that it might be possible, in conjunction with a spinning firm, to develop a distinctive kind of yarn which would given Senshū cloth some distinctive appeal, or to develop double gauzes for medical clothing. There is a passage on the need to be fully aware of every development in Parisian and American fashions, a suggestion that every respectable enterprise should have a product-development centre and that in Senshū groups of firms might establish them jointly, and a passage on the need for the highest level of skills to do such work and consequently for polishing the technical skills of those who are already working in the district, given the lack of resources to attract new talent of the highest calibre into the area.

As for the question how to make the 70 per cent of production expected to remain in traditional lines more efficient, there are two proposals: for the introduction of more automated machinery in both weaving and preparation – 'in which we are behind not only the industrial countries, but also some of the developing countries too' – and secondly, for more co-operative action, joint purchase of materials and joint sales by groups of weavers, co-operative sizing, beaming, etc.

All in all, the report gives a general impression of trying rather desperately to fight off recognition of the fact that the area is weaving a product that others can weave just as well and much more cheaply. But it does at least provide the justification for a four-year schedule of activities to be financed under the sanchi development programme – in the Senshū case jointly with two other sanchi in the same prefecture. When it was finally approved the programme was budgeted to spend about 80 million yen (about a third of a million dollars) on such activities as more surveys, exhibitions of products and PR leaflets, seminars and training programmes, market research, tests of new looms and special grants to promote weavers' exit from the industry to other 'knowledge-intensive' industries (Senshū Orimono, 1980).

It is a not unnoticed function of some of these grants that they can pay the salaries of workers already employed in the co-operative – as well as providing a source of patronage for the co-operative officials. The point made about workers and unions that the interests of representative organizations and their officials have to be considered separately from those of the people they represent applies equally to weavers and their co-operatives. And when the co-operatives become powerful means for the crystallization of political pressures, it is not surprising that governments should be sensitive to organizational interests.

It should be said, in partial amendment to the above, that for some of the *sanchi* with important export markets which they seem to have good prospects of holding – the colour-weaving gingham area, the filament weavers of the north coast, etc. – the reports produced are a little more down to earth and some of the activities seem more likely to have productive pay-offs.

The ideology of small business policy

One point in the Senshū document which is worth a short digression is the suggestion that there should be more co-operation between groups of weavers for joint purchase, joint services and joint marketing. This is, in practice, little more than ritual endorsement of a Good Thing. It is a recommendation which ignores the fact that (a) scale economies in sizing, beaming, etc., are already largely achieved by specialization; (b) the system of contract weaving, by smaller weavers sub-contracting from larger weavers, provides further scale economies by co-operative arrangements albeit in hierarchical form; and (c) for family proprietors who choose not to enter sub-contracting arrangements but continue their own purchasing and marketing, the business side is often a welcome relief to the physical tedium of keeping looms going and not something they would be keen to give up. Nevertheless, the ideology of co-operation has a strong hold in Japan.

Its endorsement in this document points to the source of a certain tension in Japanese public policy in general and industrial policy in particular which is of wider interest and has a bearing on the feature of the Japanese industrial structure described at the beginning of this essay – the enduring ties between hierarchically ranked firms.

The tension is between conflicting values. On the one hand it is the perception that these hierarchical relations are good for promoting national efficiency. (Which seems to me true: the systems works well, and one would expect it to work well anywhere – where it was manned by Japanese.) There are also strong supporting cultural traditions which approve (i) of the fittingness of arrangements wherein the more able/powerful dominate/have broader responsibilities than the less able/powerful, and (ii) of the benevolent consideration for subordinates in the hierarchy and restraint in exercising full market advantage which these hierarchies are supposed to entail.

On the other hand is the penetration of the ideology of market individualism, the principle of the equality of all individuals before the law and the price mechanism, which has a great deal of appeal, particularly when it is diffused in the form of indignant denunciation of the evils of the denial of equality – i.e. 'exploitation'.

One manifestation of this, and of the tendency to identify the individualism–equality set of values with 'modernity' is the founding, in 1977, of the Association for the Modernization of Business Relationships in the Textile Industry. The Association is an association of associations, of no fewer than 52 national associations, 30 of them concerned with production in textiles and clothing, 18 in distribution and four of them umbrella organizations. It was founded, according to its handbook, 'with the guidance and support of the Ministry of International Trade and Industry and other interested organizations', and it was intended as a kind of side-effect suppressant of what was then MITI's strong belief that the way forward for the textile industry lay in strengthening hierarchy at the expense of market – promoting the dominance of 'modern' firms either by full vertical integration or by ties of long-term contract. The Association was intended to prevent hierarchy from becoming abusive.

Its purpose was elaborated in a formal Declaration, intended to be a kind of Gettysburg Address of the textile industry, adopted at the Association's first meeting (Seni Kindaika, 1979). The first article with its resounding pledge to take every effort to modernize trading relations is hardly elucidatory, but the second becomes more specific. 'We seek to promote trading under clear terms and conditions through *written* [my emphasis] agreements for basic conditions of trade and careful invoicing of all separate transactions.' Article 3 gets closer to the 'exploitation' nub of the problem. 'We shall never use a position of economic superiority to force risks and charges which should be ours on to a weaker trading partner.' Article 4 moves on to a self-help note, a slight concession to the 'well, they only have themselves to blame. Caveat contractor. It's their own fault really' point of view. 'In order to make trading relations on a footing of equality possible, we shall each seek to strengthen and improve his own negotiating power, by finding ourselves access to rapid and accurate information about consumer markets, by developing new products and process techniques, by improving the efficiency of our production and sales.' Although the rhetorical code of the next article is difficult to break, it presumably is a condemnation of business corruption – employees of larger firms taking kick-backs or personal favours in return for awarding contracts, and the sixth and final clause sounds like a promise not to bother the courts too often in spite of all this unJapanese talk about contracts: 'We adhere to the basic principle of finding our own solutions to our own problems and pledge to move forward towards the rationalization and modernization of transactions in a full sense of our personal responsibilities.' (Another document recommends informal mediation, the prior appointment of a kind of standing arbitrator for any on-going business relationship, as the best way of settling disputes.)

It is easy to grin at the rhetoric and dismiss the whole exercise as simply an attempt to give the woodshed a bright green coat of paint without doing anything about the nasty things inside it. Nevertheless, at the margin, the campaign may well alter business practices to a degree which will be cumulatively significant.

It is doubtful whether one should attach much significance to the fact that between the Association's first two annual surveys of business practices the proportion (in a sample of over 1,100 firms) who said that they did have written contracts with their suppliers and purchasers rose from 15.9 to 18.5 per cent, though the fact that small weavers showed me some of the pro-forma contract forms distributed through their local co-operative suggests that some impact was already visible. Another co-operative was trying to start a black list of traders who had returned unwanted goods without full justification, presumably at the inspiration of the Association's campaign. (One thing the surveys revealed was a clear inverse correlation between the proportion of a supplier's trade which was governed by written contract and the proportion of 'claims' and 'returns' he had had to accept.)

The likely effect of the campaign, however, will not be to strengthen the values of equality and individualism which vaguely underlie the Association's vision of 'modernity'. It will, instead, tighten the web of hierarchical relations in the industry with the reinforcement of genuine morality, making something more real of the 'relations of trust', 'the duty of considerateness and respect for the other of the stronger party' (Confucian 'benevolence' in short), instead of allowing those slogans to be used as a cover for a one-sided exercise of power. What the Association is trying to do is to achieve the transformation in business relations which the late 1940s reforms did for labour relations in the enterprise, to achieve the bureaucratization of benevolence and the moralization of hierarchy. The first case translated in the appendix shows just how powerful can be the sanctions which the weaker party can bring to bear on the stronger party (without recourse to lengthy litigation) when the stronger party clearly transgresses the norms which the bureaucratization/moralization process has enshrined.

To return to the starting point of this digression, the attachment to the idea of co-operation displayed in the Senshū document is, like the 'modernization of trading relations', another manifestation of the value clash between hierarchy, trust and tradition on the one hand and equality, contract and modernity on the other. Co-operation – rejecting the selfishness of individualism, retaining the 'mutual consideration' part of traditional hierarchical structures, while gaining the equality advantages of the new – has enormous appeal as a way out of the dilemma. Hence the long succession of starry-eyed writings about new forms of co-operative agriculture which have appeared in Japan since the war. Hence also the ritual urging to co-operative units in weaving in the Senshū document. What Japanese writers fail to take into account is that Japanese producers do already show a capacity for drawing the line between co-operation and competition by criteria which in most societies would count as embodying a very enlightened and long-term view of self-interest. The broad range of function of the weavers' co-operatives are an example of that. But that there are further *large* opportunities for co-operation on a smaller scale as yet unexploited seems on the face of it unlikely – which is not to say that technical change may not alter the parameters which determine the value of co-operativization, as in the case of the Fujishima co-operative with its water-jet, cloth-drying and drawing-in equipment which was described at the beginning of chapter 7.

Modernization grants

The sanchi grant scheme described earlier, available for several industries besides textiles, expands an earlier scheme which was designed to promote both collective and individual-enterprise developments. This, the central arm of textile policy, is run by a special quango founded in 1967 and known in English as the Textile Industry Rationalization Agency (the name it has borne since 1974 translates more accurately, if more ponderously, as the Association for the Promotion of Structural Improvement in the Textile Industry). For much of its operations, however, it acts as agent for a similar but rather larger organization founded a little later with a much larger remit – the Small and Medium Enterprises Agency.

The 'Structural Improvement' which the textile agency is charged to promote has undergone some reinterpretation in the course of its life. The registration system for equipment in many branches of textiles introduced in the late 1950s was primarily a means of freezing capacity, with the secondary aim of encouraging the replacement of rather poor-quality equipment built during the post-war steel shortage with better subsequent vintages of the *same type* of equipment. By 1967, however, there had been significant technological breakthroughs; the rapier and other types of faster shuttleless looms and a variety of new equipment for the preparation stage were offering the possibility of substituting capital for labour, and it was the concern to promote this sort of new investment, particularly as a solution to the problem of the mass of low-productivity (and low-income) family-based small enterprises that prompted the creation of the Association, to provide subsidies for such modernization efforts.

By 1973, however, it was apparent that neither the rate of investment in the equipment, nor the structural changes it was inducing in the industry, were adequate to meet the challenge to the industry's competitiveness, and this prompted a search for some new policy departures. Those challenges were seen to be mounting more rapidly than ever before as the increasing strength of the developing economies of Asia and the rising value of the yen were reflected in the continuing loss of export markets and the import surge of 1973.

The Textile Council was the forum for working out the guidelines for a new revision of the textile industry legislation, the Law for Emergency Measures for the Structural Improvement of the Textile Industry of May 1974. The rallying slogan which recurred in the Council's report was that the industry must 'move towards a more knowledge-intensive basis to respond to the changing character of demand – for higher quality, greater diversity, and greater individual differentiation.' At the same time there was a need to reduce excess capacity (though this negative objective was always pushed into second place). The means to achieve these ends were, first, to promote the development of the apparel industry which was closest to the changing demand front (or had the best chance of creating these notional changes in demand, the report might have said but did not), and secondly – the policy which prompted the 'modernization of trading relations' antidote – the promotion of vertical integration in the industry.

The report was a little vague on the meaning of vertical integration, but the background of the thinking was that closer ties between the various stages of the production process would lead to more rapid and appropriate transmission of change in demand at home and abroad back to the early stages of the production process. (The question in the Senshū survey which revealed that a large proportion of weavers did not know the final uses of their cloth found its way into that survey precisely because of this concern.) A second consideration was that larger enterprises would be better able to invest in new equipment, and a MITI official (it was, as usual, MITI officials who provided most of the intellectual input for the Council) suggested that a further thought was that the accelerator effect which (through stock changes) magnifies the impact of business cycles as one moves upstream from garments to weaving to spinning would have less severe effects if several stages were combined in the same enterprise. The *sanmoto* converters were singled out as key actors in this process of integration, and it was envisaged that the integration should take many forms from capital participation, joint financing of product and process development units, or simply long-term sub-contracts.

The technique used in the 1974 law was to offer a variety of grants made conditional on desirable vertical integration taking place. There were cheap loans for collective activities, conditional on co-operatives merging (preferably vertically, e.g. the sizers and beamers joining with the weavers), for Product Development Centres and for all common services (like collecting and returning used yarn cones or setting up part-time junior colleges to help attract female labour).

There were also cheap loans for individual enterprises which merged to a viable size, though what counted as viable was nowhere written in the regulations: co-operative officials quoted 100 sewing machines or 300 looms as the sort of figures the officials seemed to be using as guidelines. The loans were from the Small and Medium Enterprise Agency, and were at 2.6 per cent for up to 70 per cent of initial cost, with repayment over 12–16 years (shorter periods for working capital) and grace periods of 2–3 years. The Textile Industries Rationalization Agency could further provide loan guarantees for private borrowing. Special depreciation tax allowances were also available.

The results of the law were not impressive. Vertical integration sounds like a splendid idea when you are thinking about the industry from an office in Tokyo, but the natural tendency in most of the sanchi is in the quite contrary direction – towards fragmented specialization. Nevertheless there have, apparently, been some successful projects: examples were a group of 1 weaver, 1 finisher and 8 garment factories in Fukui which developed a new pleating system for skirts, a group including a yarn texturizer, warp-maker, 17 knitters, 1 finisher and 20 makers-up which developed a branded sports wear, etc. But the take-up has been limited. The prefectural governments which acted as MITI's agents in these matters, interpreted the conditions quite strictly, and in the event only 81 projects got approved in the whole country between 1975 and 1979: their total cost was about Y60bn ($272m) of which 35 per cent came as loans from the Small and Medium Enterprise Agency (and some additional funds from the Small Business Finance Corporation.) Total expenditure, in fact, was about one-fifth of the budget target. The applications to the Rationalization Agency for guarantees of private borrowings were also at the end of 1979 running at about one-tenth of the limit of $350m for which funds were on hand.

With a further revision of the law in 1979 the regulations were loosened up a good deal in the hope of increasing the take-up. The vertical integration principle still applies, but it is possible for, say, a weaver to claim funds for re-equipping with air-jets by having, on the one hand, a long-term agreement with a converter, plus possibly a little mutual capital participation, and, on the other hand, sub-contracting arrangements with a group of smaller weavers who weave for him on contract; the latter gets him up to a suitable scale and the former gets the necessary two-stage link. A considerable number of air-jets were being purchased in 1982–3 in the Senshū area on this kind of pretext. Even so, the Agency is not, apparently, finding it easy to get rid of its money. It was carrying over a surplus at the end of 1980 nearly twice the size of its annual expenditure of Y1.1bn. (about $5m). It may be said that a good deal of the Agency's finance comes from the industry (and, of course, from interest on its unused loan funds), and the cost to the national budget in 1980 was a mere Y82m, less than half a million dollars.

Modernization of the garment industry

The Textile Industries' Rationalization Agency has recently put a good deal of emphasis on developing the garment industry, the sector of those under its purview which has shown signs of the most vigorous growth. It had been singled out in the Textile Council's 1978 recommendations as the field offering best prospects for electronic modernization, as well as fashion creativity – one form of the 'knowledge-intensiveness' very much in vogue (Seni Kōgyō Shingikai, 1978, p.29). There is much talk of the way microchip computer systems will transform the garment trade (see Nihon Orimono 1982, pp.142–6). This will happen in at least three ways: the development of on-line networks between garment firms and satellite small-enterprise makers-up on the one hand and sales outlets on the other; secondly, the development of automated multi-floor city centre warehouses for garment makers; and thirdly the computerization of mechanical processes of pattern-making, cutting out, assembly, etc. – various kinds of 'mechatronics' as such devices are called in Japan. MITI has recently been accelerating the development of what is intended to be a far-reaching scheme for the computerization of the garment industry. There had been small beginnings in national laboratories in the early 1970s, but the latest programme is planned to be one of the large-scale projects of the Agency of Industrial Science and Technology, spending some Y10bn. ($40m.) over seven years. In 1982, the first year, expenditure of something less than half a million dollars was to concentrate on the development of handling devices with the flexible servo-mechanisms necessary for accurate placing and processing of soft pliable materials with varying characteristics. The project looks forward to building a prototype automatic plant capable of a daily production of 2,000 garments in batches of not more than 10 identical garments each, and with a turn-around time from order to product of less than six days (responding to the reported steady reduction in lot size and shortening of required delivery times – now, according to MITI's analysis, typically 20-day orders for 200 garment lots). It is obvious that these plans have important implications for the developing countries of Asia which might be hoping to expand their garment exports to Japan. Once such on-line systems linking the distribution and the production system are created in Japan, the possibilities for imports to insert themselves in the process may be very considerably reduced. At the same time any wage-cost advantages developing countries enjoy may well be outweighed by new (and relatively cheap) technology. All this applies, of course, pre-eminently to the fashion end of the market, less to underwear, standard shirts, etc.

Encouragement for exit and capacity reduction

An example was given earlier of the way in which temporary recession cartels have been created in industries with a relatively high concentration of large firms as a means of dealing with over-production which is expected to be of a temporary nature. In the spinning industry such cartels were organized in 1975, 1977 and 1981.

The same device has been resorted to in the synthetic fibre industry for the four main products: nylon filament, polyester filament and staple and acrylic staple. In addition, the synthetic fibre industry was designated as one of the industries eligible for concerted capacity reduction under the 1978 Law for Emergency Measures to Stabilize Particular Depressed Industries.

The Law was designed to provide more long-term exemption from the anti-trust legislation than was allowed for under the recession cartel system. Synthetic fibres was already in a recession cartel from October 1977 and it was soon designated (along with other industries, see p.140) as eligible under the new law. After talks were held with the industry a scheme, having the force of law, was promulgated in October 1978 by MITI. It provided for the removal from production of some 16 per cent of capacity. This could be by scrapping or moth-balling the equipment (moth-balling being defined as removal of all extruders, gear pumps, metres and gauges and the motive power therefore, and concreting in their installation beds). The operation was to be completed within three months and there was to be no rehabilitation for two years. There had to be talks with the unions before measures were taken and every effort to redeploy displaced workers. Due regard had to be paid to the effect on related small enterprises and the opportunity was to be taken to strengthen links with fibre-processors. There was to be every effort to conserve energy, to rationalize the remaining production, to diversify, strengthen non-price competitiveness, and to eliminate excessive competition both at home and abroad, 'striving to create a rational sales organization based on the principles of free and fair competition'. There were no scrapping subsidies (MITI, 23 October 1978). In the event about a third of the capacity reduction was by scrapping, the rest by moth-balling.

During the three years' operation of the plan, the situation somewhat improved. The Big Nine reduced their employment by 33 per cent, their long-term debts by 19 per cent and their energy consumption per ton of output by 26 per cent. At the same time they invested something like $300m. in new equipment for energy saving, product diversification, etc., as a result of which the proportion of output represented by 'differentiated high-value fibres' rose from 16 to 22 per cent (much more for polyester filament). But, said the Committee report which recorded these figures, demand forecast had proved too optimistic and had not taken account of the effect of the second oil crisis in widening the raw-material cost gap between Japan's naphtha-based and America's natural gas-based industries. By February 1981 there was reckoned still to be 14 per cent over-capacity and on the best projections, still 12 per cent likely in 1983 (anticipating a 2.8 per cent annual growth in domestic demand, a 5.2 per cent climb in exports and 2.5 per cent increase in imports). The mandatory scheme was renewed for the rest of the life of the legislation, until 1983. Previously moth-balled equipment was to be definitively disposed of, together with an additional 3.1 per cent of capacity – thus leaving approximately 8 per cent spare capacity for unexpected up-turns with a little bit extra for the more fashion-sensitive and season-sensitive polyester-filament and acrylic-staple production (Seni Kōgyō Shingikai, 10 February 1981).

The scheme hardly leaves the man-made fibre industry as the bright spot of the Japanese economy but it does at least leave the fibre-producers operating for the most part with small profits and closer to full capacity utilization (and with a more recent average vintage of capital) than their international competitors.

For the other segments of the industry dominated by small enterprises there are two government schemes to promote capacity reduction through exits from the industry.

The heyday of the exit-compensation scheme was 1971–2 in the wake of the big political rumpus within the Liberal Democratic Party over the Prime Minister's acceptance of tightened voluntary export restrictions in talks with Nixon before a consensus had been established in Japan. Over two years, around $150m. was paid out in scrapping compensation schemes (Y54.8bn.), together with more than twice that sum as temporary cashflow supplementation for affected producers.

That episode having passed, the current schemes operated by the Small and Medium Enterprise Agency under a Law of 1976 are more modest in scope. They operate on the principle that the exit of any producer from the industry is of benefit to the remaining producers and they, therefore, should bear the cost. A weaver, for example, giving up his business, can apply for compensation equal to three times the book-value or (exceptionally) half the replacement value of his equipment.

He must apply to the local co-operative which, in effect, receives loans to buy his looms and have them destroyed (in the presence of inspectors). The loans, partly from the central, partly from local, governments are repayable over 16 years, with a 5-year grace period before repayment begins. The amount is set at 95 per cent of the entitled compensation, and the co-operative is expected to add the other 5 per cent from its own resources. However, practice – now semi-officially condoned by the Agency – is very different.

No one is prepared to accept the 'survivors are gainers, survivors should pay' principle. Consequently the co-operatives do not add their 5 per cent. Moreover, they see no reason why they should repay the loan. So they subtract 42 per cent of the loans received at preferential rates and bank it at ordinary rates in order to pay back the loan over 16 years. Then they take another 10 per cent as a deposit in case interest rate changes upset the calculations, and pay out the remaining 43 per cent to the existing weaver, with the promise of what is left of the deposit after 16 years.

It is not surprising that no one is prepared to accept the 'survivors are gainers' principle in an industry where, to begin with, the exiters' share of the total market is minute and any room left in the market by the exit of home producers is likely anyway to be taken up by imports. The real gainers, presumably, are those who export capital goods to Korea and Taiwan, and there *is* a Japanese precedent for arranging transfers from such industries to the declining industries in the petroleum import tax earmarked to compensate those who lost in the rundown of the coal industry in the 1960s. But this seems an outlandish analogy to everyone concerned with the textile-scrapping scheme. It just is not an issue for discussion. Exit compensation is a very subordinate and peripheral part of everyone's perception of a good textile policy, much less attractive to the industry representatives who negotiate these policies than more 'forward-looking' schemes of development. When the cotton scheme ran out after a year's extension in 1981, the officials of the Weavers' Federation were in no hurry to renegotiate it, although they estimated that over-capacity was back to something like 1977 levels. They waited, partly hoping that the silk weavers, generally considered to be in a worse plight, would negotiate an improved deal (OSS, 25 October 1982). When they did start to move, towards the end of 1982, their main negotiating objective was to double the permitted maximum compensation of Y450,000 ($2,000) per loom – on the grounds that the replacement cost of an automatic loom had considerably increased and was greatly underestimated (at Y900,000) in the first place anyway.

Nevertheless, expenditures under the scheme have not been negligible – about Y182bn. was made available between 1977 and 1980 ($850m.) and some 90 per cent of it was apparently used. Nearly 100,000 looms were scrapped in the cotton, silk and fibre-weaving industries according to the Agency's report, though registration decreased by only two-thirds of that figure. This represents between one-sixth and one-tenth of the total number of looms, but, of course, a much smaller fraction of capacity: very few of the scrapped looms were automatic, and most were of narrow width. There were similar reductions in fifteen other branches of the industry – doublers, sock knitters, embroidery and lace, etc.

In every case the funds were channelled through the national federations of local producers' co-operatives. One group somewhat at a disadvantage in the scheme were the beamers and sizers. As a newish speciality formed by fission from the weaving industry, they for the most part belonged to the local weavers' co-operatives and would have had to apply through them for scrapping compensation. There is, moreover, excess capacity in the beaming industry in most areas, and many would like to get out. But the weavers who dominate their co-operatives are not at all unhappy to see excess capacity in beaming, and it appears that this element of self-interest has on occasion proved stronger than brotherly co-operativeness. Beamers have been having a hard time getting their applications through. In May 1981 it was reported that 380 beamers had come together to form a national union (OSS, 14 May 1981). Thus does fragmentation and specialization proceed.

What happens to those who leave the industry in this way? One local study provides some clues. It reports on the subsequent career of some 99 former weavers who took advantage of the exit-compensation scheme in the Senshū district and had completed their formalities between January 1977 and January 1979. They had formerly been working nearly 3,000 looms with 410 family and wage workers. The survey showed, first, that there was little problem about the former employees finding other work in textiles: the area has a shortage of workers which shows no sign of abating with the slow decline in the number of enterprises. As for the owners, 17, presumably older men, reported 'no employment'; 21 had taken paid employment, and 2 had gone into local politics. But the other 59 were still their own masters, starting restaurants, timber stores, metal-working workshops, bookstores, etc. Thirteen had gone (back) to farming and 22 into other branches of textiles – sizing, twisting and doubling, wool-knitting, carpet-tufting, etc. Most of their original workforces (a proportion of them family members, of course) were still with them after their switch.

There is an additional government scheme, operated under the 1976 Law for Emergency Measures to Assist Small and Medium Enterprises to Change their Field of Business by the Small and Medium Business Agency. It provides advice and loan finance to those who need more than their exit compensation to get started in new businesses. After four years' operation of the scheme 197 transformation plans had been approved, of which 66 were for former textile firms. The finance received by the first 141 of them amounted to some Y3.7bn. ($17m.) with loan guarantees for an additional sum of approximately half that amount (*Jigyo Tenkan*, December 1980).

The policy debate

The 1979 law under which many of these assistance measures were authorized was due to expire in 1984. Its renewal – generally taken for granted – was the occasion for yet another extensive review of the state of the industry by the Textile Industry Council. Its report (Seni Kōgyō, 1983) added very little to previous diagnoses or prescriptions. Conditions were tough; change was rapid; consumer needs and demands (in home markets especially) were becoming diversified, individualized, moving upmarket and fluctuating in ever shorter cycles; hence the need for a flexible industry that can produce widely differentiated products in small lots rapidly and cheaply.

It is striking how much discussion of the appropriate strategy for textiles in Japan there is – with so little real debate. The same phrases recur: 'knowledge-intensiveness' enhancing 'information-gathering capacities', 'increasing product differentiation', 'system integration', 'getting closer to consumer needs', 'maintaining an advantage in non-price competition'. From the pronouncements of the 42-man, 1-woman Textile Industry Council to the reports of the most struggling weavers' co-operatives; from the annual policy statements of the industry associations in synthetic fibres and spinning to those of the unions, the consensus seems to hold.

Much of this talk is whistling in the dark – certainly when these phrases are repeated in the traditional weaving areas producing grey cloth shirtings and sheetings in direct competition with China. There *are* concrete prospects behind the reality, however: the prospects that Japan will keep and improve its competitive edge in the production of special synthetic fibres and chemically sophisticated ways of finishing them; secondly, that it will improve (or gain world recognition for) its fashion design capability; and thirdly, perhaps, that its applications of the microcomputer to the garment industry will greatly enhance Japan's competitive position *vis-à-vis* developing countries.

But these potential growth areas are very largely the province of the large firms which stand at the peak of the pyramids of enduring ties between large and small firms which the first part of this paper sought to describe. A lot of the small firms will be integrated into the new systems – they will learn to take their instructions from on-line visual display screens rather than from the visiting rep. But a lot will probably go under.

And by many they will not be regretted. The belief that 'modern' industry has no place for family-sized small weavers, and that the path of progress lies in their elimination in favour of corporate enterprises with proper university-graduate managers and computerized accounts and steel and plastic furniture, remains a strong one in Japan, particularly among academic economists and MITI officials. The co-operatives which represent the small family enterprises are prepared to accept the modernization rhetoric which this belief gives rise to until some concrete policy expression of that belief actually threatens their interests. For the last ten years the one policy issue which has been a matter of overt contention because it poses just such a threat, is the move, strongly supported by the academic economists and MITI officials, to abolish the registration system for looms and other textile equipment. It is against all free-market principles to provide artificial entry barriers. (It will be recalled that no new looms may be installed without the scrapping of old looms.) It confers arbitrary property rights on people who have done nothing to deserve it. (New entrants have to buy 'loom rights' from people retiring from the industry – owners, probably, of equipment of minimal value). It simply breeds bureaucracy and cheating. And the danger of over-capacity from a flood of new entrants in an industry as widely perceived to be declining as textiles is minimal.

The co-operatives, on behalf of the little man who enjoys these registered rights, and on their own behalf (for they derive considerable revenue from operating the registration system as agents of the government) fought back. The battle has been going on since 1976 and for this round of discussions the co-operatives 'went public', running a poster and petition campaign. They argued *inter alia* that if ever a technological breakthrough gave the large capitalist weaving firms a decisive advantage over the family weaver, the latter would be wiped out without controls on installing new equipment.

And in the end, they won the battle in 1983 as they had won it in 1978: the passage in the report which reaffirms a 1976 declaration of intent to abolish – 'but not yet' – is a model of tortured compromise. The political clout of the small family firm sector is by no means to be despised.

They are not, as yet, posing severe political problems, since they have not been mortally affected. In so far as the run-down in this sector is accomplished by generation change – the death or retirement of a proprietor whom none of his children succeeds – it can be relatively painless, especially in those of the sanchi in or near expanding industrial areas. In rural sanchi, however, of which there are some with high concentrations of textile producers and few alternative industries, the impact of a run-down could be much greater and of considerable political significance.

So far, however, the government is under very little pressure either to restrict imports, to provide survival subsidies, or to provide compensation to the losers.

To take imports first, the campaign at the end of 1980 and early 1981 on the part of the spinners and weavers' associations to end GSP preference for Korea and Taiwan seemed largely to have satisfied protectionist instincts. (It was chiefly symbolic, anyway – a matter of 2–3 per cent in a year when the won was devalued against the dollar by 20 per cent overnight and the yen was fluctuating against the dollar by a similar margin.) As mentioned earlier, pressure from the spinners for protectionist measures against Korea and Pakistan grew again towards the end of 1983, but there has been no sign of the government contemplating a more protectionist approach in the run-up to the next MFA negotiations. Several factors help to explain this virtuous adherence to free trade principles.

First, adherence to principles *is* part of what it is about. A report of a symposium in July 1981 (Yamazawa, 1981) and entitled 'No need for import controls to revive textiles' makes this very clear and so do many conversations in the provinces. As exporters the Japanese feel particularly vulnerable to protectionism in the USA and the EEC for good economic and race-cultural reasons discussed in the next chapter. Hence they cannot afford to give any countenance to protectionist principles. (Except, of course, in the mild temporary forms described earlier, for which it sends missions of apology to the only countries likely to understand what is going on.) A weavers' co-operative secretary, remarking on the growth of competing imports from China, said: 'Well, it's national policy to expand trade with China, and the Government says it just has to ask us to do the weeping into our pillows (naki-neiri shite morau).'

Secondly, there is an organizational factor. The natural international neighbouring links with overseas textile organizations are not with the other protectionist OECD countries, but with Asian countries. A dozen senior company executives travelled to Seoul for the annual friendly conference of the Japanese and Korean Man-Made Fibre Industry Associations in 1980. A similar number went to Taipei and they now propose to have a single trilateral conference and to sponsor joint research of South-east Asian markets (Kasen Kyōkai, 1980, p.91). On the union side, Zensen is a leading figure in TWARO – the Textile Workers Asian Regional Organization. The Zensen president was chairman of its Bombay meeting in 1977 and the secretariat is in Tokyo.

Thirdly, the main source of an expanding supply of imports is China with which, arguably, the Japanese feel a greater sense of kinship than with most foreign nations. The General Secretary of the national weaving association described a visit to China to remonstrate over the fact that in 1979–80 China had exported double its 'orderly marketing' promise. He repeated the sob story they had been given: severe famines and need for emergency food imports, extreme shortage of foreign exchange, cutting domestic consumption absolutely to the bone, genuinely distress exports, etc. 'When they tell you that sort of story, what could we say? After all, it's true. Some people's problems *are* worse.'

So there is little pressure for protection. There seems, equally, to be only very mild pressure for large sums of government subsidies, either to prolong the life of dying firms or to provide compensation to the losers. The most generous 1971–2 schemes were the cost of mishandling a particular export problem and the government consequently putting itself at a moral disadvantage. But, as indicated above, the scrapping subsidy scheme is still not predicated on the assumption of compensation *by the community* – by the consumers who enjoy the cheaper shirts or the exporters who sell their power plants to China. The 'survivors are gainers: survivors should pay' principle is still the official basis of the scheme. There was no compensation made available either for the scrapping of fibre capacity described on page 235. And it is noticeable how every policy statement from MITI, every preamble to the large volume of authorizing legislation, and every statement by the Textile Council, follows its outline of 'the way ahead' or the 'objectives for the reconstruction of enterprises' with the phrase: 'properly speaking (honrai) the responsibility for undertaking these programmes lies squarely with private industry. However, in so far as state intervention and stimulation . . . '

And it is a fact that, as will have been apparent to the reader from examples given in earlier pages, the amount of government funds spent on these schemes is far from large. The scrapping scheme, for instance, provides on average less than a thousand dollars a loom. First-year depreciation allowances for re-equipment are extremely modest. What the newsletter of the national weavers' federation calls the 'textile budget', current and capital expenditure specifically earmarked in the MITI budget for running schemes specifically for textiles and clothing, amounted to only Y310m., about $1.4m. (Men Kōren 1 February 1981, p.3). Even if one doubles this for all the benefits received by textiles under more general schemes, it is still not a large amount for an industry as extensive as textiles with such strategically placed concentrations of voters.

The explanation must lie in large measure in the success of all the national bodies (dominated by the likely survivors) in getting the modernization message across. The central thrust of all the sloganeering about knowledge-intensive, system-integrated, high-value-added and flexible responses to the increasing individuation and differentiation of consumer needs is: 'There *is* a way ahead, and if you can't find it, the fault lies within you. Take yourself to task. Reflect on your daily activities. Ask yourself: what am I doing wrong?'

And they have succeeded in getting the small weaver, bearing the brunt of a 40 per cent drop in the price of his taffeta twill, to accept that implication and feel a twinge of guilt rather than resentment.

The reader will not be surprised at this, yet another example of the famous consensus at work again. What is, perhaps, less commonly remarked is that Japanese groupishness is also admixed with a quite genuine insistence on the virtues of self-reliance.

10
Final thoughts

The starting point for this book was an attempt (part of a multi-country study by the ILO of the prospects for Third World industrialization) to answer the following question: what are the prospects of Japan 'providing space' in its markets for the exports of the developing countries by allowing comparative advantage to take its course, refraining from protecting its competed industries and allowing them to disappear?

To be sure, 'providing space, etc. . . ' is not the way the Japanese (or indeed any other people except the Scandinavian and the Dutch) are likely to put the matter – even though they are sensitive to the complaints of the Asian NICs about the imbalance in their bilateral trade. First and foremost, to most Japanese the question is: how rapidly and smoothly can we shift our human and capital resources out of low-technology, low-value-added, labour-intensive industries (which still carry the stigma of all those early twentieth-century decades of exporting 'slave labour textiles') and into more appropriate ones – the high-value-added, internationally competitive industries fitting for a technologically progressive society, and the highly taste-differentiated industries fitting for a society that is also affluent? And if they thereby further gain by importing simpler manufactures more cheaply than they can make them, so much the better. They see things that way because, as chapter 2 suggested, the 'ladder theory' of the rise and fall – or rather of the rise and rise – of nations, indeed, all theories of long-term social and economic evolution, have a strong attraction for the Japanese and are far more widely discussed than they have been in England since the 1880s. (Herman Kahn sells like hot cakes.) And they are attracted to such 'broad long sweep' theories because of their experience of rapid growth in the past and their expectation of continued growth in the future. (As this is written, the 1985–6 Budget is being framed on the assumption that real growth will be 4.6 per cent (with 1.5 per cent inflation) and will have been 5.3 per cent (1.2 per cent inflation) during 1984–5.)

Should those hopes be disappointed, should Japanese opinions switch to a general gloomy belief that the world has basically changed, and should a siege mentality set in, then there is very little underlying internationalism to counteract it – internationalism in the sense of identification with the international community, with human kind as a whole, that is, rather than in the sense of 'good neighbour' punctiliousness about international obligations – which the Japanese have in good measure.

It has been possible for the Japanese to sustain the general consensus that adjustment and the natural run-down of labour-intensive industries is a good thing, precisely because they have been quite efficient at the process, and particularly at expanding in the fields which modern technology has made the high-growth areas. Earlier chapters have tried to detail some of the contributions to these outcomes by a variety of institutions and policies and environmental factors: by Japan's educational system, providing reliable methods of 'grading' manpower, and providing high levels of attainment in the general intellectual skills needed for advanced technology; by the equity-shareholding and banking institutions, freeing corporate managers from short-term capital-market constraints and encouraging long-term development planning; by the lifetime-employment system with its effects on company loyalties and its very special pressures on firms to make every effort to diversify (other than by take-over which stockmarket conventions – though not legal provisions – rule out); by the grip which Japan's macroeconomic policy makers have maintained on the inflation problem since 1976, and their ability to maintain aggregate demand at a gently expanding level (made possible, in part, by the relative decouplement of Japan's financial markets from those of the rest of the world); by the incomes-policy-by-consensus of the Spring Offensive system which is another precondition for such macroeconomic policies; by the openness of the world's markets which has enabled Japan to translate competitive advantage into export growth, thereby both supplementing domestic demand as a stimulus to growth, and compensating for a severe worsening of the terms of trade; by the serious attention given to exports; by the fact that there has always been a *national* 'catching up' objective to mobilize something more than purely individualistic motives in the cause of investment and enterprise; and not least by all those qualities of dexterity, attention to detail, thoroughness of planning, co-operativeness and ability to bargain sensible compromises which economists can only uncomfortably acknowledge as 'cultural factors', as sources of a mysterious 'X-efficiency'.

This ability to sustain growth has been a powerful, perhaps essential, factor in making possible adjustment in the declining industries. The quite big reductions in the workforces of major companies in the 1970s – whether of the textile companies without, or of the ship-building companies with, government assistance – could not have been carried out with so little impact on the unemployment rate, and with so few political repercussions, had Japan not been a growth economy which soon made alternative jobs available. In the 1980 elections the Komeito had a slogan about 'the people's five great anxieties' which the government was doing little to meet. The five were: pensions, housing, health, education, and natural disasters – i.e., earthquakes, typhoons. Unemployment had no mention. By 1984, with overt minimum-definition unemployment creeping up to 3 per cent, fears of technological unemployment were beginning to be more openly expressed. But still it was a subdued concern. If, however, growth slowed and Japan became as preoccupied with unemployment problems as European countries, the, at present rather feeble, demands for protection would undoubtedly gather strength. And in a society run on the politics of compromise the outsider who is prepared to be tough and uncompromising can do quite well out of appeasing concessions. The farmers and leather workers have already maintained quite high levels of protection by such means. They have the advantage of organization, and of special circumstances justifying indignation and hence an unyieldingly tough stance. The farmers can bang the table secure in the knowledge that all good Confucianists know that agriculture is the backbone of the nation and all 'chun-tze' – all urban gentlemen – have felt slightly guilty about exploiting peasants since the time of Confucius (compare the British middle class and the miners in the pre-Scargill era.) The leather workers are powerful because they are mostly *burakumin*, the former outcast group, still discriminated against and imbued with a lively victim-consciousness of a kind matched only by feminists in Western societies.

All the mom-and-pop industries have something of the same potential for political mobilization if to a somewhat lesser degree, and the labour-intensive industries – like textiles discussed in earlier chapters, or ceramics or flatware – are predominantly of that kind. So far, however, that pressure has been bought off by marginal sums of compensation, and meanwhile the policy-

makers can look forward to the welfare problem gradually solv-
ing itself as mom and pop become grandmom and grandpop
and eventually fade away.

The large-enterprise industries like steel and ship-building are a
different matter. Their political route to self-preservation lies not
in raucous public indignation outside in the corridors of power,
but in hard argument with their class peers in the huddles of the
committee rooms. Their clout lies not in votes but in political
contributions. But it would be unwise to overestimate clout of
that kind; the reasoned case they make in those huddles about
what is in 'Japan's' best interest counts for a lot. 'I see my job,'
said one MITI official, 'as the protection of a healthy textile
industry, not the protection of all the people who happen at the
moment to be in the textile industry. I know the Bureau Chief
doesn't agree but . . .' The Bureau Chief, of course, is closer to the
political pressures, but such is the ethos of MITI that it is hard for a
Bureau Chief to succumb to political pressure without either
convincing his subordinates, like my friend, that there *are* good
public-interest reasons for going along, or else confessing that he
fought the good fight and lost.

And nowadays no industries inclined like the steel industry
towards protectionism (and doing its damnedest to keep out
Brazilian and Korean steel by informal means) can hope to
convince anybody of the need for protectionist measures as long
as the exporting frontier industries are under such continuous
sniper attack from the protectionists of Europe and the USA. Only
by being able to make a plausible show of being pure as driven
snow in matters of protection ('farmers, of course, well, everybody protects their farmers, and leather workers, well, that's a
special case; I'll tell you about it some time over a drink.') – only
thus can Japan defend itself.

That consideration, too, could, of course, change if depression
and the siege mentality worsen and the Japanese have so much of
their trade discriminated against that they think they have nothing much more to lose.

But until now, Japan's record in official protectionism against
low-wage-country goods – tariffs, quotas, official regulation,
NTBs – has been a good deal better than the average OECD
country, and seems likely to remain so for the short-term future.
But in terms of the resulting trade patterns, in terms of the space
actually created in Japanese markets for imports from low-wage
countries, the record looks very different. Japan's manufactured

imports from developing countries were well below the OECD average in 1980 – only 2.5 per cent of manufactured goods' consumption compared with 3.4 per cent average for eleven leading industrial countries. Though it has to be said that this is not due to discrimination against developing country manufactures in particular. Of the manufactures Japan does import, 40 per cent came from developing countries, compared with a 19 per cent average for the other eleven.

As we have seen, the reasons for the generally low level of import penetration are various. One is the willingness of people in the family-backyard, mom-and-pop industries to work long hours for very modest returns in spite of living in the middle of a high-wage economy; another is the ability of some people at all scale levels in these industries to continue to innovate – to substitute for labour-intensive production new forms of capital-intensive alternatives which also have a quality superiority, and regain their competitive edge the more readily for that reason.

But there is also another factor much more difficult to analyse – the 'natural immunity', making *official* protection unnecessary, of industries formed by a dense web of 'relational contracting' between firms specializing in different parts of the production process, or between manufacturers and trading companies, between trading companies and retailers – relationships which are backed not only by their foundation in trust and mutual obligation, but by all the things that trust means, quality guarantees and security of supply. Imports penetrate into markets, and where there *are* no markets, only a network of established 'customer relationships', it is hard for them to make headway.

That immunity does not last for ever. It might stave off a heavy cold, but fail to cope with the flu. There comes a time when the prospect of great cost savings from switching to a foreign supplier overcomes scruples about breaking relations of trust and mutual obligation, and fears of greater risks of poor quality or slipped delivery dates. But the lag is important and explains a lot about the slow response of the Japanese economy to import price differentials.

It may be, too, that the whole system is changing. Certainly the very considerable fall in debt–equity ratios and the lessening of Japanese corporations' dependence on the banks provides opportunities for more (as the Germans say) 'enterprise-egoistic' behaviour. The much discussed internationalization of financial markets may actually take place, and once the ethic of total dedication to short-term profit margins is transferred from America to those Japanese markets – financial markets – where it can operate with least hindrance, it may spread, too, to those areas of economic life which have hitherto been dominated by a 'production-oriented' rather than by a 'finance-oriented' ethic. Some observers also predict a general decline in the 'groupishness' syndrome with increasing affluence, with the wilting of the work ethic in a five-day-week regime, or just as a result of – whatever that may mean – 'westernization'. Such observers would doubtless interpret the growth of trade-association 'outsiders' in the textile import field and the diminishing effectiveness of 'administrative guidance', which an earlier chapter recorded, as symptomatic of a general trend and not just the result of the particular strains set up in the textile field where the gap between private profit opportunities and the constraints which the 'national interest' sought to impose was larger than usual.

It is a debatable issue, about which we shall know more when another ten years have passed. But we already know more than we did ten years ago, when predictions about the eventual triumph of western individualism, the break-down of lifetime employment and all the other collective constraints on market mobility, were being made with even greater frequency and confidence than they are today.

If that is indeed the underlying trend, then it is moving at a glacial pace, and requires very sensitive instruments for its measurement. In many respects, on the contrary, the old 'groupish' characteristics have been reinforced by the vicissitudes of the last decade. The lifetime employment system has, if anything, been strengthened by the addition to its institutional repertoire of a whole set of new conventions about 'how to deal with severe recession'. MITI cartels have played a central role in cutting back production in declining industries. MITI has played a more prominent part in co-ordinating long-term objectives for private corporations' industrial R & D. Problems in export markets have forced acceptance of voluntary export agreements, and hence, inevitably, the spread of export-market sharing agreements.

And in future, should one expect that the declining vitality, which the Japanese fear will inevitably accompany the rapid ageing of the population, will lead to an *increase* in thrusting individualism?

But a more powerful argument for expecting on balance that the major 'collectivist' characteristics of the Japanese system will not disappear is that the long-term secular trends seem to have been working to reinforce, not to erode them. They are not just a 'hangover of ancient (feudal) cultural traditions'. Labour markets, product markets, financial markets, were vastly more volatile – arenas for vastly more thrusting, toughly self-regarding, competition – in the early 1950s than they have since become. It is only gradually, as they have become more affluent, that the Japanese have become able to *afford* to sacrifice temporary bargaining advantage for the benefits of stability, and security, and predictability, and the assurance of quality, and the satisfaction of having friendly rather than antagonistic relations with one's fellow men.

It is even easier to believe that what we are witnessing is an unfolding of trends deeply rooted in the nature of the modern Japanese economy, when we reflect that they are, after all, trends which are equally apparent in the other industrial economies. The difference is that there they seem to have less happy results for efficiency and growth. They are, these days, frequently denounced as 'rigidities'. It is precisely the 'retreat from market risk' apparent in the leading capitalist economies – the tendencies towards oligopoly, tenured job security, union monopolies, increasing state underwriting, if not actual provision, of industrial capital – which is denounced as the sort of market imperfection responsible for deepening stagflation. And the favourite recipe for a restoration of dynamism is to try to reverse these trends, to undo oligopoly arrangements, enforce the principles of fair trade acts, break union monopolies, break the institutional constraints which prevent wages from 'finding their own level' and make labour mobile and market-responsive again.

Japan, by contrast, has grown to be the second biggest western economy precisely by incorporating these features which are deplored elsewhere, as integral functioning elements of its system of 'organized capitalism'. It has seen the shape of the future and made it work.

One condition for that recipe to work is that the gains from trust and co-operation – the elimination of a lot of time-wasting intransigence and unpredictability and fear of cheating from market bargaining relations, especially labour relations – should compensate for the reduction in the spur of competition. Perhaps it is also a condition that there should be some cultural substitute or supplement for profit-seeking individualism to ensure that trusting co-operation is not just co-operation in the mutual assurance of a quiet featherbedded life, but is co-operation for *improvement*, for innovation and growth. Japan finds that substitute partly in traditional beliefs about a human duty for self-improvement, rooted in Confucianism and steadily reinforced by educational and political institutions since the seventeenth century, and partly in national sentiment – in the sense, sharpest among those doing business with foreigners but diffusing from them throughout the society, of being engaged in a shared *national* enterprise to make Japan a powerful and respected member of the comity of nations.

It may be that these alternatives are not available to us in Britain, and that we do have no choice, if we want economic dynamism, but to accept the prescriptions of orthodox economists and seek to give markets back their nineteenth-century vigour. Get rid of our 'rigidities', they would say, and reverse these century-old trends towards oligopoly and cartelization, the substitution of administration for market, the increasing protection of individuals from the consequences of the failure to be competitive.

But is the advice realistic anyway? No government has espoused these principles more assiduously than the British government of the last six years, both because it believes in them as the recipe for economic dynamism, and for the Hayekian reason that they see it as the only road to a free, and therefore good, society. And yet, how much impression has it made on those century-old trends? Has it proved possible to lower the welfare minimum or make substantial inroads on the structure of social security? Has the government in any way reduced selective, discretionary state assistance for industrial innovation? Has it been able to do anything about the fact that real wages of those in work in the private sector continue to increase a good deal faster than productivity, except deeply to deplore it? It has sold a good proportion of our monopoly state corporations off to private shareholders, but has it been able to reduce their monopoly power? Has it even managed to reduce the share of national income which passes through the government's hands?

The answer, of course, to all of those questions is 'no'. Perhaps, as intelligent people like Galbraith and Shonfield have persuasively argued, these century-old trends are so deeply rooted in the unfolding of technological development and the rising standard of affluence that there is no easy way in which they *can* be bucked. If only as a second-best alternative, then, it would be wise to ponder the Japanese example and ask ourselves whether we too might not do better by accepting that there is no road back to competitive individualistic atomized markets, and that we had better learn to live with organized capitalism.

That need not mean that we have to become Japanese, absorb the Confucian ethic, or raise our sense of national identity to Japanese levels. What it does mean is that we should ask ourselves whether there are not other ways in which some of the things which Japanese institutions and traditions achieve for the Japanese might be obtained by other methods, other institutional arrangements, more consonant with our own traditions. If close co-operation and consultation between managers and workers seems to be a precondition for rapid innovation in manufacturing firms, and if it is difficult to achieve this, given our adversarial traditions, what forms of industrial democracy or workplace decision-sharing might substitute for the easy acceptance of bureaucratic hierarchy which facilitates co-operation in Japanese firms? If we cannot have, and do not want, lifetime employment to be the norm, if we want to preserve a more mobile system with the greater personal freedom which that provides, can we at the same time devise schemes which would give British employers the same incentive to invest in training their employees as the lifetime employment expectation gives Japanese employers? If the crucial aspect of the Japanese system of financing industry seems to be the way in which it facilitates long-term planning and investment, and reduces preoccupations with next year's bottom line, is there any way in which our own financial institutions could be amended to achieve the same effect, without necessarily modelling our stock exchange on Japan's? If inflation control in Japan crucially depends on institutionalized wage leadership and a nationally simultaneous pay settlement date, does that not suggest the wisdom of re-examining the many suggestions that have been made for introducing synchro-pay in Britain?

These are some of the ways in which an examination of Japan's society and economy, precisely because it is even more different from ours than most of the other foreign industrial economies we hear about, can possibly help us, too, to make our rigidities more flexible. They will be examined in the companion volume to this one, *Taking Japan Seriously*.

Appendix: Labour disputes

Here are two examples from a compilation by Zensen under the title *Do not let this suffering be set at nought*. The two of the nineteen case studies chosen show the one a relatively successful and the other a relatively unsuccessful 'struggle' by the union. It will be obvious that the companies' version of events might be somewhat different.

1 The Osaka Spinning Company case

It was on 13 November 1972 that the Osaka Spinning Company, a middle-sized firm, suddenly approached the labour union (membership 200, Chairman H. Tanaka) to announce that it proposed to close the firm since it could not see any prospects of keeping it afloat. It transpired that they had already applied to the government for the 'buying-out' scrapping subsidy for all the spindles and arranged for sale of the factory site on which it had already accepted a deposit. All the workers were to be re-employed in another factory also owned by the same owner, Mr Sakamoto, the Sakamoto Spinning Company.

They called this a 'proposal'. It was more like a 'declaration'.

The union was in a relaxed mood having just finished its general meeting two days before. It was like cold water in a sleeper's ear. 'It's about time they stopped ignoring the union' was the general feeling. In a mood of anger we quickly established a committee together with the local Zensen officials.

The firm had been established in Senshū in 1925 and taken over in 1954 to become part of the Sakamoto group. It was a flourishing firm at the time of these events operating about 50,000 spindles and producing yarn worth about a hundred million yen a year. The first meeting of the 'rationalization problem' committee took the line that, although a reasonable settlement would have been possible if matters had been started early enough, the right thing for the union to do was to struggle for reconstruction of the firm. This was the start of a hundred days of conflict. In all there were nine collective bargaining sessions at which the sparks flew.

Extracts

Union: Why was the company so secretive about applying for a scrapping subsidy? You did it six months ago in April.

Company: We are extremely sorry about that: we just put off mentioning it. It was just that the future looked so bad that we started talks with the relevant authorities.

Union: Didn't you know that you can't make an application for a scrapping subsidy without the union's agreement? You just can't do it.

Company: Yes, in fact we have only just found that out recently. We would be grateful if you would give that consent.

Union: You have the nerve to stand there having sold off the equipment without breathing a word of it to us and then ask us to give our retrospective approval! Just fold your hands across your breast and think for a minute. Have you people got *any* conscience?

Company: Well, we would be very grateful if you would agree now.

Union: Why don't you go and wipe the sweat off your face and come back in half an hour's time?

Company: . . .

Union: Didn't you know that in our contract factory closure comes among the items for *consultation* between the company and the union, not for prior notification.

Company: Yes, we know that.

Union: If you know, why is it only now you are starting to talk. You should have thought of it earlier. You're breaking the contract. The contract is the constitutional basis of industrial relations.

Company: It is precisely because there is a contract that we are now discussing the matter with you.

Union: You must have gone soft in the head or something. Listen, 'prior consultation' means the following. Just clean your ears out and listen. (The union leaders banged the table as their anger redoubled. It was fierce enough for ashtrays to get knocked off and broken.)

You sell the site, you sell the spinning machines, and what's left? There is no way that talking about it can put us through a U-turn. To say that you are now carrying out this prior consultation is unforgiveable. That's not prior consultation.

Company: . . .

Union: It's no good just sitting there. Come on, say something.

Don't you feel any responsibility? On the one hand you are applying for the scrapping scheme, and on the other hand, in April, you are taking on new 15-year-old girls.

Company: We just can't see our way to a profit . . . The deal for the site is already concluded. There's nothing can be done about that now.

Union: That's not what we are asking you about. We are asking you about how you are going to take responsibility for your breach of the labour contract.

Company: Well, what do you think we ought to do?

Union: Well, that's what we are asking. Just answer us seriously. Can't you imagine what it feels like to be employees to get this kind of news just at the end of the year?

Company: But the company has made arrangements for everybody to be re-employed at Sakamoto Spinning quite nearby. Nobody's going to be out of work or lose anything. We can't understand why you union people are so upset. We're extremely sad that all this had to happen . . .

Union: It's all very well for you to say that there is a new job waiting right next door. But it is not so simple as that. Our members came to work in Osaka Spinning. How would you like it to be moved around on a chess board just like a pawn? This is the firm we joined and the firm we are fond of and the firm we want to spend our lives working in. In any case, the union at Sakamoto Spinning belongs to the [left-wing] Sohyo Federation, not the Zensen. It's not so easy as the company thinks.

Company: Well, we're very sorry, but we have no intention of trying to re-build Osaka Spinning.

Union: Then let me ask you about the debts. On the one hand you say you've got Y900m. of debts, but then on the other hand we hear that you've given Y1,400m. as a contribution to this local school, the Senshū Gakuen [probably the part-time school awarding nursery-school teachers' certificates to attract teenage-girl labour]. What's all that about?

Company: Well, that contribution had been decided long before these latest events. Half of it, anyway, is not in cash but in land for the buildings. Moreover, it is the owner's personal property.

Union: Personal property it may be, but how do you understand the mentality of an owner who makes that kind of massive donation, when his employees are going to lose their jobs?

Company: We just want to make it clear that the donation has nothing to do with the present issue.

Union: How can you say that? Under some circumstances the personal property of the owner becomes company property. The owner went to Korea and established the finest spinning company in the whole of the East. It looks to us as if it was the cost of all that investment which has put Osaka Spinning in the red.
Company: I can assure you that not a single farthing of Osaka Spinning money went into that Korean factory.
Union: We cannot know the truth because we cannot examine the details of the accounts, but it is certainly our impression that a proportion of the firm's debts come directly from this venture in Korea.

The switch to a conditional struggle

So the discussion went along on parallel lines and in no way could we get the company to think of restructuring the firm. Zensen gave its full support to the Osaka Spinning Union in its conflict with the company. December 26 was the day chosen for the first twenty-four hour strike, and the whole site of the factory was a milling mass of union members and supporting groups from outside. There were three other similar one-day strikes, the last on February 6.

In the interval the rationalization committee tried various ploys, aimed at getting the company back on its feet. In the first place, we went to the building company which had contracted to buy the site and explained the position, stressing that we were in no way responsible for the company having taken the decision to sell, and that we were refusing to co-operate in the hand-over. This caused considerable consternation to the two firms and amounted to considerable pressure on Osaka Spinning, since under the contract it would have had to return the Y600,000,000 deposit with 100 per cent premium for breach of contract.

Secondly, we went to the Japan Spinning Industries' Association through which the scrapping applications have to be channelled, to explain our position and to ask that the application should be arrested in mid-course. The Association agreed to this (the application being in breach of regulations), but earnestly requested us to reach an amicable solution.

We also worked hard on public relations and got the case widely known through the local press, which got the company in a state of some anxiety, but not enough to get them to change their mind about closure. On one occasion there was a small happening, as after a demonstration outside the head offices of

Sakamoto Spinning there was an unplanned invasion of the offices which were occupied for about an hour.

Meanwhile the union members were also beginning to waver. It was already 90 days since the firm had approached the union and there seemed absolutely no prospect of being saved. There was a growing feeling that the union ought to change tactics, give up the total victory objective and seek to impose the best conditions. The members of the committee had to think long and hard about whether they were going for an absolute challenge or a conditional challenge; whether they could carry their members with them for an absolute challenge. Finally, on February 7 there was a mass meeting of all union members and the decision was taken by an overwhelming majority to switch to a conditional struggle. The demands put to the company as conditions for severance of employment were as follows:

1   The company should pay four times the 'employer's convenience' entitlement of severance pay under the firm's retirement bonus scheme.
2   There should be a payment of one month's wages in lieu of notice.
3   There should be an additional payment of Y150,000 per person as a farewell goodwill gift.
4   There should be a payment of 'apology money' to the union of Y50m.
5   The company should pay the expected summer bonus equivalent to 2.3 months' wages.

As for transfer to Sakamoto Spinning, everyone who wished to go should be accepted and should be guaranteed full continuation of his present pay scales. For those who did not wish to go to Sakamoto Spinning there should be tripartite efforts by the union and management and Zensen to find them jobs.

The company, having claimed all along that discussions should be about conditions, received these demands with some astonishment, claiming that in total they would amount to about six times what the company was obliged to pay under the 'employer's convenience' clause of the retirement bonus scheme. It is certainly true that generally speaking in such negotiations over severance bonuses Zensen had held out for about two to two-and-a-half times the entitlement. Our first claim for four times was intended as an expression of our anger at the way the management had treated us, as a lesson to other firms, given the likelihood of similar rationalization plans elsewhere in Senshū, and as an admonitory gesture to the firm in the hope that they would reconsider their pre-modern belief that there is no problem that money can't solve.

The company insisted that it had no legal obligation to pay a month's salary in lieu of notice, since it had already given three months' notice, but the union clung to this provision as part of its attempt to establish new conditions for severance. We put in the farewell goodwill gift as 'an expression of apology for what the company had done to employees who for so many years had been working so hard in the dust and grime of a spinning factory.' The damages to the union were by way of recompense for having broken the provisions of the labour contract.

The distance between Osaka Spinning and Sakamoto Spinning was only about one kilometre. The company took the line that those who transferred to Sakamoto Spinning would be treated in all respects as continuing employment with 100 per cent guarantee of previous rights so that there should be no question of paying them severance pay. They drew parallels with people of other firms who after a plant closure had had to go across rivers and across mountains to quite new districts to continue a job. We insisted that the employment contract was with Osaka Spinning and that that was the point to hold on to. We suggested finally that, while those who went to Sakomoto Spinning should receive all the other entitlements, as far as the severance bonus proper was concerned, the exact entitlement, rather than four times that amount, should be paid and paid into the Pension Fund at Sakamoto Spinning.

A painful atmosphere but some satisfaction

The negotiations took until February 26 and for the last stages the Chairman of the Zensen spinning section and of the Osaka region came to join the negotiators. The final settlement was as follows:

1   The severance bonus should be 3.6 times entitlement.
2   There should be one month's pay in lieu of notice.
3   The farewell goodwill gift should be Y135,000 per person.
4   Damages to the union would be paid amounting to Y24m. and the distribution left entirely to the union.
5   The summer bonus would be paid at the rate of 1.47 months' pay for leavers, 2.2 months' pay for those joining Sakamoto Spinning.

There were further provisions that everyone who wished it could get a job in the Sakamoto group and would be guaranteed all rights, except that those who joined subsequently after taking their severance bonus would be counted as new employees. Those who wished for jobs elsewhere would be helped by the three parties (firm, union and Zensen) and if anyone over 35 was still unemployed after a month he would be given a final settlement payment of Y70,000.

The total sums due to union members were Y450 m. which, since the severance bonus entitlement was Y96 m. amounts to 4.7 times entitlement. Reigning at the final meeting to report the settlement was a generally sombre mood – 'at last we are at the end of the road' – but at the same time there was a mingled sense of satisfaction that we had nothing to regret about our struggle. The company closed on March 21 and the union was dissolved on May 27. Forty-four men and 27 women moved to Sakamoto Spinning and 129 took their severance pay. Most of the teenage girls took their money and went home.

2 Daishin Spinning Company: unions working together

The double punch
At 9 a.m. on 23 September 1974 Mr Kitagawa, chairman of the trade union at Daishin Spinning Company in Handa, Aichi Prefecture, knocked anxiously at the door of the managing director's room to find him looking extremely pained. 'I want you to tell me frankly how the company is doing.'

The managing director explained that he had tried every approach to the parent company and done his level best but things were going from bad to worse. As he spoke he suddenly stood up. He knelt down with both hands on the floor. 'Chairman: I don't know what to say or how to apologise to you. It is a terrible situation. It is beyond the scope of anything I can handle.' And he burst into tears.

'So it's closure.' Chairman Kitagawa felt the blood freezing in his veins. Nevertheless, he managed to get the words out. 'I am sorry, but if all you have to say about matters as grave as this – that are going to rock the foundations of my members' lives and those of their families – if all you can say is that you can't find words to apologise, I am afraid that is not good enough. We shall stand shoulder to shoulder to defend our livelihood. What I must ask you as the chief person responsible for this firm is to think hard about your social responsibility and to put the very last ounce of your effort into finding a solution.' He left and went back to his office and called his committee together.

There had been plenty of reasons for thinking that the company was in trouble since the beginning of the year. It had been established in 1946. It specialized in wool and worsted spinning and had 17 knitting machines in addition. There were 1,300 employees and capital of Y450m. It had ridden on the post-war booms to rapid expansion, only to come up against the troubles which hit the woollen industry from the late 1950s onwards.

The company had acquired huge loans and it began to suffer from overmanning and eventually came under the supervision of the banks. Then, in 1964, Tōyō Spinning Company decided to put some capital into it and try to reconstruct it. The joint efforts of managers and workers were finally rewarded in 1972 at the time of the international rediscovery of natural fibres, and the company finally managed to get rid of its accumulated debts. Then came the double punch of the dollar shock and the oil shock, blows from which a company which had exploited every ounce of its latent saleable assets in the rationalization process was left reeling. Yarn prices below its costs of production put it steadily further in the red.

What the union did
In 1974 the union took every opportunity in the joint consultation meetings to press the company hard on prospects for the firm. The company evaded the issue on the grounds that it was too early to make pronouncements, that terms were still being discussed, etc. In September the union heard that the company had begun an evaluation of all its realizable assets. It realized that there was no time to lose and that it must demand top-level meetings.

The reaction of the executive committee when they heard the news from the Chairman Kitagawa was predictable: 'We really knew it was coming.' But they soon pulled themselves out of their mood of sombre fatalism and determined that they must do everything that could be done in the situation so that they would have no cause to regret their handling of the matter at the end of the day. They set to appointing an emergency committee of about 30 composed of section chiefs and foremen among the men and some leading women. After the meeting the three chief officials (chairman, deputy chairman and general secretary) set off for the Zensen headquarters in Tokyo to see the officials of the woollen section. There they were told that there was little Zensen could do to prevent the firm going on to bankruptcy and the important thing was to make absolutely certain that the workers got their dues. It was decided that a strategy would be worked out at the prefectural headquarters and meanwhile the leaders were given case studies of earlier bankruptcies and the pamphlet on how to deal with rationalization measures.

Their hearts were heavy as they came back. The next day was the fourth-Saturday-in-the-month holiday and the following day Sunday. Never had days passed more slowly. They had no idea what to do and yet a burning feeling that they ought to be doing something.

On the Monday they went to the prefectural headquarters of Zensen. The district chairman suggested that they might try asking the Democratic Socialist Party to see if they couldn't put some pressure on the banks. He telephoned to the party chairman in Tokyo to ask him to see what he could do. Thirty minutes later came the return call. He'd been in touch with the top managers of the Tōkai Bank and there was due to be a meeting the next day. The managers of Tōyō Spinning Company and Daishin Spinning Company were going to the bank, and the bank promised that they would do the very best they could. For the union officials that phone call was like reaching out of the dark and finding themselves clutching a straw.

The prefectural headquarters put them on to their consultant lawyer to whom they took the copies of the company's accounts that they had received. As they expected, every realizable asset had already been taken as a security by the banks and there was simply nothing left. The lawyer's advice was that in a situation like that there was not much point in taking a tough line: the best thing to do was to hope to negotiate an amicable settlement.

On October 3 the company asked for a formal works consultation meeting and there suggested closure and termination of employment for everyone on the 30th of the month. The union declared its opposition to closure and immediately called a meeting of the emergency committee which set up its plans for an opposition struggle and drew up a petition for the continuance of the firm for all the workers to sign. The officials then went off to Osaka to meet the Secretary General of Zensen, who was on a visit there, to ask for strong support from the Federation. The next day there was a rally of all union members at which a resolution was passed condemning the closure proposal. The union offices became so full of press reporters that the officials hardly had time to consult with each other.

Collective bargaining sessions were held but they got nowhere. The union claimed that everything should be done to continue the firm, even if it did mean large-scale redundancies, whereas the company simply repeated that with yarn prices below costs of production there was no way they could carry on.

Uncompromising struggle or conditional struggle?

A few days later one of the union members came rushing into the union offices, pale with excitement. Ten large trucks had arrived and were beginning to load up all the stocks, both of yarn and raw wool. If the raw wool was taken away there would be no more production. Once production stopped, then closure was inevitable. The union executive made immediate preparations to set up a picket line to stop the loading and immediately got on to the managers and told them that, if they went ahead, the union would have to take emergency measures involving the use of physical force. The company was startled. The work was stopped and the trucks went away. This had a considerable effect in impressing on the employees the insensitivity of the company and the importance of the union. Meanwhile at the Zensen headquarters in Tokyo a Daishin Spinning taskforce was set up and one of the headquarters' organizers came to stay on the spot.

In the collective bargaining sessions the company began to show a little more sympathy. They proposed that they should defer a decision until the 11th and that both sides should see what they could do to save the company. The union officials immediately took off with the petition signed by all their members and went to the parent company Tōyō Spinning, to the Tōkai Bank and to the Mitsubishi Trading Company, and they also paid visits to the prefectural and the municipal parties to ask for their backing. None of this got them very far.

By this time a number of union members were beginning to say that the best thing to do was to get the matter settled while they could still draw severence pay rather than face the prospect of being thrown out with nothing in the end. An all-out struggle or a conditional struggle? The officials went on having sleepless nights.

As the 11th arrived without any gleam of light on the horizon, the union decided that the time to accept the *fait accompli* had arrived. A meeting of all union members agreed to the proposal that they should concentrate on discussing the severance conditions. Distressed as they were at the prospect of the firm closing, this decision took a great load off the union officials' shoulders.

There was an enormous amount of information and consultation work to be done. How could one ensure that the girls who were studying part-time could continue their studies? What chances of re-employment for older workers? Every personal case was different. There were those who wanted to draw out the money they had in the workers' savings bank because of a rumour that it would be taken by the liquidator. There was a union member who had for years been nursing a grudge against the senior manager and insisted that he wasn't going to leave without the chance of beating him up. Patiently the officials had to explain that the overwhelmingly important thing was to bring the negotiations about severence conditions to a successful conclusion.

The union demanded 2.3 times the statutory severance bonus, an emergency payment of two months' wages, and a severance allowance of one month's wages. It pressed the management hard to show its sincerity and to agree to these, the union's final demands, as an appropriate expression of apology. The company's offer a few days later was for a tiny 1.7 per cent increment over the severance bonus entitlement – a total payment for all the workforce of only Y456m.

The union reacted strongly, but the management kept repeating that, as a result of the rationalization process, the company was absolutely without assets. The severance bonuses would have to be paid with funds supplied by Tōyō Spinning, the parent company, and Tōyō Spinning itself was having to find 3,000 people to accept voluntary redundancies. In the circumstances they said this was absolutely the best offer they could make. It was clear that the Daishin Spinning management had lost its capacity to manage.

Appeal to the parent company union
On October 19 there was a mass meeting of union members at which it was accepted that there had to be negotiations with the parent firm and that the chief official for the union should be given full authority to negotiate on everybody's behalf. There were some who wanted a chance to approve the outline to the

settlement before it was reached, but they were persuaded to go along with the majority.

It was evening before they could leave for Osaka and their first stop was the headquarters of the Tōyō Spinning Company union. Sugano, the union president promised to do everything he could and that measure of encouragement meant a great deal to the union officials who were beginning to feel desperate. A meeting was arranged with the Tōyō Spinning managers to whom they described events so far and put the case for a more generous settlement. They were told that Tōyō Spinning had great problems of its own, and that it would be impossible to agree to all their demands. However, they promised to respond as far as was in their power and come up with something that evening. The Daishin management was already on its way to Tōyō Spinning headquarters.

The union officials went back to the Tōyō Spinning union headquarters and meanwhile President Sugano made his own approaches to the Tōyō Spinning management. At 11 o'clock in the evening word came from the labour relations' director of Daishin Spinning that he wanted a personal meeting with the union chairman. The message was: 'Look. This is not a bargaining ploy but the end of the road. We can offer you 10 per cent above entitlement but I'm afraid anything more would be impossible.' Chairman Kitagawa rejected the offer flat telling him that no way could he go back to Handa with a figure like that and warned him that the next day busloads of workers would be coming up to Osaka to put on the pressure. The director muttered that he would have to think about it. When they got back to the Tōyō Spinning union there was a call from the union offices back home which were still fully manned, sustained by a supply of rice dumplings from the girls in the dormitories. 'Stick to your guns' was the message.

President Sugano came back to ask: 'Tell me. What is your absolute bottom line?' Thirty per cent on entitlement; Y650m. was the answer. 'Mm.' President Sugano folded his arms in thought: 'Okay. I can't say you'll get what you want but I'll do the very best I can.' By this time it was three in the morning.

Presently President Sugano came back. 'I've been in touch with the managing director and tried everything I can, but I'm afraid 23 per cent on entitlement – 600 million – is absolutely the limit of my negotiating power. Do you think you could take that offer back and discuss it?' The three chief officials felt on the one hand that, having got that far, they would like to push it just a little bit further, but on the other hand it seemed to them that it was a figure that they could probably sell to their members and did at any rate make their journey to Osaka worthwhile. So they decided to accept.

The formal meeting with the company was quickly over. But when the managing director put out his hand to seal the agreement Chairman Kitagawa did not feel like taking it. 'We've still got to get the approval of our members.' After courtesy visits to the Tōyō Spinning management and to the union they rushed back to Handa. The union approved the compromise without questions or objections. It was 23 days since Chairman Kitagawa had been summoned to the managing director's office.

Lowering the burden

There was still work for the union to do: helping to get new jobs. As expected the greatest difficulties were for the older men. Many ended up in jobs where they could only equal their former pay by doing 30 to 40 hours' overtime a month, or else small non-unionized firms where the boss unilaterally decided wages and conditions. Some of the girls found jobs nearby from which they could continue to attend their night school. Others gave up their studies and went home. On the 30th the union held its Dissolution General Meeting followed by the farewell party. Chairman Kitagawa and the managing director shook hands and then, the emotion overbrimming, embraced. There was no anger, no distrust. Finally, by November 20, the girls returning home had left in their special buses. The dormitories were empty. With the exception of one who was convalescing from an illness, the girls who were changing jobs had all been found positions. As he walked past the dormitories once ablaze with lights and saw them now wrapped in silent darkness, it came to Chairman Kitagawa for the first time with full force: this is the end of the affair.

Bibliography

Boltho, A. 1985: 'Was Japan's industrial policy successful?' *Cambridge Journal of Economics*, vol. 9, June.

Caves, R., and Uekusa, M., 1976: 'Industrial organization' in Patrick and Rosovsky.

Destler *et al.* 1979: I.M. Destler, H. Fukui and H. Sato, *The textile wrangle: Conflict in Japanese-American relations*, Cornell University Press.

Dore, R.P. 1983: *A case study in technology forecasting: The Japanese Next Generation Base Technologies Programme*, London, Technical Change Centre.

Dore and Taira 1984: Dore, R.P. and Taira, K., *Structural adjustment in Japan, 1970–1982*, Geneva, ILO, 1986.

EPA 1981: Keizai Kikakuchō (Economic Planning Agency), *Keizai hakusho (Economic White Paper)*.

EPA 1982: Keizai Kikakuchō (Economic Planning Agency), *Nihon Keizai no genkyō (The present state of the Japanese economy)*.

FT: *Financial Times*, London daily.

Fukui-ken 1981: Fukui-ken Chūshō Kigyō Jōhō Sentaa (Fukui Prefecture Small and Medium Enterprises' Information Centre) *Fukui-ken no seni sangyō seisan no ugoki (Production trends in the Fukui textile industry)* March.

Fukui Textile 1982: *Fukui Textile News*, 20 January.

Goldberg, V.P. 1981: 'A relational exchange perspective on the employment relationship', SSRC Conference, York, mimeo.

Goto, A. 1981: 'Statistical evidence on the diversification of Japanese large firms', *Journal of Industrial Economics* 29, iii, March.

Gyōsei 1982: Gyōsei Kanri-chō (Administration Control Agency), *Paatotaimaa no genjō to mondaiten (Conditions and problems of part-time workers)*.

Hirschman, A.O., 1970: *Exit, voice and loyalty: Responses to decline in firms, organizations and states*, Harvard University Press.

Hōrei, yearly: Hōmusho (Ministry of Justice), *Hōrei zensho (Annual collection of laws and regulations)*.

Ikeda 1984: Ikeda, Y. 'No need to apologize: Explaining Japanese industrial policies', *Speaking of Japan*, February.

Japan Institute of Labour 1979: *Employment and employment policy*, Tokyo.

JIB 1982: Nihon Kōgyō Ginkō, Sangyō Chōsa-bu, (Industrial Research Department, Japan Industrial Bank), *Nihon sangyo no shin-tenkai, (New developments in Japanese industry)*, Tokyo, Nihon Keizai Shimbunsha.

Jigyō Tenkan 1980: Chūshō Kigyō Jigyō-dan, Chūshō Kigyō Jōhō Sentaa

(Small and Medium Enterprises' Agency, Information Centre) *Jigyō tenkan jirei jōhō (Changing one's field of business: case studies)* No.24, December.

Johnson, Chalmers, 1978: *Japan's Public Policy Companies*, Washington DC, American Enterprise Institute.

Johnson, Chalmers, 1982: MITI *and the Japanese miracle: The growth of industrial policy 1925–1975*, Stanford University Press.

Kagaku-Gijutsuchō 1981: Kagaku-Gijutsuchō (Science and Technology Agency) *Kagaku Gijutsu Hakusho: (Kokusai kikaku to kongo no kadai) (Science and Technology White Paper: International comparisons and the problems of the future).*

Kampō daily: *Kampō (The Official Gazette).*

Kasen Kyōkai: Kasen Kyōkai, (Man-made Fibres' Association), *Kasen Handobukku (Man-made Fibres Handbook),* annual.

Kasen Kyōkai 1980: Nikon Kagaku Seni Kyōkai (Japan Man-made Fibres' Association) *Gyōmu-Hōkokusho (Annual Report).*

Keizai Kikakuchō, see EPA.

Kokuzeichō 1983: Kokuzeichō, Sōmuka, *Zeimu-tōkei kara mita hōjin kigyō no jittai. 1981 (The state of Japanese enterprises as seen from tax statistics: A 1981 sample survey).*

Kōsei, 1981: Kōsei Torihiki Iinkai (Fair Trade Commission) *Kōsei Hakusho (Fair Trade White Paper),* annual.

KR: Nihon Seisansei Hombu (Japan Productivity Council), *Katsuyō Rōdō Tōkei: chingin kōshō no shihyō (Practical labour statistics for wage negotiators)* annual.

Kubota 1980: Akira Kubota, 'The political influence of the Japanese Higher Civil Service', *Journal of Asian and African Studies,* XV, 3–4.

Kuroki Toshio 1982: 'Jetto fukyō o arau' ('The truth about the jet depression') in *Nihon Gosei Seni Shimbun (Japan Synthetic Fibres Daily),* 22 February.

KY: Keizai Kikakuchō (EPA), *Keizai yōran (Annual digest of statistics).*

Magaziner, Ira C. and Hout, Thomas M. 1980: *Japan's Industrial Policy,* London, Policy Studies Institute.

Menkōren ten-daily: Nihon Men Sufu Orimono Kōgyō Rengōkai (Japanese Federation of the Cotton and Staple Fibre Weaving Industry). *Men sufu orimono jōhō (Cotton and Staple Fibre Weaving Information Bulletin)* three times a month.

Ministry of Labour 1984: *Rōdō tōkei yōran (Abstract of Labour Statistics).*

MITI Seikatsu 1977: MITI, Seikatsu-Sangyō Kyoku, Seni Kōgyō Kōzō Kaizen Jigyō-Kyokai (MITI Consumer Goods' Bureau and the Textile Rationalization Agency), *Atarashii seni-sangyo no arikata (The textile industry of the future).*

MITI yearly: MITI, Tōkeibu, *Seni Tōkei (Textile Statistics),* annual.

MITI Tōkeibu December 1971, December 1976: MITI, Tōkeibu, *Dai 4 kai Kōgyō Jittai Kihon Chōsa Hōkokusho (31 December 1971) Seni Kōgyō (Fourth Basic Survey of Industry of 31 December 1971: Textiles);* and also fifth, ditto, of 31 December 1976.

MITI 1978: MITI, *Nairon Chō-seni seizō-gyō no antei-keikaku (Plan for the stabilization of nylon filament production and ditto for polyester staple and filament, acrylic staple)*, 23 October.

MITI 1980a: Sangyō Kōzō Shingikai (Industrial Structure Council) *Hachijū-nendai no tsusan seisaku bijion*. Partially translated as: *A vision of trade and industry policy for the eighties*.

MITI 1980b: Sangyō Kōzō Shingikai (Industrial Structure Council), *Hachijū-nendai no sangyō-kōzō no tembō to kadai (The industrial structure of the 1980s: Outlook and problems)*.

MITI 1981: *Chūshō kigyō kakusho (White paper on small and medium industries)*, annual.

Mombushō 1979: *Kyōiku-shihyō no kokusai-hikaku (International comparisons of educational indicators)* Tokyo.

Nakagawa and Ota 1981: Y. Nakagawa and N. Ota, *The Japanese economic system: a new balance between intervention and freedom*. Tokyo, Foreign Press Centre, (translated from M. Baba and K. Masamura, eds, *Sangyō shakai to Nihonjin*, Tokyo, Chikuma, 1980).

Neef, A. and Capdevielle, P. 1980: 'International comparisons of productivity and labour costs', *Monthly Labour Review*, December.

NBG monthly: Nihon Bōseki Kyōkai (Japan Spinners' Association), *Nihon Bōseki Geppō (Japan Spinners' Monthly)*.

Nihon Kaihatsu Ginkō (Japan Development Bank), *Chōsa*, 47 (Bessatsu), September 1981.

Nihon Orimono 1980: Nihon Orimono Chūō Oroshishōgyō Kumiai Rengō kai (Japan Federation of Central Cloth Wholesalers' Cooperatives) *Shūsanchi apareru no kasseika jōken (Conditions for the revitalization of garment wholesalers)* 1980.

NIRA 1979: Mitsubishi Sōgō Kenkyūjo (Mitsubishi General Research Institute) for NIRA. *Nikkan ryōkoku o chūshin ni shita kokusai-bungyō no arikata (On the international division of labour between Japan and South Korea)*.

Nōritsu Remmei 1979: Zen Nihon Nōritsu Remmei (All Japan Efficiency Federation) *Rōdōryoku idō ni kansuru jittai chōsa hōkokusho (Report of survey research on labour mobility)*, March.

OECD 1979: *The impact of the newly industrializing countries on production and trade in manufactures*, Paris.

Okimoto, D.I., Sugano, T. and Weinstein, F.B., eds. 1984: *Competitive edge: The semi-conductor industry in the US and Japan*, Stanford University Press.

Okumura 1982: 'Masatsu o umu Nihonteki keiei no heisa-sei'. Ekonomisuto 6 July 1982, translated as 'The closed nature of Japanese intercorporate relations', *Japan Echo* 9; iii.

Okumura, H. 1984: *Hōjin shihon shugi (Corporate capitalism)*, Tokyo, Ochanomizu Shobo.

Okun, A.M. 1975: 'Inflation: its mechanics and welfare costs', in A.M. Okun and G.L. Perry, eds., *Brookings Papers on economic activity*, 1975: 82.

Okurashō: Okurashō, Shōkenkyoku (Ministry of Finance, Securities Bureau), *Hōjin kigyō tōkei chōsa (Statistics on corporate enterprises)*, annual.

OSS: *Osaka Senken Sokuhō (The Osaka Textile Research Express)* daily newspaper.

Pascale and Rohlen 1983: R. Pascale and T.P. Rohlen, eds, 'The Mazda Turnaround' *Journal of Japanese Studies* 9, ii, Summer.

Patrick, H. and Rosovsky, H., eds, 1976: *Asia's new giant*, Washington DC, Brookings Institution.

Prindl, A. 1981: *Japanese Finance: A guide to banking in Japan*, Chichester, John Wiley.

RH: Rōdōshō; *Rōdō Hakusho (White Paper on Labour)*, Tokyo, Rōdō Kyōkai, annual.

Rōdōshō 1984: Rōdōshō, Daijin Kambō, Tōkei Jōhōbu, *Rōdō seisansei tōkei chōsa hōkoku (Labour productivity statistics)*, 1982.

Sanshin 1981: Sangyō-Kōzō Shingikai, Aruminiamu Bukai (Aluminium Sub-committee of Industrial Structure Committee), *Tōshin (Report)* 9 October.

Schonberger, R.J. 1982: *Japanese manufacturing techniques: Nine hidden lessons in simplicity*, New York, Free Press – Macmillan.

Sekiguchi, S., 1981: *Nihon no sangyō chōsei (Industrial adjustment in Japan)*, Tokyo, Nihon Keizai Shimbunsha.

Seni Kindaika 1979: Seni-torihiki Kindaika Suishin Kyōgikai (Council for the Modernization of Trading Relations in the textile industry), *Seni-torihiki kindaika suishin (The promotion of modernization of textile trading relations)*.

Seni Kōgyō Shingikai 1978: Sangyō Kōzō Shingikai (Textile Industrial Council and Industrial Structure Council), *Kongo no seni-sangyō no Kōzō-kaizen no arikata (On the structural improvement of the textile industry)*.

Seni Kōgyō Shingikai 10 Feb 1981: Seni Kōgyō Shingikai (Textile Industry Council) *Sōgō bukai gōsei seni shōiinkai hōkokusho (Report of the Synthetic Fibres' Sub-committee of the General Board)*.

Seni Kōgyō Shingikai 1983: (Textile Industry Council), *Tōshin: Atarashii jidai no senisangyō no arikata nitsuite: Senshinkoku-gata sangyō o mezashite (Report. A textile industry for a new age. Aiming for a structure of advanced-country type.)* 31 October.

Senshū Orimono 1980: Senshū Orimono Kōzō Kaizen Kōgyō Kumiai (Senshu Weavers' Industrial Co-operative for Structural Improvement, with two other co-operatives), *Osaka men, sufu orimono sanchi shinkō keikaku (Plans for the revitalization of the Osaka cotton and staple fibre weaving district)*, March.

Senshū Orimono 1979: Senshū Orimono Kōzō Kaizen Kōgyō Kumiai (Senshū Weavers' Industrial Co-operative for Structural Improvement) *Katsuro kaitaku chōsa shidōjigyō hōkokusho (Report on guidance activity arising from the survey of pioneer ventures into the future)*, March.

Shinohara, Miyohei 1982: *Industrial growth, trade and dynamic patterns in the Japanese economy*, Tokyo: Tokyo University Press.

Shizuoka-ken 1981: Shizuoka-ken Hamamatsu Seni Kōgyō Shikenjo, Shizuoka-ken Shōkobū Jiba-Sangyō-ka (Hamamatsu Textile Research Station and Prefectural Industrial Bureau, Local Industries'

Branch), *Shizuoka-ken no Seni Kōgyō (The textile industry in Shizuoka Prefecture)*, April.

Shokugyō 1980: Shokugyō Kenkyūkai, Nihon Rōdō Kyōkai, (Occupational Research Association and Japan Institute of Labour), *Koyō chōsei no jisshi ni saishite no rōshi kyōgitō no jittai ni kansuru chōsa (Field studies of management-labour negotiations over the implementation of employment adjustment measures)*.

Shonfield, A. 1983: *The use of public power*, Oxford University Press.

Shōya, K. 1978: *Kinu orimono sanchi no genjō to mondaiten (The present conditions and problems of silk-weaving areas)* Momoyama Gakuin Daigaku, September.

STN: Rōdōshō (Ministry of Labour), *Shitsugyō Taisaku Nenkan (Yearbook of measures to deal with unemployment)*, annual.

Sumiya Mikio 1978: *Nihonteki koyō seisaku no tembō (Prospects for Japanese-style employment policy)*, Tokyo, Nihon Keizai Shimbunsha.

Suzuki, H. 1984: 'Industrialization in the Republic of Korea and the Small and Medium Enterprises in Japan'. *Japan Foundation Newsletter*, II, vi.

Taira, Kōji 1980: 'Colonialism in Foreign Subsidiaries: Lessons from Japanese Investment in Thailand', *Asian Survey*, 20, 4 April.

Taira, Kōji 1983: 'Japan's low employment: An economic miracle or statistical artifact', *Monthly Labour Review*, 106, July.

Takenaka Heizō 1982: 'Coherence in capital investment policy: A key to higher productivity' in Programme on US–Japan Relations, Centre for International Affairs, Harvard University: *US-Japan relations in the 1980s: Towards burden sharing*.

Tanaka Hirohide 1979: *Shōgai koyō kakumei, (The revolution in lifetime employment)*, Tokyo Diamond Publishing Co.

Tenryūsha 1979: Tenryūsha Orimono Kōgyō Kyōdō Kumiai, *et al.* (Tenryūsha Weavers' Co-operative and five other Co-operatives), *Betchin, kōruten orimono sanchi shinkō keikakusho (Plans for the revitalization of the velveteen and corduroy weaving area)* October.

Tomizawa 1980: Tomizawa Konomi, *Apareru sangyō (The apparel industry)* Tokyo, Tōyō Keizai Shimposha.

Tōyō Bōseki 1980: Tōyō Bōseki Keizai Kenkyūjo (Economic Research Institute of Tōyō Spinning Company), *Seni kōgyō (The textile industry)* Tokyo, Tōyō Keizai Shimposha.

Tōyō Keizai 1982: *Kaigai shinshutsu sōran (Guide to firms operating overseas)*, annual.

Tsūsanshō (Tsūshō Sangyōshō), *see* MITI.

TWTG: Tōyō Keizai, *Tōkei Geppo (Monthly Statistics)*, monthly.

Uekusa, Masu 1982: *Sangyo soshiki-ron (The theory of industrial organization)* Tokyo, Chikuma-shobo.

Williamson, O.E. 1975: *Markets and hierarchies: Analysis and anti-trust implications*, New York, Free Press.

Yamazawa 1981: 'Seni sangyō no saisei ni yunyū seigen wa hitsuyō nai' ('No need for protection to revive textiles'), *Tōyō Keizai*, 4 July.

Yonezawa Yoshie 1981: 'Zōsen-gyō no sangyō-chōsei', ('Industrial adjustment in ship-building') in Sekiguchi.

Yoshioka 1978: Yoshioka Masayuki: *Seni Sangyō wa ikinokoreru ka (Can the textile industry survive?)* Tokyo Nikkei Shimbunsha.

Zensen 1980a: Zensen Dōmei (Federation of Textile Workers' Unions) *Kono kurushimi o muda ni sumai (Let's make sure all that suffering was not for nought)*, October.

Zensen 1980b: Zensen Dōmei, *Dai-36-kai Teiki Taikai Hōkokusho 1 (Report to the 36th Annual General Meeting)*, September.

Zensen Dōmei 1981: Zensen Dōmei (All Japan Federation of Textile Workers' Unions), *Survey of the textile industry*, mimeo.

Index